Asking and Telling

*A Collection of Gay Drama
for the 21st Century*

Asking and Telling

*A Collection of Gay Drama
for the 21ˢᵗ Century*

Six Scripts by
DAVID DILLON
JOHN M. CLUM
GUILLERMO REYES
NEAL BELL
SAMUEL ADAMSON
STEVE MURRAY

Edited by
JOHN M. CLUM

Garden City, New York

ISBN 0-7394-1619-7
Printed in the United States of America

CONTENTS

EDITOR'S INTRODUCTION

This anthology bears witness to two important facts about gay drama in the twenty-first century: First that it is indeed alive and well, and second that, like much important new theater, it is local. These plays were produced in the small theaters that have become the seedbed of contemporary serious drama, small non-profit theaters in large and small cities across America and in London. In a way, the book is also a tribute to these adventurous theaters that are willing to nurture new writing. Many of these theaters are run by gay artists and depend on the gay community as their core audience. Many, like Bailiwick Repertory in Chicago and Manbites Dog Theater in Durham, North Carolina have annual festivals of queer theater.

David Dillon's *Party* had its first production a decade ago at Chicago's Bailiwick Repertory, an exciting theater now eighteen years old with two intimate performance spaces. Bailiwick offers a varied repertory, but has a special interest in serving Chicago's deaf community and its gay and lesbian community. Bailiwick offers an annual Pride Festival of lesbian and gay theater every June and July. *Party* moved from a successful run at Bailiwick to Los Angeles and New York for successful long runs and has spawned a number of sequels. It returns to Bailiwick for an anniversary production in the fall of 2000.

On one hand, *Party* is successful commercial fare, offering its audiences laughs and nudity as its characters play a version of Truth or Dare. In an era in which good comedy is a rarity, *Party* is a special delight. In the context of the history of gay drama, *Party* is a nineties sequel to Mart Crowley's 1968 play, *The Boys in the Band*. In Crowley's play, a group of New York gay men gather to celebrate the birthday of one of their friends. In the course of the evening, they play a truth game that, like the games in Edward Albee's *Who's Afraid of Virginia Woolf?*, succeeds in humiliating everyone. What else could one expect from the self-hating basket cases Crowley offers his audience? Dillon's characters are anything but self-hating. Even the Catholic priest is comfortable with his sexuality. The truths Dillon's characters get at through their game playing connect the men rather than divide them. *Party* is also a healthy celebration of male nudity and eroticism. Nudity has long been a staple of gay theater. Like everything else about *Party*, it's good clean fun.

My short play, *Dancing in the Mirror*, was first performed as part of the *Pieces of the Quilt* project of the Alma Defina Group in San Francisco. Sean San Jose, the project's artistic director, decided in 1994 to create a dramatic equivalent to the AIDS Quilt. The dramatic quilt San Jose has woven now consists of forty short plays by writers including Edward Albee, Lanford

Wilson, Craig Lucas, Maria Irene Fornes, Naomi Izuka, and Erin Cressida Wilson. The plays can be put together in a number of combinations or performed together in a dramatic marathon. They have been performed in hospitals, clinics, schools, libraries, theaters, community centers, and outdoors, and have raised over $50,000 for AIDS organizations.

Guillermo Reyes, a native of Chile, has lived in the U.S. since he was nine. He has an M.F.A. in Theater from the University of California at San Diego, one of our best centers of theater training. *Deporting the Divas*, Reyes's second major play (the first, *Men on the Verge of an His-Panic Breakdown*, has been successfully performed all over the U.S.) was first produced at Celebration Theatre in Los Angeles, which has developed a number of important gay theater works. After a run at Borderlands Theater in Tucson, Arizona (Reyes is playwright in residence at Arizona State University), the final version of the play opened at Theatre Rhinoceros in San Francisco, one of the oldest and most active of gay theaters. The progress of Reyes's play through some of the best small theaters in America is typical of the fate of the most adventurous American drama nowadays.

Deporting the Divas is part love story, part fantasy, part social satire, set on the border between Mexico and Southern California, but also set on the borders between Chicano and Anglo, gay and straight. Like all great satirists, Guillermo Reyes manages to offer hard truths in a manner that is pleasing and constantly surprising.

Neal Bell's *Somewhere in the Pacific* had its premiere at Manbites Dog Theater in Durham, North Carolina. Durham might seem an odd place to open a play by a highly acclaimed playwright who has won an Obie for Lifetime Achievement, but Bell has had a long, productive artistic collaboration with Duke University based director, Jody McAuliffe. Housed in a former printing company, Manbites Dog, founded in 1987 by Artistic Director Jeff Storer (also on the Duke faculty) and Managing Director Ed Hunt, has focused on cutting edge contemporary drama and performance with a particular interest in developing new work. Manbites Dog Theater also offers an annual festival of lesbian and gay theater.

Somewhere in the Pacific takes place on a cargo ship transporting sailors and marines to Japan during the final days of World War II. Dreams of violent death, memories of past betrayals, and sheer terror overwhelm the young men as they make what they think will be their last voyage. The permeable border between male comradeship and sex the military tries so hard to maintain keeps breaking down as intimacy is the only viable way of forgetting briefly the terror of war. Bell's powerful, highly original play zigzags back and forth in time as the ship zigzags to evade Japanese torpedoes. Don't expect a realistic war story. *Somewhere in the Pacific* is more like a dream.

Samuel Adamson's *Clocks and Whistles* premiered at the Bush Theatre at the far end of Shepherd's Bush Green in West London, an unlikely place for a center for exciting contemporary drama. The Bush was the birthplace of Jonathan Harvey's *Beautiful Thing*, that sweet love story of two teenage boys on a low-income housing estate that became a hit film, and of other major works of gay and straight theater. One enters the Bush through the Fringe and Firkin pub, climbs a narrow wooden stairway, checks for fire exits (useless) and enters a tiny playing space with cushioned risers on two sides. First timers at the Bush have to get used to being so close to their neighbors. Lean back and you rest against the knees of those in the next tier of risers. Eventually everyone gets into the intimate, festive spirit of the place.

Clocks and Whistles is the perfect Bush play. A debut work by a playwright in his twenties, it speaks of the sexual manners and mores of twenty-somethings in contemporary London. At its center are two relationships: the friendship of Henry and Anne and the love of Henry and Trevor. Anne wants more from Henry than he is capable of giving her or she is capable of returning. Henry and Trevor's love dare not speak its name, not because of legal or moral sanctions, but because of fear of commitment. This is not a gay play—the word gay is not mentioned—but a play about a network of social and sexual relations in a society disinclined to categorize desire. In its own economical way with prose as spare as that of Pinter or Mamet, *Clocks and Whistles* is the contemporary equivalent of a Restoration comedy.

Actor's Express in Atlanta is the love child of Chris Coleman, Georgia's answer to Orson Welles. Coleman produces, directs, acts, sings, and writes on occasion. His theater began in 1988 in a church basement, moved shortly thereafter to a small, Spartan space near Atlanta's funky Little Five Points neighborhood, and is now more comfortably settled amidst restaurants and galleries in the King Plow Center, an arts complex carved out of an old plow factory on the west side of this bustling, sprawling metropolis. Actor's Express presents a variety of work old and new, but none has been as successful as Steve Murray's *Rescue and Recovery*, which opened for a limited run in early July, 1999, and was still running in November. A New York production is now planned.

One of the aspects of contemporary gay film that particularly disturbs me is the misogynist pairing of a handsome, "together" gay man with a homely, dysfunctional straight woman (think of Tori Spelling in *Trick*, for instance). This convention implies that gay men cannot forge solid friendships with other gay men or non-neurotic women. The grotesque depiction of the women also implies a kind of masculine superiority. Steve Murray's *Rescue and Recovery* depicts a far more complex male-female friendship. The action begins with the breakup of Dr. Cameron Trace's marriage after he confessed to an affair with a male nurse. Though Janie, his ex-wife, no longer wants to be married to Cameron, she hopes they can have an ideal ex-husband and wife relationship. Amidst all the men who come into Cameron's life, his wife remains his only real friend until he betrays her once too often. In Murray's play, it's the gay man who is dysfunctional, but in ways that hold a mirror up to the foibles of a lot of contemporary men, gay or straight. Like *Clocks and Whistles*, *Rescue and Recovery* is a brilliant social satire; funny, sexy, and frighteningly on target.

Asking and Telling is evidence that gay drama is still thriving and that, if Broadway is becoming more Las Vegas than a center of good drama, venues in other American cities remind us that there are still a lot of fine playwrights working. I am also constantly in awe of how many fine actors and directors there are all over this country. Terrence McNally once wrote that he works in New York because that's where all the good actors are. He's wrong. The best productions I have seen of his plays were on the other side of the Hudson River. You're as likely to get a brilliant performance in Atlanta, Baltimore, or Indianapolis as you are in New York.

I have grouped the plays into three sections: "Parties," for obvious reasons, as you shall see; "Borders" for the plays of Guillermo Reyes and Neal Bell, which focus on maintaining and destroying false boundaries; and "Negotiations" for the plays of Samuel Adamson and Steve Murray which center on the making and unmaking of human connections. Since I have written at length about most of these plays in my book, *Still Acting Gay: Male Homosexuality in Modern Drama*, I have invited the playwrights to introduce their own works. Reading these plays will only give you a partial sense of the theatrical pleasures and power they offer. Talk your local theater into producing them so that you can get the full effect.

My thanks to Mark Glubke for supporting and publishing this collection. Thanks, too, to the playwrights and their agents—Bret Adams, Joyce Ketay, Carl Mulert, Mitch Douglas, Sebastian Born—for allowing these fine works to be published here. To the love of my life, Walter Melion, for helping me "pitch" this anthology and to Michael Flamini, the closest thing to a fairy godmother I have known, for cooking the fine dinner at which it was pitched on that cold Chelsea night, and for transforming my professional life. Finally, thanks to e-mail, which makes all things possible for us writers and editors.

PARTIES

PARTY

by David Dillon

Party was first produced by Bailiwick Repertory, David Zak, Executive Director, at the Theatre Building in Chicago on November 7, 1992 with the following cast:

Kevin	Jim Brown
Ray	Ted Bales
Philip	Robb Williams
Brian	Kellum Lewis
Peter	Nic Arnzen
James	Sal Iacopelli
Andy	Sam Sakharia
Directed by	David Dillon

Party opened off-Broadway on April 14, 1995 at the Douglas Fairbanks Theatre, 432 West 42nd Street, New York City, New York, produced by Michael Leavitt, Fox Theatricals, Leonard Soloway, Peter Breger, Jerry Frankel, Dennis J. Grimaldi and Steven M. Levy, with the following cast:

Kevin	David Pevsner
Ray	Ted Bales
Philip	Larry Alexander
Brian	Kellum Lewis
Peter	Tom Stuart
James	Jay Corcoran
Andy	Vince Gatton
Directed by	David Dillon
Set	James Noone
Costumes	Gail Cooper-Hecht
Lighting	Ken Billington
Sound	Tom Clark
Production Stage Manager	Bruce Greenwood
Assistant Stage Manager	Eric Bernat

Dedication

I'd like to dedicate *Party* to Elizabeth Marquis and Carolee Pearce, Harold Bush, Mary Lou Mosteller (who is *fabulous*) and to the many Party Boys, but especially the first magnificent seven.

AUTHOR'S INTRODUCTION

The last thing I expected to do in September of 1992 was write a play. While I always knew that someday I would write, I envisioned it to be later on in life, so the notion wasn't anywhere near the surface of my consciousness.

I had directed a gay play that summer as part of the Pride Series at Bailiwick Repertory in Chicago. It was a contemporary drama about two brothers, one gay, one straight, one dying of AIDS and the other too homophobic to cherish his brother's last days. I liked the play very much, the issues were powerful and moving and it was well received. So well received that Bailiwick's Executive Director, David Zak, called me in September to ask if I would be interested in directing another gay themed play for a six-week slot running late nights in November. He even went so far as to tell me I could choose my own script (with his ultimate nod of approval, of course). I agreed instantly.

I began reading. I read two or three scripts a day. I read submissions that David had received at the theater, I bought some plays I wasn't familiar with and I skimmed an anthology or two. In less than two weeks, I read in excess of forty scripts.

Some of them were very good, many were hopelessly ordinary and a few were, of course, appalling. After reading a dozen of them or so, I was suddenly struck by something extraordinary—every single play I had read shared one very startling trait. Once it dawned on me and the significance of it sank in, I was stunned. Without exception, every one of the plays I'd read dealt with how difficult and painful it is to be gay. I think that was precisely why I had not been drawn to any of them. I didn't go into this process knowing it, but I realized I had tired of all the "issue" plays we'd been steeped in for so long. It had been years since I had gone to see a gay play and simply laughed. I couldn't remember the last time I smiled up at a stage with the fond recognition that I knew those people, that I was seeing a piece of my world and loving the fact that it *was* my world. I had suffered losses, I had watched loved ones die and there were people close to me who were grappling with being positive and enduring the pharmaceutical merry-go-round as an unpleasant but by now familiar fact of life. But, it was also profoundly clear to me that we did not live the nightmare twenty-four hours a day. We often went for days . . . weeks . . . without ever mentioning "it." It did not define us and it did not rule us. Yet, each time I went to the theater to see a gay play, I felt bombarded with only the worst parts of our lives. I knew in that instant the sort of play I wanted to find and I went on a quest. I rejected the weight of a dark and unbelievably sad decade and wanted, more than anything, to say something positive. I wanted, very simply, to say that in spite of everything, it's fabulous to be gay and I set out to find a play that would make that statement.

I never found one.

If I thought it was unbelievable that the first twelve or fifteen plays I read were all about the anguish of gay life, imagine my dismay in finding the thread unbroken after forty plays! Not one single script celebrated the joys in gay life. Not one play would have convinced a straight audience that a gay man could be something other than wretchedly miserable. And, perhaps most important, not one of them validated what I knew was one of the most cherished parts of my life—being a gay man.

Play after play examined illness, AIDS, death, homophobia, bashing, hate crimes, suicide, families disowning their gay children, and every form of discrimination and victimization imaginable. If they dealt with sex, it was dark and seedy sex and every relationship was either abusive or full of deceit. It was as though we had discovered some divine nobility in being victims. I began to wonder if we had actually made any real strides since Stonewall, for if we had, how could our voices be so relentlessly dark?

Let me clarify one point. Each of the issues these plays explored were and are perfectly valid subjects about which to write. Many of the scripts were very good and deserved to be produced. But, I was resolved to present the flip side of gay life, the part of the story that was not being represented and not being celebrated as far as I could see. I asked myself what I would want to see as an audience member. I knew that I wanted it to be a comedy. Laughter is not only a great healer, it is something that, when experienced in a group, creates a shared, intimate and equalizing sense of belonging. I recalled the time I first saw *The Women* in a movie theater with an entirely gay audience one Sunday afternoon when I was still in college. It was the first time in my life I genuinely felt that I belonged to a large body of people with whom I could enjoy the shared sensibilities that had always made me the alien before. I loved being gay that day. Though it's easy to neglect it, I think it's important to replenish that spirit on a steady basis.

I isolated what I considered to be the most positive things I associated with gay life, knowing, of course, that my truths would not be everyone else's truth, but I needed a clear point of view. I wanted to say that our friendships are very important to us, that we can have healthy relationships, that we are more honest about sex than any other cultural sub-group, that we are capable of genuinely enjoying ourselves and each other, that we have a keen appreciation for the arts and for pop culture, that the camp sensibility is a divine gift, and that we have incredible taste. Hell, we're so fabulous, we discovered Bette Midler!

I also wanted something unabashedly sex positive. The eighties had cast a gloom over sex and I thought it was time we reclaimed our libidos and recognized that, while the virus may be bad, sex is good. For me, sex has always been a sort of celebration of being gay and being male and I hoped to capture that essence in something sex positive without being sleazy or pornographic. (This was certainly one role the nudity would play in the show, along with its metaphorical purpose in posing the question of when we are most vulnerable. However, my political motives regarding nudity were equally strong, but my dissertation on male nudity in arts and entertainment forms could fill the remainder of this volume, so I will save it for another occasion.) I began to think of how I could combine all these elements situationally and what structure I could utilize to call them all into play.

That's when it hit me.

A couple of months before, I had been to a party of about six gay male friends and we played "Truth or Dare." Madonna's movie had come out the year before and had sparked a resurgence in what we had all dismissed as a high school game years ago. I think I was at three parties that year where we ended up playing it. At any rate, this most recent one was a truly wonderful evening. We had great fun, we laughed incessantly, we learned a lot about each other, we each confronted and broke down a mild barrier or two, we definitely became closer as a result and, oh yes, we all ended up naked. But nothing sexual happened, which was actually pretty wonderful. I had remembered thinking after that party how it sort of summed up for me all that I love about being gay. It seemed to define and celebrate who we were as gay men. Sure, during the course of the game, some questions were asked which brought to the surface less happy times, but the point was, if any of us had troubles, they were *human* troubles, not *gay* troubles. We were a group of guys for whom being gay was not a problem in the least.

So, I decided that if I could not find a play that said what I wanted to say that I would write my own. The idea that I could make my statement in its entirety and in my own voice was exhilarating. I decided to take the situation and the characteristics of the real life party I'd been to and apply them to a fictional group of characters, relationships and situations. So, while *Party* would bear little resemblance to its real-life inspiration in a factual sense, I hoped I would be able to capture the spirit that we had all experienced.

I had been recovering from the break up of an eight-year relationship that year and I was staying at the time with my wonderful friends Beth and Carolee in their house in Berwyn (a Chicago suburb). I lived in the downstairs which was quiet and had a desk and a computer, so I isolated myself and began to write.

Four days later, I had my first draft. I gave it to David Zak, he thought it was "a hoot," he made a couple of excellent suggestions, I did a rewrite and we were holding auditions less than two weeks from the day I started writing the play—that's how fast it all went. I was blessed to find a wonderful, dedicated, and brave cast and we started to work with no idea whatsoever of how we would be received. It was a bit scary for all of us. And, as I've always said, the only thing worse than being in a flop is being naked in a flop.

We opened for our six-week run in November of 1992 and with extensions at Bailiwick and then a commercial transfer to another theater, the original production of *Party* ran for over two years, closing on New Year's Eve, 1994. It opened in New York in the spring of 1995 where it was greeted more enthusiastically than we'd ever imagined, another company opened in Los Angeles that fall, in London in 1998 and in many other cities in various countries since moving on from its Chicago roots. It has been an amazing odyssey, though not always a joyous one, unfortunately. There is definite truth to the old "be careful what you wish for" caveat. Yet, I can never look back and not be grateful for a number of things. The opportunity Bailiwick and David presented to me back in 1992 is the stuff playwrights dream about. I found a first cast who dedicated themselves to the play's message so that their audiences couldn't help but see their truth. And, without the very genuine heart they brought onstage with them, an ensemble comedy with a bunch of (naked) guys romping around at a party would be walking on very thin ice. For, though I am the first to admit that *Party* is a light and frilly affair, I have always been deadly serious about its message and by a wonderful stroke of luck, I found seven guys who felt exactly the same. We truly believed that, in our own way, we were making a political and a radical statement by saying "Goddamnit, we can be gay **and** be happy!" Those seven guys were an army of commitment and what I owe to them is incalculable.

Oh, and I feel lucky in one more way, too. If even just *one* of those forty scripts I read had been funny and positive . . .

DAVID DILLON
Los Angeles, 2000

Characters

KEVIN   Very late 20s to late 30s. Attractive, but not overly gorgeous or gym-perfect. A theatrical director also currently working in advertising—directing commercials and industrials. He teaches theater classes as well. Recently ended a seven-year relationship. Is sensitive, funny, and intelligent. The perfect husband.

RAY   30–40ish. A priest. Is very comfortable being gay. Has a pretty active libido which he manages to keep contained. Very loose, funny, outrageous. Teaches theater and arts appreciation in high school. Kevin's best friend for thirteen years. *Not* a queen. His sense of humor contains elements of camp, but it is *imperative* that we believe he could function in a parish and that parents would feel comfortable having him teach their children. His humor is a humor of words and ideas, he is *not* nellie or mincing. It is always a challenge for the actor playing Ray to walk this line, but it is the essence of his character that the actor succeed. Costume Note: He should *not* wear priest garb. A turtleneck and dark jacket work best depending on your climate.

PHILIP   Late 20s–30s. Owns a travel agency. Attractive and very easygoing. Masculine, but in a very natural way, not playing butch or trying to be "straight acting/appearing." Everybody's best friend. Great sense of humor, extremely likeable. Sexually, he is a Top.

BRIAN   Mid to late 20s. A dancer/singer/actor. Has a great body (particularly his butt, which is quite remarkable) and he dresses to show it off. Very "out." Can be a little flip and jaded. *Loves* sex. Is a *huge* bottom and looks upon sex as a fabulous celebration of being male and being gay. Lives for fun, but is responsible about how he pursues it. Great sense of humor.

JAMES   Late 20s–40. A leather Top. Butch. Attractive. A little too serious at times, needs to lighten up. Proud to be gay, but shuns feminine gay stereotypes. Has no appreciation for gay pop culture, so it may seem at times that he has little in common with some of the others at the party. Not true, though. Deep down, a strong sense of friendship binds all these guys together and James is no exception. He may love to spar with Ray, and he may think Ray's obsessions with things like musical theater are a nightmare, but there is very real caring under the surface. Has a quiet strength—even when he is quiet, the wheels are always turning. Costume Note: James should look like a leatherman without beating the audience over the head with it—black boots, Levi 501s—either black or worn blue—and a leather motorcycle jacket when he comes in depending upon climate works just fine. A black leather cockring is also a good touch.

ANDY   21–22. Very cute. Somewhat naïve, but only due to inexperience and not being exposed to things—he is not stupid, just unworldly, so he's slow on the uptake. Likes to have fun but is easily shocked. A college student studying acting. Shy and innocent.

PETER   22 years old. Very attractive, but maybe or maybe not in a conventionally perfect way. A great smile. A former student of Kevin's, now his roommate (platonic). Currently in college with Andy (he wants to be a set and costume designer) and interning with a local opera company. The defining term for Peter is "charm." Always smiling, always laughing, always a great audience for everyone around him, he is the ideal boyfriend/lover for every gay man. He is in love with Kevin, but he has never let on to anyone. He is intelligent, extremely mature for his age, and enormously together for such a young person.

Author's Notes

It has always been my intention that *Party* be set in the city in which it is being performed as I think the play supports that immediacy and familiarity nicely and audiences always seem to respond warmly to this indirect connection with the guys onstage. For publishing purposes, we have selected the New York version of the script, but the references are adaptable to any locale.

It is *very* important to understand that these characters are *very* comfortable with being gay. For these guys, being gay is *not* a problem. If they have troubles in their lives, they are human troubles, not gay troubles. They are never ugly or bitter with each other. Any bitchy humor comes from a place of affection, not of underlying issues. This level of comfort allows them to enjoy a sense of humor and rapport that is very specifically gay, yet not necessarily nellie or queeny. This is not to say that they cannot call upon these characteristics when they desire to, it merely does not define them. It is not without their awareness that they apply these sensibilities.

Some stage notes are given regarding when characters drink, smoke, and ad lib, but in general, the play should be treated as a party. The actors should be encouraged to move around, whisper, laugh, drink, have munchies and generally create as natural a party atmosphere as possible. They should have *fun*. The choices of music and major stage directions should be treated as part of the script and should not be changed without the author's consent.

As ensemble is the essence of this show, the curtain call is to be an ensemble bow. No one is to be given a solo or "star" bow. For production purposes, you may consider this a directive which is part of the script. Further, though it should, I hope, be obvious, it is stated here that the curtain call for this play is *not* to be done in the nude. The actors are to be covered for their bows. The bows in Chicago, New York, and Los Angeles were always to the disco version of "Don't Cry for Me, Argentina" by Festival. The author recommends the use of this music in order to unify the spirit of all productions, but this is not at all required. This cut is available on CD.

Party is not to be performed either in an amateur or professional situation regardless of whether or not admission is charged, without an executed license agreement and the payment of appropriate royalties. Contact the author's representative regarding obtaining a license.

Be aware that in addition to obvious infractions such as changing dialogue, changes such as adding an intermission, having any actor not do the nudity the script calls for or altering the specific music choices without written permission shall be considered a breach of your license agreement and is actionable.

Setting

The living room of Kevin's apartment

Time

Tonight

Party is to be performed with no intermission.

The living room of Kevin's apartment. It may be a rehab or a high-rise, but it should indicate that its owner is not a starving artist. There is a sofa, a large square coffee table, an easy chair and a bar with a small refrigerator, among other furnishings. There should be subtle or not-so-subtle touches that say gay or "show business," but everything should be tasteful without being queenie or froofy. In New York and Los Angeles, one wall was covered with a series of seven "Sweet Charity" posters—Gwen Verdon (her original and the second Anniversary Broadway poster which was of a different design), Chita Rivera (U.S. National Tour), Juliet Prowse (London), Debbie Allen, Ann Reinking and Donna McKechnie (revivals). Obviously, not every production needs to or can do this, but something along those lines is a fun idea. There are two entrances/exits—the front door and a hallway leading off to the bedrooms, kitchen, john, etc. After house announcements (if you do any) or at the end of pre-show music, The Weather Girls' "It's Raining Men" plays. It should play for a minute and a half or so before the lights begin to fade. The music fades out in the black and the first verse (not the intro—the first verse—beginning with the lyric "You're the top, you're the Coliseum. . . .") of the Lincoln Center revival recording of "Anything Goes" bumps up with the lights and plays throughout the scene. It is suggested that the music level be strong at the beginning and gradually fade once dialogue begins so as not to overtake the actors. At rise, Kevin is at the bar, mixing shots in a pitcher—slammers or kool-aids or some other sort of fruity red thing. He finishes the mixing, perhaps tastes it. When he is done, he moves the pitcher to the coffee table. Ray enters from the kitchen carrying two bowls of snacks.

RAY (*from off*): Sweetie Darling! (*Entering*) I found these in the kitchen. Are they okay?

KEVIN: That's great.

RAY (*he places them on the coffee table. He then takes a Sun Chip from one* *of the bowls, tastes it and grimaces*): Ugh—these Sun Chips are terrible! They taste like French Onion flavored gravel on toasted cardboard. Who would eat this crap? (*He throws the chip he just took a bite out of back into the bowl on the coffee table*)

KEVIN: James and Philip like them.

RAY: I hate healthy people. Lemon chicken Chelsea fags who don't smoke, don't drink—always health, health, health. It's a nightmare.

KEVIN: James is hardly a lemon chicken fag. And Philip drinks.

RAY: Yeah, but he goes to the gym, so it cancels out all the good the alcohol does. Is it too late to run out for some Ho-Hos or Ding Dongs? Something with a little salt or sugar or fat?

KEVIN: Calm down, darling. I didn't forget about you. There's garbage food too. I got your favorites.

RAY: You mean . . . ?

KEVIN: Be right back.

RAY: Oh, goody, goody!

KEVIN (*indicating some ashtrays*): Will you put the ashtrays out for me?

(*Kevin goes off to kitchen. Ray puts out the ashtrays, lights a cigarette and mouths or sings with the recording, perhaps doing a little Patti LuPone homage. Kevin re-enters with a bowl*)

RAY: My babies! My jewels! My Bugles! (*He grabs some bugles snacks from the bowl and puts them on his fingers like long fingernails. With a wisp through his hair and a cross of the eyes, he does a little Streisand*) "People . . . people who need people . . ."

KEVIN: Knock off the Barbra and get me the shot glasses.

RAY: Where do you keep them?

KEVIN: I left them on top of the dishwasher.

(*Ray exits to kitchen. Kevin continues to straighten up. He grabs some small couch pillows, fluffs them and starts to place them on the sofa, asymmetrically. Ray re-enters with a tray of shot glasses which he places on the coffee table*)

RAY: Here you go, darling.

KEVIN: Thanks. (*Remembers something and darts off to kitchen*)

(*Ray passes the couch and blanches. With a roll of the eyes towards the off-stage Kevin, Ray switches the pillows to make them symmetrical. Kevin re-enters with another bowl of munchies for the coffee table*)

RAY: Where's Peter? He *is* joining us tonight, isn't he?

KEVIN: He had to work till eight. He should be home soon.

RAY: He is such a cutie. I hope someone makes me kiss him or something.

KEVIN: You'd better behave tonight or you're gonna go to hell. Didn't you take a vow of chastity?

RAY: Of course I did. But I also took a vow of obedience. So, if someone tells me to kiss the boy, you can see my predicament. (*He lies across Kevin's lap*)

(*The doorbell rings*)

KEVIN: Get off me you skinny old queer. (*He goes to press door buzzer*)

RAY (*going to turn off stereo*): You better be nice to me tonight or I'll make you tell everyone the story about your secret nickname.

KEVIN: You wouldn't dare!

RAY: Wouldn't I?

KEVIN: Then I'll tell the story about you getting caught running that wet altar boy contest at the rectory.

RAY: What? I never did that!

KEVIN: Yes, but who will they believe?

RAY: Evil! Evil, vicious and nasty!

KEVIN: Do you want something to drink?

RAY: Sure . . . I'm easy. How about some white wine?

KEVIN: Isn't that a little predictable for you? (*He goes to the bar to pour Ray some wine*)

RAY: Only if it's blessed.

KEVIN: That's all you ever drink anymore. I think they brainwashed you in priest school.

RAY: I happen to like wine. (*There is a knock at the door*) And it isn't called "priest school."

(*Kevin goes to answer the door. Philip enters*)

KEVIN: Philip!

PHILIP: Hey, Kevin. (*Hugging him*) How's it going? Ray! (*Hugging him*) How are you?

RAY: Oh, I'm exhausted from helping Kevin get ready. It was grueling! Shot glasses, pillows, flowers, ashtrays, posters, Sun Chips—it was a nightmare.

(*Doorbell rings—Kevin presses buzzer*)

KEVIN: Maybe for once this bunch'll actually be on time.

PHILIP: Who all is coming?

KEVIN: Well, besides us, Peter, Brian, James, and a friend of Peter's from school named Andy who you haven't met yet.

PHILIP: Oh, a new addition. Cute?

KEVIN: Yeah, but he's kind of young. (*To Ray*) So, be nice! He took one of my classes at the Studio last year. He's a real sweet kid, but he's a little shy and I don't think he's got a lot of gay friends. So, Peter and I thought it would be a good idea to invite him tonight.

PHILIP: Great!

KEVIN (*to Philip*): What can I get you to drink?

PHILIP: Beer?

KEVIN: Coming right up. (*He gets Philip a beer from the refrigerator and gets one for himself. He gives Philip his beer then goes off to the kitchen*)

PHILIP: So, what's new with you?

RAY: Same old thing—teaching, lecturing, saving souls—the usual. Oh, they want me to do a *"20/20"*—what will probably be a very heated debate on capital punishment and they want a representative of the church to discuss the old "eye for an eye" versus "Thou shalt not kill" argument. God, I hate those things—it's like abortion—everyone has such strong opinions and sometimes it's hard for me. I have to bite my tongue because I don't always agree with our "official" position on things.

PHILIP: So, where do you stand personally on capital punishment? Pro? Con?

RAY: Oh, I'm for it, but only under certain select circumstances.

PHILIP: Like what?

RAY: Well, I think it should only be applied to people like Manson, Gacy, Jeffrey Dahmer, Geraldo Rivera, and most Republicans. Other than that, I'm strongly opposed.

(*Knock at the door. Ray goes to answer it*)

PHILIP: I'd throw in Kathie Lee too if I had a vote.

RAY: Oh, absolutely! She is so fucking perky she drives me crazy! (*Ray* *opens door. Brian enters carrying a brown grocery bag)* Brian! How are you, love?

BRIAN (*hugging Ray*): I'm fine, you sleazy whore, you!

RAY: That's *Father* sleazy whore to you, you little tramp.

(*As each of the guys enter, the placement of hellos and hugs they will do with each of the others should be what works for your staging*)

KEVIN (*re-entering*): Brian!

BRIAN: Kevin! (*Handing Kevin the bag*) Here—I brought some beer.

KEVIN: You didn't have to do that. It's my turn . . .

BRIAN (*cutting him off*): Oh, shut up. I knew Ray would be here, so I worried about you running out of stuff.

RAY: You are too amusing. I haven't had this many genuine laughs since *Ishtar.*

KEVIN (*to Brian*): Do you want one?

BRIAN: Yeah.

KEVIN: I have some cold ones in the fridge. I'll get you one of those and put these in.

BRIAN: Cool.

(*Kevin loads Brian's beers into the fridge and pulls a cold one out for Brian*)

PHILIP (*to Brian*): So, what are you working on now?

BRIAN: *42nd Street.* Again. This'll be my fourth time. I swore I would never do that show again. Last time I sprained my ankle on one of those fucking dimes and had to go to physical therapy. Oh, but you should have seen the guy they sent me to. Tony. Yum! A dick as big as a baseball bat.

PETER (*entering through the front door*): Have I missed anything yet?

BRIAN: Peter!

RAY: Not a thing, sweetie. We were just discussing . . . sports equipment with Brian.

PETER: How is everyone? (*Going to each of them—hugs, etc.*)

RAY (*hugging Peter*): Don't you look cute tonight?

PETER (*hugging Ray*): Always for you. (*Going to Philip*) And speaking of cute . . . (*Hugs him*)

PHILIP: Hi, Peter. It's good to see you again. I keep missing you whenever I'm over.

PETER: I know. I'm almost never here. My work schedule has been really crazy, and I'm interning this semester and designing a show at school.

KEVIN: I didn't think you'd get here for another half hour or so.

PETER: Yeah, for once I actually got out on time. (*Goes to Brian*) Hey, how are you?

BRIAN: Fabulous.

KEVIN (*to Peter*): You want something?

PETER: Oh, it's okay, I can get it. Be right back. (*Goes off to his bedroom—doorbell rings—Kevin goes to press buzzer*)

BRIAN: Kevin—how's it working out with Peter?

KEVIN: Perfect. I was a little apprehensive about having a roommate, but I kind of like having someone around again.

PHILIP: I could never live with someone unless I was married to them. It's too hard to be yourself when someone's always around.

RAY: Are you and Peter planning on getting married, Kevin?

KEVIN: No! He's just a real nice kid. We got to be really good friends last year while we were working on that benefit. I like him, and we get along really well. Besides, I'm *never* getting married again.

BRIAN: Never say never.

PHILIP: Yeah, who knows? It's always when you aren't looking for it that you find it.

RAY: Oh, leave him alone. He's not ready for another relationship yet. It's been all we can do to make him forget about what's-his-name.

BRIAN: Matt?

RAY: Ssssshhhhh! Don't remind him. He'll get all depressed and we'll have to hide all the sharp objects and listen to Piaf all night.

PETER (*Peter re-entering with a beer*): Piaf?

RAY: A tragic French chanteuse. Dead, you know. (*On "dead," he flicks his ashes on the floor in a Bette Davis move—this distresses Kevin*)

PETER: I know who Piaf is. I meant, what about her?

PHILIP: Nothing. Just one of Kevin's favorite singers, that's all.

PETER: I didn't know that. I love Edith Piaf. I've never heard you listen to her.

RAY: We've tried to wean him away. It isn't good for his moods. He starts moping around, dressing in black, and throwing bread crumbs to all the sparrows. It's positively depressing.

(*Knock on door. Kevin goes to answer it*)

KEVIN: Can we drop this?

RAY: Not on your life.

(*Kevin opens door. James and Andy enter*)

JAMES: Hey, look what I found hanging around downstairs. (*Indicating Andy*)

RAY: My God, leave a door open in this neighborhood, and you never know what you'll find.

KEVIN (*going to them*): Hello, boys. (*Kisses James*) Hi, sweetie. (*Kisses Andy*) Come on in and say your hellos. Oh, and, everyone, this is Andy. Andy, that's Ray, Brian and Philip, you already know Peter, of course. And you've just met James. (*As Kevin introduces Andy to each of them, they wave, say hi, etc.*)

ANDY (*afraid they may have taken James seriously, Andy nervously tries to explain himself*): I wasn't hanging around downstairs, we were just coming in at the same time.

(*They all stop momentarily, not sure what to make of this and do a bit of a take to each other before Kevin breaks the silence and the guys all say their hellos and kiss and hug*)

KEVIN: What can I get you guys to drink? James? Iced tea?

JAMES: If you've got it.

KEVIN: Andy?

ANDY: I guess a beer.

KEVIN: Regular or lite?

ANDY: Oh, it doesn't matter. Lite, I guess.

KEVIN: You got it.

(*Kevin busies himself getting their drinks. The guys all settle in. There is a silence when everyone's attention is focused on Andy as the new kid on the block. In particular, Ray examines him to the amusement of the others*)

RAY (*suddenly breaking the silence and startling poor Andy*): So, Andy, we understand you go to school with Peter.

ANDY: Yeah, except I'm not graduating this year. I still have another one to go.

PHILIP: And you took one of Kevin's classes?

ANDY: Yeah. Acting for film. I'd never taken a camera class before.

JAMES: So, is this everybody?

PHILIP: Looks that way.

BRIAN: What about Bob?

RAY: He and Sean are out of town. It's just us tonight, babycakes.

BRIAN: Oh, right. They went to D.C. Did they end up driving or flying?

PHILIP: Flying. We got them a great rate.

RAY: I hate flying. I much prefer to drive places. You get to see the country that way.

PHILIP: I will never drive a long distance with you again as long as I live.

RAY: I am a perfectly charming travel companion. What are you talking about?

PHILIP: You were unbearable when you and Kevin and I drove to Philadelphia.

KEVIN: Oh, don't start on the Philadelphia trip.

PETER: What happened?

RAY: Absolutely nothing. The three of us drove down to visit Sean—that was before he moved to New York. I thought we had a lovely time.

PHILIP: We did. Except that you didn't stop singing the whole way there. You made me crazy. And then, in Newark, I almost killed you.

RAY: Oh, I'd forgotten about Newark.

ANDY: What happened in Newark?

PHILIP: Well, it wasn't actually *in* Newark. It was while we were driving *through* Newark. See, Ray had insisted on us all having lunch together before we left. So, we met at a little coffee shop, had a bite, and then took off.

PETER: So?

PHILIP: So, what does Ray order for lunch? Chili. Extra hot. Now, is that the sort of thing you'd order for lunch before being cooped up in a car for hours?

RAY: Who was thinking?

PHILIP: So, just as you'd expect, all of a sudden Ray lets loose with the most ferocious gas leak you've ever encountered. And not just one, but a whole string of them. It was the first time in modern history anyone ever had to open up their windows in Newark for fresh air.

(*They all laugh*)

BRIAN: Why are farts so funny?

PHILIP: You wouldn't have been laughing that day, believe me.

KEVIN: We were striking matches for the next ten minutes.

RAY: I hardly think one little mishap makes me a terrible traveling companion. Philip, I am very hurt.

PHILIP: Oh, sure you are.

BRIAN (*seeing pitcher*): Hey, what's that?

KEVIN: Shots.

PHILIP: Oh good. I think we should do a dozen or so before we start.

ANDY: I've never played this game before. It makes me nervous.

BRIAN: Oh, it's fun. You'd be surprised how much you learn about people. You talk about things you usually don't talk about, you let down your inhibitions, you get close to people. I think it's fun.

PETER: I'm with Andy. I'm scared of you guys.

PHILIP: Why?

RAY: Because you're a bunch of evil, vicious, immoral perverts who are going to make them do terrible things. (*Pause*) I hope.

PETER: Who made up this game?

BRIAN: This chick I did *A Chorus Line* with. We even had real decks of cards made. So, I suggested it for tonight.

ANDY: So, you guys do other things too?

KEVIN: We do something different every time we get together. Like, last month we had a "celebrity" party.

JAMES: Oh, I hated that game.

RAY: Why? I loved it!

JAMES: Of course you loved it—you won. You put in all those hard names like Coco Chanel and what is that woman's name? Stich? Stretch?

RAY: Elaine Stritch you philistine!

JAMES: Right—like we should all know Elaine Stritch.

RAY: She was the original Joanne in *Company*, she was in the concert version of *Follies* at Lincoln Center, she did *Showboat* on Broadway . . .

JAMES: Oh, forgive me! Like we should all know that!

BRIAN: I knew her.

KEVIN: Yeah, but you're in the business. It may be a little obscure for a normal crowd.

RAY (*indignantly*): She was in *Cocoon II*. She played Mia Farrow's mother in the movie *September* . . .

PHILIP: Oh, that wasn't the worst one though. What was that one name you put in that no one but you could even pronounce?

JAMES: Oh, right. I forgot about that one. What was it?

RAY (*haughtily*): Maria Ouspenskaya.

JAMES: I rest my case.

RAY: I cannot help it if you do not know some of the leading figures in the history of film and theater.

JAMES: Leading figures? Maria what's her name?

RAY (*to James*): Well, what about you putting in all those sports figures? Like anyone in this bunch knows any football players. Well, except, of course for Dick Butkus. Somehow that name always stuck with me.

JAMES: Oh, I am so sorry that your knowledge of public figures is so limited. I think that a world class athlete is as valid a name as some show tune diva no one's ever heard of.

RAY: Show tune diva! You ignorant buffalo!

JAMES: Nellie snob!

BRIAN: You guys are not going to settle this argument, so just kiss and make up so we can move on. This is getting boring.

RAY: (*to James*): Come on, kiss, kiss.

JAMES: I wouldn't kiss you if you were the last hole on earth.

RAY: Bitter, bitter, bitter! Really, Darling, you must do something about your people skills.

(*This banter, though it may sound harsh, is not ugly—it's the way they talk to each other—nothing more, nothing less*)

BRIAN: Alexis! Crystal! You're both pretty! (*Getting down to business*)

Okay, first, I think we should all do a shot to officially get the party started. Any objections?

PETER: No—only I think I need a tumbler of shots to be ready for this.

ANDY: Okay by me.

KEVIN (*starts pouring shots for everyone*): Brian, why don't you do the rules and I'll pour.

BRIAN: Okay. It's really easy. The game is called "Facts and Fantasies." There are twenty-five cards in this deck. Some say "Fact," some say "Fiction," some say "Fantasy," and some say "Flip." We decide who goes first. That person then picks anyone in the room and tells them to draw a card. When you draw, though, keep it to yourself—don't show it to us. If you draw a "Fact" or "Fiction" card, tell us you drew a "Fact" card. Then, the person who picked you asks you a question. If you *did* draw a "Fact" card, you have to answer the question truthfully. If you drew a "Fiction" card, you answer the question, but you lie—you make up an answer and try to fake us out. Then, when you're done answering, we all guess whether you told the truth or lied. *Then*, you show us the card. Of course, if it's something about the person you already know, you shouldn't vote.

PETER: How do you know for sure that they're being honest if they say their answer is true?

BRIAN: You're always honest in this game. It's like Truth or Dare. There's something about it—this honor thing—you just can't lie. It's weird. Anyway, so if you draw a "Fantasy" or "Flip" card, just tell us you drew a "Fantasy" card. Then, the person who picked you gives you a fantasy to act out. If the card you drew *was* a "Fantasy" card, *you have to do it*. If the card you drew was a "Flip" card, you get to make somebody *else* do the fantasy—even the person who gave it to you if you want.

ANDY: And you have to do it no matter what it is?

BRIAN: No matter what it is.

PETER: You can't like, pass or something?

BRIAN: Nope. They can tell you to do whatever they want, and you have to do it.

KEVIN (*passing out shots*): Okay—shots are ready.

PETER: Thank God!

RAY: Ah, let's see . . .

(*Everyone but James takes one. Andy looks for one to give James*)

JAMES: I don't drink.

RAY: A toast. To . . .

KEVIN: To . . . us!

(*They all clink glasses—James toasts with his iced tea*)

PETER: Cheers.

RAY: Up your bum!

KEVIN: You're a sick man.

RAY: Whatever . . .

(*They all drink. After the toast, they all settle in. Ray lights a cigarette*)

ANDY: That's good. What is it?

KEVIN: Just some fruity thing they make at the bars.

BRIAN: I love those fruity sissy drinks. You drink them like they're nothing and then they hit you—bam! A couple more, and somebody may be able to take advantage of me.

KEVIN: A couple more and everyone may be able to take advantage of you.

BRIAN: Whoo! Gang bang after the game! We'll go in ascending order of size, working up to the biggest. Who's first?

(*Kevin points to Ray, which Ray does not notice at first. When he does, he smacks Kevin*)

PHILIP: Like anyone would answer that question.

BRIAN: Okay. I'll just have to find these things out for myself.

PETER: Okay, so getting back to these rules—are there any limits or anything? I mean people just can't tell you to do anything?

BRIAN: No limits.

JAMES: None?

BRIAN: Well, I mean, if someone tells you to murder someone, you obviously aren't going to do it. I mean, no limits within reason.

JAMES: How do you define reason?

ANDY: Yeah. Like things could get pretty wild. Aren't there limits, like— sexually?

BRIAN: Not really. Well, I guess it could be going too far to tell someone to blow everyone here.

RAY: Not necessarily.

BRIAN: I don't think you need to worry about it. The game can't really go further than everyone wants it to. So, if it's a conservative group playing, it's pretty tame. If everyone is a major sex fiend, then who cares anyway?

RAY: I vote we play the sex fiend version.

JAMES: You're a priest!

PHILIP: That's true. There should be some special rules for Ray. If you think something is beyond your limits—religiously—then you should be able to pass. (*To the group*) Don't you think?

BRIAN: No!

PETER: No fair! He gets to pass and no one else can?

KEVIN: Hey! Ray has taken vows. I think that's fair. But only him.

RAY: Well, thank you, Pat Robertson. I can take care of myself, I'll know what's okay and what isn't. You all don't have to play vice squad.

PETER: So, who goes first?

PHILIP: I think Kevin should go first since it's his house.

JAMES: Sounds fair.

PHILIP: Is that okay with everyone?

(*They all indicate it's okay*)

KEVIN: Let's see. Umm . . . Okay, Philip. Draw a card.

PHILIP (*with a slight wince, he does*)**:** It's a Fact card.

KEVIN: Okay. We'll do something innocuous first. Philip, what's the most embarrassing thing that ever happened to you?

PHILIP: The most embarrassing thing . . . Let's see. (*Thinks*) Oh, okay. Well, I was in college, and I wasn't out to my family, but I did have a boyfriend at school. Well, my birthday was coming up, and it fell on a weekend that year, so my family invited me home to spend my birthday. And, I asked if they'd mind if I brought a friend home with me—that way my boyfriend Richard could come with me. So, they said fine—and, so we left after our last class on Friday, and got to my folks' house Friday night. Now, my parents had told me that they had plans that night, but we'd all do something on Saturday. So, when Richard and I got there, my parents were on their way out the door, but my Mom told me she'd put some chicken in the oven for us for dinner. She had set the timer in the kitchen and said it would go off in an hour and that I had to take the chicken out right away then or else it would burn, so I should listen for the timer. So, anyway, they left, and Richard and I immediately went up to my bedroom. Well, we were having this incredible sex—for what must have been a long time—because we heard the timer go off in the kitchen. For a minute I thought—"Fuck the chicken, let it burn," but I knew my

Mom would kill me when she got home, so Richard and I stopped what we were doing to get the damn chicken. Well, we were being really silly, so he got on my shoulders and we ran down the stairs—laughing and screaming, both of us with raging hard-ons, and flew through the swinging doors into the kitchen—and, there is my entire family (*the guys gasp and roar*) parents, grandparents, aunts, uncles, cousins even—all shouting "Happy Birthday!" You should have seen their faces when they got a load of the two of us—Richard on my shoulders, stark naked, dicks to the sky. I thought I'd drop dead right there. I thought my grandmother would too. The poor thing just sort of fell screaming into the deli tray. I was totally mortified.

RAY: Well, there is a bright side—at least you never had to sit them down and say "I have something to tell you."

PHILIP: No, that night sort of did the trick.

BRIAN: Jesus! Well, okay—now, do you think he was telling the truth or bluffing?

KEVIN: Oh, that's right. We have to vote now. Well, I guess he *could* be lying.

PETER: Oh, I don't think so. It was pretty detailed.

KEVIN: Yeah, but, I've known him a pretty long time. If that had really happened, I think I would've heard that story by now.

BRIAN: But where would he have come up with that?

JAMES: Ah, but bluffing is the point of the game. I think he was lying.

RAY: Really? I believed it. (*To Philip*) You poor dear.

BRIAN: Okay—hands. How many think he was telling the truth? (*Andy, Peter, Ray, and Brian raise their hands*) Four. Okay, James and Kevin— you think he's lying?

JAMES: Yup.

KEVIN: Yeah, what the hell.

BRIAN: Philip? (*Does drum roll*)

PHILIP: (*revealing Fiction card*): Suckers!

RAY: How did you make that up?

PETER: I was sure that really happened.

PHILIP: It did. (*Brief pause*) Just not to me. It happened to Mark Peterson, my old college roommate, except in his story it was his girlfriend.

JAMES: His girlfriend had a hard-on?

RAY: You used someone else's story? What, we get to plagiarize our old school chums? Oh, goody—how Joe Biden.

PHILIP: Now, I get to go. Brian—draw a card.

BRIAN (*He does*): Fact.

PHILIP: Who would you say is the sexiest guy you've ever been with?

BRIAN: The sexiest? God, there have been so many!

RAY: Narrow it down to the top few hundred and then just pick one. (*Brian thinks for a bit—hems and haws*) Don't you have this on disk somewhere?

BRIAN: Okay, okay—I think it would have to be this guy I kind of knew in college. He was gorgeous—real big and hunky. I have never seen a body like his—this massive chest and huge arms. I'd see him around the gym or on campus, and I'd just melt. I was head over heels for this guy.

KEVIN: Well, that's a switch for you. Usually it's heels over head, isn't it?

BRIAN: Not back then. I was still relatively inexperienced.

RAY: How old were you? Nine?

BRIAN: Are you gonna let me tell this?

RAY: Sure, pumpkin.

BRIAN: So, I was obsessed with this guy. Well, there was this one dirty bookstore downtown. It had both straight and gay stuff, but it had booths in back, so guys used to fool around and cruise the booths. Well, I went in every once in a while—I was a horny nineteen year old—and this one day, who do I see back there but *this guy*. I thought I'd die. So, he passes by me and he opens the door to a booth, and as he's going in, he looks back at me and motions at me with his head. So, I follow him in and he undresses me—real slowly—and I can't believe I'm standing there naked with this god of a man. But what was really incredible is, he picked me up by the waist—lifted my body off the floor and gave me the most amazing blow job I've ever received—all the time just holding me in the air in front of his face, moving me in and out of his mouth. I have never felt anything like that feeling. I mean, can you imagine the kind of arms this guy must have had? And after I came, he put me down, hugged me, said "thanks" and that was it.

JAMES: I would say that's pretty sexy.

KEVIN: Works for me.

RAY: I have a boner.

BRIAN: So, true or a lie?

KEVIN: I don't know. He could have made that up.

RAY: Actually, I think he stole it from a porn film. Wasn't that Ryan Idol and Joey Stefano in *Homo Alone II—Lost in a Bookstore*?

PHILIP: No. You're thinking of *Guess Who's Coming On Dinner*—and it was Rex Chandler, not Ryan Idol.

RAY: Oh, I think you're right. Well, I still think he stole it.

BRIAN: Votes?

KEVIN: Okay. Truth? (*James, Andy, and Peter raise their hands*) Three. Fibbing? (*Kevin, Philip, and Ray raise their hands*) A tie. (*To Brian*) Well?

BRIAN (*showing Fact card*): Oh, ye of little faith.

RAY: Slut! Bookstores at nineteen?

BRIAN: Okay, Kevin. Pick a card.

KEVIN: Please let it be something easy. (*Picks card*) Oh, God. It's a "Fantasy" card. (*Everyone cheers. Ray jumps up in excitement*)

RAY: Give him something really good, like doing an erotic dance interpretation of Petula Clark's "Downtown."

KEVIN: Do that and you are dead meat.

BRIAN: No, I'll make it something interesting, but easy. It *is* our first Fantasy, after all.

ANDY: This is scary. (*Everyone looks at Andy*)

BRIAN: All right. Kevin. Pick someone you are attracted to and make out with him for thirty seconds. And, I mean, *really* make out.

(*As this is the first Fantasy, the guys all cheer and keep the excitement level going all the way through the section*)

RAY (*young Bette Davis*): Well, I'd like to kiss ya, but I just washed my hair.

JAMES: Well, Kevin? Who's it going to be?

KEVIN: I don't know. Maybe you should ask Andy. (*He shows a Flip card*) I'm flipping this to him.

ANDY: Me???

JAMES: Oh, you are cold!

KEVIN (*playfully and affectionately, not throwing Andy to the wolves*): What? He needs to loosen up, right? What better way? It's like throwing someone in a pool to teach them to swim.

ANDY: Oh, please. I'm not ready yet. (*This may make him nervous and he* *may wish to hide under the couch, but this should not be seriously traumatic for him)*

PHILIP: Sure you are. It'll be a good ice-breaker for you. So, who do you want to pick? I should warn you that Ray has hoof and mouth disease. It may be a good idea to stay away from him.

RAY: You are such a hemorrhoid!

PETER: Come on, Andy—we all have to go sometime.

ANDY: Oh, God, this is embarrassing.

KEVIN: Don't be embarrassed. It's just a kiss. So, who do you want to pick?

ANDY: I don't know. It's weird if it's one of you I know, and it's weird if it's one of you I don't.

RAY: Yes, yes, yes—weirdness abounds. You have no argument there.

BRIAN: Well, who do you feel most comfortable with? Or who do you think is the sexiest? You could go either way.

JAMES: Or, you could make it easy for him and make him make out with *everyone* for thirty seconds.

ANDY: NO! No, I'll decide. Let's see. (*He looks around at everyone, trying to choose*) Brian, do you mind?

BRIAN: Hell, no. I haven't turned down a kiss since second grade.

PHILIP: So, get with it you two. Who has a watch with a second hand?

JAMES: I do. I'll time it.

RAY: Now, don't go cheating or anything. They're supposed to kiss for a full thirty seconds, so let us know when a minute is up.

BRIAN (*to Andy*): So, come on, hotlips.

ANDY (*getting up and going to Brian*): I feel so weird doing this.

JAMES: You guys ready?

ANDY (*he positions himself, standing over Brian who is sitting in a chair*): Is this okay?

BRIAN (*who happens to be eye-level with Andy's crotch*): Fine by me.

JAMES: Okay, ready . . . go.

(*Andy bends down and he and Brian begin to kiss, then Andy lowers himself down on Brian's lap and they build in passion till they're really into it—it becomes really sexy. A couple of the guys perhaps move closer or circle them to get a better look and they all respond with general whistling and other mature things*)

PHILIP: Go for it, Andy!

RAY (*singing*): "I think I'm gonna like it here." (*From* Annie)

JAMES: Look at that!

RAY: Animals, that's what they are!

KEVIN: Hey! Watch the hands.

PETER: Watch the chair. It's IKEA.

JAMES: Okay. 5, 4, 3, 2, 1. Okay, stop.

(*But they don't—Andy and Brian continue to kiss*)

RAY (*pulling Andy off of Brian*): Hey, stop!

(*Andy's a little embarrassed, but proud of himself. Brian's unfazed, but content. The guys applaud*)

KEVIN (*to Andy*): I knew you could do it. See, that wasn't so bad, was it?

ANDY: No. It was fun.

JAMES: So, who takes a turn now? Kevin or Andy?

BRIAN: Kevin flipped to Andy, so it's Andy's turn now.

PHILIP: Pick someone, studmuffin.

ANDY: Okay. You. (*To Philip*) Pick a card.

PHILIP: I've already done one.

BRIAN: Doesn't matter. There's no order. You can pick whoever you want. Draw.

PHILIP: Okay. (*Draws card*) It's a Fact.

ANDY (*with some confidence now*): Okay. Tell us about your first sexual experience.

PHILIP: Okay. Let's see. I guess I was about sixteen. I had dated in high school, and had sex with a few girls . . .

(*Ray lets loose a nauseated heave or moan*)

KEVIN (*to Ray*): You shut up. You're so judgmental.

RAY: Just kidding. (*Turns and makes an "ick" face at the other guys*) Eeeeeeuuuuuuuuuuu!!!!!!

PHILIP: My first time though, was at a party, and there was this girl—Kathy was her name—and she really started coming on to me. And she was cute. I mean, I knew I liked guys, but I wasn't out—I was just in high school—so I had to play along with that "liking girls" stuff. But Kathy was really cute. I mean, I really was attracted to her. So, we kept flirting and like feeling each other up all night. She was rubbing my dick even, and I stuck my hands down her blouse—I even fingered her under her skirt. (*Ray moans and feigns nausea*) So, that night, we just did it. It was incredible. She was a little animal. She just sat right down on it and got wild.

RAY: You're trying to kill me.

PHILIP: Actually, the sex was really great.

RAY: Thank you very much. That was very interesting. NEXT!

PHILIP: What's really interesting is that, after we all got out of college, Kathy became this real severe leather dyke—motorcycles and everything.

PETER: You fucked a leather dyke?

PHILIP: Well, she wasn't one at the time. She was just this cute little high-school girl.

RAY: Yeah, a cute little high-school girl who looked like Marlon Brando in *The Wild One*. Okay, enough about Dutch boy here sticking his fingers in the dyke. Next!

KEVIN: We have to decide if he's telling the truth first, remember?

RAY: Oh, who would make that up? Stephen King? I say it's the truth. It's too disgusting to be made up.

JAMES: It is not disgusting, will you shut up? I think it's the truth too, Philip.

KEVIN: Everybody who says true? (*They all raise their hands*) Philip?

PHILIP (*holding up Fact card*): Guilty. Can't fool you guys.

RAY: It was the bit about the fingers. No one would add a detail like that unless they'd actually lived through it.

PHILIP: Actually, I rather enjoyed it. Don't knock it till you've tried it.

RAY: Oh, I'll get right on that.

KEVIN: Philip, your turn.

PHILIP: Oh. Right. Ray—Draw.

RAY (*excitedly*): Me? (*With a look "Upwards" and a "Luck Be a Lady" intensity*) Come on, Mama needs some new shoes! (*He draws a card*) A Fact. Damnit.

PHILIP: Good. Here's something I've always wanted to ask you. Why did you become a priest?

JAMES: Good question.

RAY: Oh, God, how boring.

KEVIN: Because the convents kept turning him down.

RAY (*a death-ray glance at Kevin, then*): Seriously?

PHILIP: Yeah, seriously. I think it's interesting.

RAY: Okay, seriously. Why I became a priest. Well, Oprah, it was like this. (*Finally being straightforward*) See, I was not a happy kid. Family life was fine, I just never felt like I belonged to the rest of the world. I grew up in a very working class neighborhood where bowling was the big cultural event of which to partake, but from as early as I can remember, I loved the arts. I'd go to the Whitney or the Metropolitan every day after school. I'd look at the paintings in the museums and wonder what sorts of people they were who created them. I'd spend hours in the music section of the library teaching myself about musical theater. I'd go through the record albums and listen to every Broadway show I could find. I especially loved Jerry Herman. I listened to *Dolly*, *Mame*, *La Cage* and *Dear World* until I knew every word to every song. It gave me something I never found anywhere else. It's like I knew who I was when I was looking at art and listening to music. Unfortunately, my love for the arts and the fervor with which I pursued my hunger for them was not easily understood by my contemporaries. I was an outsider at school, made fun of. Also, I guess I was pretty obviously gay even. And the more I tried to blend into the woodwork—hoping they wouldn't notice me, the more they came after me. I could deal with being ignored, but I was terrified of being tormented. Well, there was one boy in my school—Joe Ivanovich—who suddenly became aware of me in my junior year and proceeded to make my life miserable. I couldn't go anywhere, make any move, without Joe there to taunt me or to embarrass me in front of the other kids. I used to go home and cry and ask God why he made me so different, why I couldn't be more like Joe Ivanovich so everyone would like me or at least leave me alone. Then I'd ask God why he wasn't listening to me. Anyway, I was terrified of this boy who seemed to hate me for no reason I could understand. It was the first time in my life I was faced with irrational hate. I always thought you needed a reason to hate someone. I'd never hurt Joe

Ivanovich, I'd never done a thing to him—why should he hate me so? Well, I got through high school—barely—but it was a very unhappy time for me. I spent every day scared and believing that I was somehow responsible for bringing all this on myself. Then, not four months after we'd graduated, Joe Ivanovich was killed in a car accident. He'd been a pretty wild kid, so no one was very surprised. But I was so happy! I was actually overjoyed that this horrible creature was dead. Then, all of a sudden I caught myself. I thought—you are celebrating the end of someone's life—a young person's life. And I think it was that day that I promised to do two things with my own life. First, I wanted to teach art and arts appreciation. But more importantly, I wanted to be there for any kid like me who needed someone to make them realize that they are okay as they are. I had always been very religious, so I couldn't think of any better way to live my life than to bring both God and a sense of self-worth and self-respect to young people like me in need. Being a priest seemed to be the best way I knew to keep those promises to myself. I don't mean this to sound lofty and noble, because Lord knows I'm not, but it's what I believe in. So, that, in a rather painfully large nutshell, is why I became a priest.

ANDY: I think that's wonderful. Thank you.

JAMES (*sincerely, to Ray*)**:** Yeah, I do too.

KEVIN: Well, I can't vote, because I know the answer. Besides, as if it isn't obvious, does anyone not believe that Ray was answering truthfully? (*General nos from the group*) Well, Ray? Show and Tell.

RAY (*displaying a Fact card*)**:** Ta-da! It's a Fact! Wow! Why does everyone always want to know priestly things? I *have* had a real life, too, you know. So, my turn. Let's see. Who shall I torment now? James, love, draw.

JAMES: And I was just being nice to you. Now, nothing nasty, Father Time. (*He draws a card*) Good. A Fact card.

RAY: Shit. I was going to make you feed me grapes in a lovely tropical sarong while you fanned me. Well, we can save that one for later.

JAMES: Just ask your question.

RAY: All right. James, have you ever paid for sex or been paid for sex?

PHILIP: Whoa. Some good dirt.

RAY: Well, have you ever done either one of those things?

JAMES: No.

RAY: Darn. I thought we'd get some good dish.

BRIAN: Wait a minute, we don't know if he's lying yet.

RAY (*there is hope yet*): That's right! He could be lying! Are you lying?

JAMES: I don't know. You guys gotta vote first.

KEVIN: I think he's probably telling the truth. I don't think he'd ever have to pay for it, and I don't think he ever hustled . . .

BRIAN: I think you're right. I say true.

KEVIN: Anyone else?

PETER/ANDY/PHILIP: True.

KEVIN: Ray?

RAY: I'll say true too, I guess.

KEVIN: James?

JAMES (*slowly revealing card—it is Fiction. He is smiling*): Fooled you.

KEVIN: Oh, my God.

RAY: I don't believe it. I really hit on something. Philip, call the *Enquirer!*

PHILIP: James!

RAY: Well, which was it? Paid or been paid?

JAMES: I don't have to tell you. I answered your question. You said had I ever done either of those things, and yes, I have done *one* of them. But, you didn't say which one, you said *either*.

BRIAN: He's right.

RAY: Damn! Well, whoever gets James next, find out!!

PHILIP: Well, Mata Hari—it's your turn.

JAMES: Brian. Draw.

BRIAN: Yes, sir. (*He draws a card*) It's a Fantasy card.

JAMES: Alright, this isn't so bad. Brian—moon us.

BRIAN: Moon you?

RAY: Yes, yes, yes. Take down your pants and show us your butt!

JAMES: I think everybody knows what mooning is.

BRIAN (*disappointed that it's not racier*): That's a *fantasy*?

RAY (*pitifully*): For some of us, dear.

BRIAN: Okay.

(*And so he does. It is important that there is no effort to hide anything from the audience. Not that Brian has to moon directly at them or anything, but it makes the performance of the play self-conscious if you make a special effort to soften anything for their sake. Brian stands up, and with no hesitation, lowers his pants and moons the group. They all cheer and clap, etc.*)

KEVIN: Ladies and gentlemen! The Bermuda Triangle! Ships have gotten lost in there!

BRIAN: Not ships, just sailors. Can I *please* pull my pants up now?

RAY: Like those words have ever come out of *his* mouth before.

(*Brian pulls his pants back up and bows*)

PHILIP: God, dancers have the best butts.

BRIAN: Okay, Philip—draw a card.

PHILIP: But I've already gone *twice*.

BRIAN: Yeah, but you got questions both times. I want to see you draw a *fantasy*.

PHILIP: Well, maybe I'll get a question again. (*Draws—his luck has run out*) Fantasy.

BRIAN: All right! Philip—it is my fantasy to see you play the rest of the game in your underwear.

PHILIP: My *underwear*?!?

BRIAN: You got it.

PHILIP: The whole game?

BRIAN: Hey, you're lucky I'm letting you keep your underwear!

KEVIN: He does have a point.

BRIAN: Come on, take it off.

PHILIP: I'll get you for this.

BRIAN (*flirtatiously*): I hope so.

(*Philip rises and takes off all his clothes but his underwear. He does this in a very straightforward manner, not erotically*)

PETER: If anyone makes me do this, I'll kill them.

KEVIN: You don't really think you're going to avoid it all night, do you?

PETER: If I'm lucky.

ANDY: Shit, I'm not wearing any underwear.

RAY: Well, that'll teach you. Didn't your mother ever tell you to always wear underwear? What if you were in an accident and they had to rush you to the hospital and they had to undress you and there you were with no underwear on? What would the doctors and nurses think?

(*Philip has now undressed down to his underwear*)

PHILIP: There. Happy?

BRIAN: I'm getting there.

RAY: Very, very nice. Philip, I approve.

PHILIP: Oh, thank you so very much.

RAY: De Nada. (*Indicating a place on the couch next to him*) Sit near me.

(*Philip grabs a teddy bear that is sitting off to the side and holds it in front of him as he sits. He will keep the bear and play with it during the rest of the show*)

PETER (*regarding the bear*): Be careful with Googie. (*A reference to Rita Moreno's character in* The Ritz)

PHILIP: My turn. Okay, let's see. Andy—draw.

ANDY: Oh no, not me. Remember, I'm not wearing any underwear.

RAY: I think we've established that, already.

ANDY (*drawing a card*): Whew, it's a Fact.

PHILIP: Fact. Okay. Andy—what is your favorite sexual act?

ANDY: My favorite sexual act? It depends who I'm with, I guess.

BRIAN: Cop out.

ANDY: No it's not. I like different things with different people.

PHILIP: Just in general—all things being equal—what do you like to do best with a guy?

ANDY (*pause*): Okay. I think I'd have to say kissing.

BRIAN: Kissing?

RAY (*raising his hand*): Fiction!

PHILIP: That's not a sex act.

ANDY: Yes it is!

BRIAN: Andy, sex acts usually means sucking, fucking, beating off, 69 . . . but kissing?

ANDY: Yes. For me, that's a sex act. I mean, it's part of what you do together isn't it?

BRIAN: Well, yeah, but so is choosing stemware!

ANDY: So, that's my favorite thing. I think kissing someone is sexier than sucking their dick.

(*There is a huge gasp from the group and they freeze in shock for a moment*)

RAY: Oh, Chino—make it not be true. Make it not be true! (*Maria in* West Side Story)

BRIAN: Remind me never to marry you.

KEVIN: Wait a minute. I think kissing counts. If that's his favorite thing, that's his favorite thing.

PHILIP: But, I said *sex act*. Kissing's more romantic, not sexual. I mean, you do it while having sex, but I don't consider it a sex act by itself.

PETER: But that's you. Maybe for Andy it is sexual. I think he answered the question.

JAMES: Enough. Okay, he answered the question. Now, is he telling the truth?

PHILIP: I'd have to say that's a fib. I mean, kissing?

KEVIN: How many think it's a fake out? (*Ray, Brian, and Philip raise their hands*) And how many think it's the truth? (*James, Kevin, and Peter raise their hands*)

RAY: Oh, come on.

KEVIN: No, I think he meant it. Well, Andy?

ANDY (*showing a Fact card—not sure if he should be embarrassed or not*):
It's true.

RAY: Well, now I've seen everything.

JAMES: Leave the guy alone. (*To Andy*) Don't listen to them. Go on, your
turn.

ANDY: Okay. Kevin. (*Kevin draws*)

PETER: Excuse me, but what am I, chopped liver?

KEVIN: Oh, Peter hasn't been picked yet. Okay you're next. I'll pick you.

ANDY: Oh, I'm sorry. I wasn't keeping track.

PETER: That's okay.

KEVIN: I picked a Fact card.

ANDY (*thinking*): A Fact . . . fact—oh, I've got it. Who in this room, if anybody, have you slept with? (*The guys like this question*)

KEVIN (*with a little shock that this came from little Andy*): Andy!

ANDY: What? Shouldn't I ask that?

(*The guys en masse reach out to Andy to indicate that this is okay—perfectly
okay*)

PHILIP: No—perfectly legitimate question, Andy.

RAY: You're doing a beautiful job.

PHILIP: Kevin—your answer?

KEVIN: I'm just surprised is all. Okay, Andy. The only person I've ever
slept with here is James. (*James, Ray, and Philip exchange knowing
looks*) It was just once—God only knows how many years ago—well, before I met Matt. We slept together the first night we met, but it didn't
go very well. There was just something about it that wasn't quite right.

Neither of us ever really knew why it didn't work because it was one of those wonderful nights, you know, when you first meet someone and you stay up all night talking. I really had a great time with him. Anyway, we ended up becoming friends after that and never slept together again. In fact, it's weird now to think of us ever having had sex, because we're so close. We were definitely meant to be friends and not lovers. But, when I think back on it, that night really meant a lot to me. (*He smiles and there is a pause*) So, votes?

(*There is a vocal indication of True from Peter, Andy, and Brian. Ray, Philip, and James don't vote, and no one presses them to—it just sort of goes unnoticed*)

ANDY: What was your card?

KEVIN: (*revealing a Fiction card*) Fiction.

RAY (*feigning surprise*): Well, *quelle surprise!*

ANDY: It was a lie?

PETER: God, I believed it. It sounded so real.

KEVIN: It *was* real. It just wasn't James.

(*There is a moment of confusion before Philip speaks*)

PHILIP (*fondly*): Thanks. It meant a lot to me, too.

(*Kevin gives Philip a hug or a kiss on the forehead*)

RAY: Oh, look. It's Hope and Michael from *Thirtysomething*.

JAMES: Your turn, Kevin.

KEVIN: Peter—draw.

PETER: Finally! (*Draws a card*) It's a Fact.

KEVIN: Fact. Hmmm. Okay. Peter. What is your favorite childhood memory?

PETER: Childhood memory. That's a creative question—I like that.

RAY: Oh, how warm and fuzzy!

PHILIP (*maybe smacking Ray*): I *like* that question!

RAY (*the* Barney *song*): "I love you, you love me . . ." (*He gags and Philip smacks him or puts a pillow over his face*)

PETER: Oh—I've got it! I was about ten—is that early enough?

KEVIN: Sure.

PETER: Okay. Well, a year or two before, my parents had taken me to a revival house to see the film version of *My Fair Lady*. My folks had been worried I might be bored but I just sat riveted to the screen. I loved every minute of it. I totally fell in love with Audrey Hepburn. She was just perfect. Her eyes, her voice, her look—she was so elegant but she was so real too. From then on, I watched every Audrey Hepburn film I could find.

RAY: Oh, she was fabulous. *Breakfast at Tiffany's* is my favorite. George Peppard was unfortunate, of course, but she was fabulous! I've always kind of thought I had her neck—don't you think?

PHILIP (*a look at Ray, who is seeking validation but Philip just deadpans him and then turns to Peter*): You were saying?

PETER: Well, a couple years later, my family took a trip to Washington, D. C. My father had business there, so we all went because my parents thought it would be educational for me to see the capital. We stayed at this really ritzy hotel—on Dad's company. There was always something going on there—banquets and dinners and people in tuxes and gowns, limos lined up outside. And this one night I had gone down to the store off the lobby to get a candy bar. And as I was waiting for the elevator to go back up, there were three people ahead of me. Two men and a woman. They were all dressed up—tuxes and stuff, but their backs were to me so I didn't see their faces. We got in the elevator and I wasn't paying attention, I was unwrapping my candy bar or something, when I heard the woman say, "Don't let me forget to reschedule that interview for Thursday." I will never forget it. "Don't let me forget to reschedule that interview for Thursday." I knew that voice. The second I heard it, I knew it was her. I turned around and there was Audrey Hepburn—in the same elevator as me. She was a little older, but she was still gorgeous! Those eyes, that smile, that neck. When I turned around, she looked at me, right in my eyes, and she smiled and said, "Hello, what's your name?" My mouth dropped open. She talked to me. I blurted out my name and told her I had seen all of her movies and that my parents had taken me to see *My Fair Lady* and I just kept rambling on and on and she just kept smiling and asking me questions. I told her that seeing her play Eliza made me decide that I wanted to go into the theater or the movies because I wanted to be a part of all that excitement and magic. As I said that, we stopped at her floor and as she got out of the elevator, she put her hand under my chin, looked in my eyes and said, "It's been a pleasure meeting you, Peter. Be happy." And then she kissed me on the forehead and walked off the elevator.

(*There is quite a pause as the bigness of this moment sinks in*)

RAY (*suddenly breaking the silence*): Oh my God! You met Audrey Hepburn!!! She kissed you?

PETER (*nodding*): There was some UNICEF function going on in the hotel. So, I guess she was there to speak or something.

BRIAN: Wow. Audrey Hepburn.

PETER: I'll never forget how wonderful she was to this little kid. She was so sweet and genuine.

RAY (*with dead and firm seriousness*): That is a fabulous story. And I'm going to vote true because I really need to believe that that really happened.

BRIAN: Me too. (*To everyone else*) You guys?

(*Everyone indicates True*)

PETER: It's a Fact.

RAY: Yay! I knew it.

KEVIN: Great story, Peter.

RAY: I loved her! When she died, I sat in a dark room for two weeks humming "Moon River" and asking God that if he had to take someone from that film, why couldn't he take Mickey Rooney instead.

PETER: James, draw a card.

JAMES (*he does*): Shit. Fantasy.

PETER: Fantasy. Oh, God, my first Fantasy. I've never had to think of a Fantasy before.

KEVIN: Use your imagination.

PHILIP: I have some rubbers if you need them.

PETER: Quiet for a minute. I can't think. I'm really bad at this. I want it to be something good. Let's see . . . all right, I've got it. Oh, this'll be fun. James—we're going to pretend that you're Aladdin. And, my fantasy is, I want to see you sit on your Genie's lap and tell him the three things you most wish for. But, since your Genie is a dirty old man, you have to strip down to your underwear, sit on his lap, and ask him in the most seductive way you can for your three wishes.

KEVIN: Peter!

PHILIP: Well, he's catching on to things pretty fast. Wait a minute—who's the Genie going to be?

PETER: Well, let's see . . .

RAY (*jumping up and with an air of desperate urgency as if he will die if he does not get to do this*): Oh, I will pay you any amount of money you want if you choose me. Please—I will never ask you for anything ever again if you just do this one little thing for me. Pretty please?

PHILIP: Well, he did say the Genie was a dirty old man, you are the obvious choice.

RAY: I will even abide all of your nasty cracks if I can just have the pleasure of having James humiliate himself on my lap in his underwear. (*To*

Peter) I'll give you anything you want. Money, novenas, my *Wonder Woman* lunchbox, anything!

PETER (*to shut him up*): All right, all right! You can be the Genie!

RAY: Yay! I'm lighting a candle for you first thing tomorrow.

PHILIP: Well, now I won't be the only one exposed. I'll have company.

JAMES: Oh, you'll have company, but it won't be me. (*He displays a Flip card*) It'll be Brian.

BRIAN: What?

RAY (*furious*): What? What? What? After all that you don't have to do it? No fair! I gave away my *Wonder Woman* lunchbox for nothing?

JAMES: Hah! Serves you right!

RAY (*mimicking James*): Hah! Serves you right!

BRIAN: Wait a minute. I'm not wearing any underwear. Just a dance belt. (*Ray considers that maybe this won't be so bad after all*)

PETER: Okay. Sit on your Genie's lap in your dance belt.

PHILIP: Good answer. Good answer. And don't you think he should have to stay that way for the rest of the game?

PETER: Yeah, okay. You have to stay that way for the rest of the game.

BRIAN: *The rest of the game?* (*Standing up and undressing*) Love to!

RAY: Okay, everybody—make room for Genie.

(*The guys give Ray more room on the sofa—and do the* I Dream of Jeannie *theme as Ray folds his arms and does the Jeannie blink/nod*)

PHILIP: I love dance belts. They're one of God's greatest inventions.

BRIAN (*he has finished undressing*): Okay, ready, Genie?

RAY: Ready, little boy.

(*Brian sits on Ray's lap—Ray makes sure Brian sits on his hand*)

RAY (*pulling his hand out from under Brian's butt and feigning shock*) Hey!! Give me my ring back!!!! And while you're at it, I think I had a bracelet on . . .

BRIAN: Cute.

RAY: So, Prince Abooboo, your wish is my command.

(*Throughout this, Brian does his best to drive Ray crazy in a fun way, and he succeeds. Ray's bluff has been called and he squirms—again in a fun tone— and the guys love every minute of it*)

BRIAN (*rubbing his hands up and down Ray's chest and arms*): But, Genie, don't I have to rub you first to make you come out of your lamp?

RAY: Aladdin, darling, you keep doing that and something funny is going to happen in Genie's lap and we'll lose our "G" rating. Now, I can grant you three wishes. And remember—I can't kill anyone, make anyone fall in love with anyone, or bring anyone back from the dead. So, what do you wish for?

BRIAN (*seductively*): Well, first I'd like a (*starts doing revolutions on Ray's lap with his butt and milking each adjective slowly and sugges- tively*) great, big, fat (*finishing the sentence quickly*) starring role in a new Broadway show written just for me! (*The butt revolutions have sped up now*)

RAY (*slaps Brian's back to stop him, then as if he is dizzy*): It's like the tea cup ride at Disneyland.

BRIAN: Then, I'd like a beautiful, big, hard, black . . .

RAY: Oh, my God.

BRIAN: . . . Mercedes convertible with all the options. (*Building on the se- ductive, sexual play with Ray*) And, last, I want a gorgeous, hunky, sexy

International Male model with a dick of death to do anything I want him to. (*Brian is lost in the ecstasy of a pretend orgasm*)

RAY (*after Brian is finished—to the others*): Sort of makes you wonder what he's like on Santa's lap, doesn't it?

BRIAN (*with Betty Boopish flirtation*): Now, that's not asking too much, is it Mister Genie?

RAY: Would you settle for six weeks at the Gaeity, a subway token, and a date with Charles Nelson Reilly?

BRIAN: Not on your life! Am I done now?

(*The guys applaud Brian*)

RAY: Done. (*Aside to the others*) And I thought *Showgirls* was tacky. (*To Brian*) Your turn, Cupid.

BRIAN: Ummm . . . Kevin—draw.

KEVIN (*he draws*): There is a God. Fact.

BRIAN: Okay. Question, question. Shit. I'm much better with fantasies.

RAY: That's a *real* shocker.

BRIAN: Oh, okay. What is the cruelest thing you ever did to anyone?

KEVIN: The cruelest thing? I've never been cruel.

BRIAN: Oh, come on. Everyone's done something shitty to someone some time in their lives.

KEVIN: Not that I can think of . . .

BRIAN: There's gotta be something . . .

KEVIN (*thinks of something*): Well, I don't know if this is what you're talking about, but I had this friend—his name was Craig—and he was in the hospital dying, and his lover Kurt called me and told me that they didn't expect Craig to live through the night, and he had asked to see me. So, Kurt was calling to ask me to come to the hospital—but I didn't go. (*Pause*) I don't know why—maybe I had just had too much and didn't think I could take it, I don't know. But, then, the next day, after he died, I just felt so guilty, so selfish that I couldn't go to say goodbye and it was the last thing he wanted from me. So, I guess that would be it.

(*There is a long pause. No one really knows what to say*)

PETER (*finally*): Wow. I think he's telling the truth.

RAY: Oh, honey. I remember how upset you were after he died, I just never knew that was the reason.

BRIAN: Okay. How many think it's true? (*Peter, James, Andy, Brian, and reluctantly, Ray raise their hands*) And who thinks he's lying? (*Philip raises his hand*) Five to one. Kevin? Was it the truth?

KEVIN (*revealing Fiction card*): Are you kidding? Of course not! What do you think I am? (*There is a moment of incredulous silence as the guys get over the shock of having been so successfully duped*)

RAY: Well, thank God. You asshole!

KEVIN: What? I was supposed to make something up, right? I can't help it if it says Fiction!

PETER: That was too real for me.

JAMES: Yes, Kevin. Very convincing.

PHILIP: But not convincing enough. I knew you'd never abandon a friend.

KEVIN: Well, thank *you* at least for having some faith in me.

BRIAN: I didn't realize you were such a good actor.

RAY: Your turn, Miss Streep.

KEVIN (*to Peter*): Okay, draw.

PETER: Me?

KEVIN: Yes, you.

PETER (*he draws*): Fact. Now, don't be mean to me. I'm still recovering from the last one.

KEVIN: I won't. How many times a week do you masturbate?

PETER (*he is shocked, and protests, but is also a bit amused*): Excuse me! I don't think that's any of your business.

KEVIN: We're playing a game! What did you think that people were going to ask you, your favorite color?

PETER: Well, no, but that's so . . . personal.

PHILIP: I think the boy is beginning to catch on.

PETER: Well, I don't know. I don't count. Besides, it's different all the time.

KEVIN: An average then. In a typical week, approximately how many times do you jerk off?

PETER: I can't believe we're talking about this. That's a very private thing.

RAY: Get over it, Myrna. Besides, we're all friends in this room. We'd never judge you. (*Gives him an evil grin*)

PETER: Okay, let me think. (*Counts in his head*) I don't know . . . maybe fifteen.

KEVIN/RAY: *Fifteen??*

PETER (*innocently*): What, is that a lot? I mean, sometimes it's less, and sometimes it's more.

RAY: *More?!?*

BRIAN: You go, girl!

RAY: Well, there certainly are things to be said for your early twenties.

PETER: So, what does the jury have to say?

BRIAN: I say he's telling the truth.

ANDY: Me too.

BRIAN: Ray?

RAY: Oh, God, I hope he's lying.

BRIAN: But what's your vote?

RAY: Oh, hell, I'll agree with them. True.

BRIAN: James?

JAMES: I think he's lying. There's something about that innocent act— "What, is that a lot?"—I think he's bullshitting.

KEVIN: I agree. Bluffing.

BRIAN: Philip?

PHILIP: I think it's true. I remember my college days.

BRIAN: Okay, four for and two against. And the answer is . . .

PETER (*showing a Fiction card*): I lied.

RAY: Oh, good, I don't feel so bad now.

PETER: Usually it's more than fifteen.

RAY/KEVIN: MORE??

KEVIN (*with an arm toward presenting Peter*): I'd like you all to meet my roommate, Peter Portnoy.

ANDY: Huh? I thought his name was Malone.

RAY (*they freeze with a look of absolute shock*): Forget it. Waaaayyy before your time. (*To Kevin*) Oh, God, you just have to keep me away from young people—they make me feel so damn old. (*To Andy*) Tell me, Andy, and I'm not being facetious here, but do you even know what say, Stonewall was?

ANDY: Sure. (*A little unsure*) That's that thing in England that they can't figure out how it was built, right?

RAY (*Ray screams and falls on the floor*): I'm melting! (*He does* not *do Margaret Hamilton, we all know this quote*)

KEVIN (*helping Ray up*): Your turn, Peter—get us out of this.

PETER: James—draw.

JAMES (*drawing*): Uh oh. Fantasy.

PETER: Oh, I like those.

PHILIP: Be careful, James, I think he's getting into this.

PETER (*without missing a beat*): Okay, James—show us your dick.

PHILIP (*impressed*): All right, Peter!

(*The guys applaud and cheer*)

RAY: See? It's always those young innocent types you have to watch out for.

KEVIN: All right, James, whip it out!

BRIAN: This I want to see!

JAMES: Serves me right for thinking this group would have anything else on their minds. You're sure that's your fantasy?

PETER: For now. Come on. Take it out.

PHILIP (*starting a chant that the others join in on*): Free Willy! Free Willy!

JAMES (*standing up and starting to unzip*): Okay. Here you are you assholes. (*Pulls out his dick—the guys all cheer*) Satisfied?

KEVIN: More than acceptable, I'd say.

BRIAN: The first penis of the evening! (*They all cheer again*)

KEVIN: Well, things are starting to get interesting around here now. Thank you James.

BRIAN: Hey, what about me? I showed you my ass! (*Ray and Kevin share a laugh*)

RAY (*pointing to Brian*): Get her! (*To Brian*) Oh, honey—who hasn't seen your ass? Frankly, who hasn't had your ass?

BRIAN: Excuse me, but I do have standards.

KEVIN: Oh, what standards? You'd do it with anybody.

BRIAN: I would not! I draw the line at Ernest Borgnine!

(*Ray does a spit take or grimaces*)

RAY (*in disgust*): Aaaahhh! Moving on!! Moving on!!

JAMES: Okay. Peter—draw.

PHILIP: Oops. Someone's going to get even.

PETER (*drawing*): Uh oh. Fantasy.

JAMES: Okay. My fantasy is, I'd like to see you go up to the person you'd most like to go to bed with in this room, tell him what you'd like to do with them, and then give them your most passionate kiss for forty-five seconds.

(*Reactions from gang—they are loving this*)

PETER (*horrified*): You can't do that!

JAMES: Oh, yes I can.

PETER: Oh, God, I can't. Please give me something else.

JAMES: Nope. That's it.

ANDY: Gee, what's so bad?

KEVIN: I don't know. But there must be something. Come on. No one's going to attack you. We're all friends. Right guys?

RAY (*holds up his hand as if he's flashing nail polish a la* The Women) Yeah. Jungle Red.

BRIAN: Time's running out, babe. Who's it gonna be?

PETER: Shit. I really don't want to do this.

PHILIP: Come on. You have to.

PETER: Okay. Just give me a second.

JAMES: Okay. I'll time it. (*To Peter*) Tell him what you'd want to do with him, and kiss him passionately for forty-five seconds.

PETER: Oh, God.

BRIAN: Go on. Who is it?

(*Peter prepares himself and after a suspenseful silence, Ray breaks it with . . .*)

RAY: Oh, the suspense is killing me. It's positively Hitchcock! I feel like Tippi Hedren outside of the schoolhouse. "Run, children, run!" (*And then as if he sees a dead body on the stage floor*) Oh, my God—it's Suzanne Pleshette!

PETER: Come on—I'm trying.

JAMES: Go ahead. We're waiting.

(*They are all anxious—wondering who it is. Peter gathers his nerve and slowly discards. Finally, and suddenly, he turns to Kevin*)

PETER: It's Kevin.

RAY (*shocked, then rising with glee*)**:** Well, *quelle surprise* again!

ANDY: Kevin??

PETER (*to Kevin*)**:** I'm sorry.

JAMES: Okay. Now, what do you want to do with him?

PETER: All right, all right. Give me a second. (*While he prepares himself, the guys all move in closer so as not to miss a thing. During the following section, they huddle and almost chew their nails as they listen*) Okay, Kevin. I think you're very attractive. I've . . . liked you for a long time, and I'd love to go to bed with you.

JAMES: More specific. What would you do in bed?

PETER: Hang on. I'm not done yet. First, I'd like us to have a quiet evening together—like a date. Just the two of us. We'd go to dinner some-place quiet and romantic, take our time, have a bottle of wine and talk about everything we don't know about each other. Then, we'd go for a long walk and hold each other and talk some more. Then, we'd come home, put on some soft music and go to bed. I'd want it to last for hours, starting with lots of holding and kissing and touching. I'd explore every inch of your body with my mouth and tongue, and you'd explore mine. Then, I'd take you in my mouth and lick you and suck you until you were ready to explode, but I wouldn't let you come yet.

BRIAN (*almost as to himself*)**:** Oh, no, not yet!

PETER: We'd go on making love like that until we couldn't take it any-more, then I'd want to feel you inside of me. We'd start out gently and build until we came together in one of the most wonderful orgasms we've ever had, and then we'd fall asleep in each other's arms.

(*Peter takes Kevin's face in his hands, and begins to kiss him—softly at first, then very passionately*)

BRIAN: Well, that gave me a little chubby!

PHILIP: Tell me about it.

JAMES: I don't know, it was a little too lovey-dovey.

BRIAN: Oh, I don't think so. It was romantic, but it was sexy.

RAY: You can't expect James to understand. His idea of a romantic encounter is exchanging first names with some guy he just peed on.

BRIAN: God, look at them go!

PHILIP: I'll bet they both have woodies.

BRIAN: I would.

RAY: Isn't their time up yet?

JAMES: Not quite.

RAY: Well, cheat, then, for Christ's sake! This isn't fair!

JAMES: Okay. (*It's time*) Stop.

(*They break apart*)

RAY: Well, I imagine things are going to be pretty interesting around this apartment from now on.

BRIAN: I'll say.

PETER: I need another drink.

KEVIN: I need another drink and another shot.

BRIAN/PHILIP: SHOTS! (*They start to pour*)

RAY: I wonder how many new romances have started from this game? So many things we keep hidden deep down inside until they have to be dragged out of us.

JAMES: Sometimes nature just needs a little boost to get things going. He'll thank me for that one day.

(*Peter looks at him, then at Kevin. He knows James may be right*)

BRIAN: Here we are. (*They pass shots around*)

ANDY: What should we toast to this time?

RAY (*big—with a sense of teasing celebration which, of course, only embarrasses Peter and Kevin*): To the happy couple!

KEVIN/PETER: RAY!

PHILIP: How about to all the things we have yet to learn about each other before the night is out?

RAY: Well, if that's not a frightening thought, I don't know what is, but what the hell. To all our deep dark secrets!

BRIAN: To our secrets! (*They all clink and drink*)

KEVIN (*privately, to Peter*): It's okay. We'll talk later, all right?

PETER: I'm sorry. It's so embarrassing. I'm sorry. I didn't want . . .

KEVIN: It's okay. (*Hugs Peter—not romantically, just to say it'll be okay*) Really.

(*Throughout the rest of the game, Kevin and Peter will occasionally look at each other. Kevin isn't quite sure of his feelings, but maybe . . .*)

BRIAN: God, those are good. Be right back. Don't start again without me. (*Brian runs out of the room to the john*)

(*Kevin starts clearing away some of the empty beer bottles to take them to the kitchen. If needed, he can bring out more when he returns*)

RAY: So, Peter, what are all these projects you are working on? What are you mounting (*with a pointed look at Kevin, which Kevin does not notice*) next?

PETER: Well, I'm taking two classes this semester because I'm also interning with a small opera company. They're pretty small budget, but they do pretty good work. And I'm designing a show at school this year—I'm doing sets for *Evita.*

RAY: *Evita!* I LOVE that show! If there was one role I was *born* to play, that is it. (*His arms up in the* Evita *pose*)

KEVIN (*returning from kitchen*): Evita? You? (*He laughs*)

PHILIP: You want to play Eva?

RAY: Absolutely. And I would be fabulous! I want to be the first man to play Eva. I mean, if Mary Martin and Cathy Rigby can play a little boy, and if Sarah Bernhardt can play Hamlet, why not? God, I'd kill to play that role! I love that show!

ANDY: So do I. I listen to the soundtrack all the time.

RAY (*the very thought makes him cringe, but he struggles to remain calm and patient*): You do? (*Dryly*) Why?

ANDY: Why what?

RAY: Why do you listen to the soundtrack all the time? I thought you said you *liked Evita.*

ANDY: I do.

RAY: But Madonna can't *sing Evita.*

KEVIN: Ooops, here we go. (*He runs off to the john*)

ANDY: Oh! No, I have the soundtrack from the *play*—with Patti LuPone and Mandy Patinkin . . .

RAY (*Ray freaks—putting his hand over Andy's mouth*): Don't speak. Don't speak. (*Dianne Wiest from* Bullets Over Broadway)

PHILIP (*jumping up to run out to the john too*): I'm outta here.

PETER: Wait for me. (*Before they exit, a last look to Andy*) Poor little guy. (*They are gone*)

RAY (*the guys who have gone to the john return at various times throughout the following, so Ray does indeed have an audience beyond poor Andy*) Darling, darling, darling child. Let me educate you. It is only your age and sweet disposition which prevents me from becoming apoplectic, for you have just demonstrated one of my biggest pet peeves. (*Takes a breath to calm down*) You see, when you watch a movie, you are seeing the result of a recording. The film records the visual image which is the *visual* track and the music you hear is recorded on a *separate* track—the *sound* track. It is the playing of these two tracks simultaneously and in sync which allows you to see an all talking, all singing, all dancing movie musical. And that is why when you buy a recording of a movie musical, you are buying and listening to the *sound track.* Now, on stage, where the music is performed *live*, there *is* no soundtrack. So, the cast goes into a studio and records a (*with emphasis*) *cast album.* What you have is the "original Broadway cast album" of *Evita, not* the "soundtrack." (*The guys wearily applaud—they have heard this sort of tirade before and they think Ray has finished*) *But,* since you brought it up,.(*the guys moan*) I'm *glad* you have the Broadway recording. At least you know what the score *should* have sounded like.

PHILIP (*who has returned from the john in enough time to hear Ray's last few sentences, then addresses Ray*) Hissss! Booo! (*he liked Madonna*)

RAY: Oh go hiss-boo yourself! Look, I'm as big a Madonna fan as anyone here. I couldn't call myself a homosexual if I weren't. But, if you ask me, when a composer has to completely rewrite his score because his star can't sing it as written, then someone is miscast. I went to see it. Every time she opened her mouth to sing I said to Kevin "who's she whispering to?" If they wanted the music to sound like that they could have made the film fifteen years earlier with Olivia Newton-John. But the bottom line really is that no one will *ever* be able to sing that score as well as Patti. I'd like to see Glenn Close try to step into *that* one.

(*A momentary pause while everyone tries to figure out if he's done. Also, they are afraid of saying the wrong thing or encouraging him even more*)

ANDY (*grasping, then finally, hoping he can at least bring up something positive about this film*): Yeah, but Madonna looked great. (*Thrilled that* *this can end on a positive note, the guys all applaud Andy—they agree. All but Ray, that is, who just glares at them)*

RAY: She *looked* great??? She *LOOKED* great??????? God, what a bunch of fags. (*This last comment may be a simple observation or be filled with faux despair, but it should* not *be serious or ugly)* Lucille Ball looked great in *Mame*, too—although they used enough Vaseline on her camera lenses to jerk off Cincinnati for a year—but I *still* don't want to hear her sing! She sounded like Joe Cocker! Well, the one good thing I can say about Madonna is at least she wasn't the *worst* choice they could have made. (*To the older guys)* Remember years ago they talked about Barbra for the movie?

ANDY: Barbra who? (*This stops the room cold—everyone freezes)*

RAY (*in shock*): Did you just say "Barbra who"? Okay. Lesson number two. Our stage and screen goddesses do *not* need last names. Barbra, Judy, Liza, Bette, Bett*e*, Liz, Carol, Chita, Bernadette, Diana, Patti, and Angela are always Streisand, Garland, Minnelli, Midler, Davis, Taylor, Channing, Rivera, Peters, Ross, LuPone, and Lansbury. Write that down. *Barbra who???* You could have your fag card taken away for a slip like that.

ANDY: Wow, I'm sorry, Ray, I didn't mean anything . . .

RAY: Oh, that's all right, darling.

ANDY: That's all very interesting. You seem to know so much.

RAY (*primping*): Oh, yes, well . . .

KEVIN (*to Andy*): Andy—don't you have to hit the john?

ANDY: Oh, yeah . . . be right back. (*He goes out)*

(*Ray notices that the guys are all staring at him)*

RAY: It was important!

PHILIP (*to Ray*): Well, you sure made an impression on young Andy. Are all your students so mesmerized?

RAY (*proudly*): Most are. I have this gift. (*Southern—doing Blanche*

DuBois) "Give me a boy at an impressionable age, and he is mine for life."

KEVIN: Ray, that's from *The Prime of Miss Jean Brodie*, that's not Blanche DuBois.

RAY: Yeah, I know, but I can't do Scottish.

BRIAN (*flirtatiously*): How are you at French and Greek?

PHILIP: Do you ever think of anything besides sex?

BRIAN: No.

PHILIP: Good. I like that in a person.

KEVIN: Maybe you are so obsessed because you don't get laid enough. When was the last time you got some?

BRIAN: Last night.

PHILIP: Last night? Who?

KEVIN: Who were you with last night?

BRIAN: How should I know? I don't have eyes in the back of my head!

(*Andy returns from john*)

KEVIN: Okay, is everybody ready? Can we get on with the game? I forgot. Where were we?

RAY: Diamonds, daisies, snowflakes (*pointing to Peter*) THAT GIRL! (*This was the lyric for the theme song for the TV show* That Girl, *but he should say it not sing it*)

KEVIN (*embarrassed*): Oh, right. Peter.

PETER: Okay James—draw.

JAMES (*drawing*): Fact.

PETER: A question. All right. What's your favorite kinky thing to do?

RAY: Oh, God, forgive him, he knows not what he does.

JAMES (*he is amused by this—that his sex life is so shocking to them when it is perfectly normal for him*): My favorite "kinky" thing? Let me think. Well, I guess it would have to be water sports.

KEVIN: Water sports?

BRIAN: Gross!

RAY (*moaning*): Oh. I'm feeling the ratatouille we had for lunch at the rectory today.

ANDY (*not understanding why they are having a negative reaction*): God, swimmers have *great* bodies. (*Once again, he stops the room cold—they are in shock*)

JAMES: You *are* kidding, aren't you?

ANDY (*innocently*): What?

BRIAN: Andy, water sports doesn't mean swimming.

ANDY: What does it mean?

BRIAN: It means peeing on someone or being peed on.

ANDY (*now Andy is scandalized*): No. Really? Gross!

RAY (*to Andy*): You must be very quiet now.

KEVIN: Well, I'd say that qualifies. If it's true. Who thinks true? (*They all raise their hands. Some reluctantly and distastefully*) Unanimous. Well?

JAMES (*showing Fiction card*): Schmucks! There are things I like way more than that.

PHILIP: Damn, you had me going.

RAY: Well, I for one, am relieved. (*He realizes only after saying this that there is a pun in there—he is delighted with himself*) Get it? "Relieved?" (*They just stare at him*) Tough room.

JAMES: Brian—draw.

BRIAN (*drawing a card*): Fantasy, of course.

JAMES (*pleased*): Oh, good. Brian—86 the dance belt. Off. For the rest of the game.

(*Whooping and hollering and general approval from the guys—Philip high fives James*)

RAY: Thank you, James. I take back everything I've ever said about you.

PETER: What kind of card do you have, Brian?

(*They realize it may be a "Flip" card, but Brian smiles and reveals a Fantasy card—they breathe easily*)

BRIAN: Well, thank God—this thing is killing me. But remember—look but don't touch.

PHILIP: Yeah, that's the next fantasy.

BRIAN (*as he gets ready to begin*): What? I'm supposed to do this without any music?

(*The guys sort of look to each other—Ray starts to sing "The Trolley Song"—they find this very funny—except Brian*)

BRIAN: Shut up! I was hoping for something a little sexier.

RAY: So were we. (*Brian feigns indignation*)

(*The guys begin to hum and bump "The Stripper." Brian proceeds to remove his dance belt. As he is indeed an exhibitionist, he does this with no inhibition, and in a very sexy way. They heckle him and cheer and generally ad lib their approval. At one point, Ray jumps up and yells "My name* is *'Gypsy,' what's yours?" When Brian has finished, he strikes a pose and bows*)

PHILIP: Yeah!

(*The guys all applaud Brian. The applause dies out, and Ray is still clapping. When he realizes he is alone, he stops*)

RAY: I think I'm gonna have an aneurysm.

PHILIP: Okay—Brian—it's your turn now.

BRIAN: Let's see, who do I want to get?

KEVIN: Uh oh, look out.

BRIAN: Kevin. Draw.

KEVIN (*moaning but picking a card*): Fantasy. Shit.

BRIAN (*quickly*): Good. Take Peter's underwear off with your teeth.

KEVIN and PETER: What?

BRIAN (*slowly and with emphasis*): Take Peter's underwear off with your teeth.

PETER: But that means I'll be naked. (*They all stop dead in their tracks and look at Peter*)

RAY: Sharp as a tack. Nothing gets past you, Sylvia.

BRIAN: Right. And you have to stay that way for the rest of the game.

PETER: What? Don't I have a say in this? It's not my turn, why should I get naked?

BRIAN: Because I said so. It's legal. After all, Kevin didn't have to give his permission for you to kiss him earlier.

KEVIN: Brian—can't you give me something else? Something that doesn't involve . . . someone else?

BRIAN: Nope.

KEVIN: Peter, I . . .

BRIAN: It's not up to him. Go on.

PETER: Oh, why not? (*He starts to undress. He takes everything off but his underwear*)

KEVIN: (*to Brian*): I'll get you for this.

BRIAN: All's fair in love, war, and nasty party games.

RAY (*pathetically*): What I want to know is, why don't I get good ones like this?

PHILIP: Oh, you still could. The night is still young. Besides, you haven't drawn a "Fantasy" card yet.

RAY: Yeah, but I've only had one turn! (*He looks accusingly at everyone*) And besides, I'd probably get something stupid like "stand up and cluck like a chicken." No one's ever going to give me the underwear with the teeth one.

JAMES: That's because everyone's afraid you'll drool and burn holes in the carpet. (*Ray lunges at James—the others hold him back*)

(*Peter has finished undressing. Turns to offer himself to Kevin*)

PETER: Okay, go to it—I'm all yours.

KEVIN (*showing his fantasy card and discarding it*): This is about the most embarrassing thing I've ever done in my entire life.

BRIAN: Relax. Just enjoy it. And, remember, no hands. Just your teeth.

(*They should position themselves profile to the audience so we can see the action, but with Peter facing the guys. Kevin kneels down in front of Peter who is standing*)

KEVIN: Well, here goes.

(*Kevin begins to position himself. Just as he is about to bite down on the bottom of one of the legs, Ray jumps up*)

RAY: "As God is my witness, I'll never be hungry again!"

(*Kevin falters, gives Ray a dirty look, which Ray returns with a smile. Kevin repositions himself and begins at Peter's leg openings—the guys do the Jaws theme music and Kevin, starting with one side, pulls his shorts down a bit, then moves his mouth to the other leg, brings it down the same distance, and then goes for the middle and pulls them down the rest of the way*)

PHILIP: Very good work, Kevin. You showed great style and technique.

KEVIN: Thank you.

ANDY: Gee, this is fun. (*He collapses in laughter and the guys all look at him*)

JAMES: Well, two down, five to go. (*The guys stop in their tracks—Andy suddenly stops laughing—they all look at him again*)

RAY (*to Andy*): Not so funny anymore, is it, little sister?

KEVIN: Let's see now—who hasn't been picked in a while?

RAY (*Ray frantically waves his arms*): Hello!

KEVIN: Okay, Ray—we'll give you a chance to draw a Fantasy.

RAY: Thank you, thank you. (*Draws a card, looks at it, and is frantically ecstatic*) YES! Fantasy! I got a golden ticket! (*Willie Wonka*) Whose underwear do you want me to take off? (*Ray bites at the guys—he looks at Andy*) We could mime yours.

KEVIN: Ray! I can't make you do that. You may lose your dentures. Besides, I have to think of a priestly Fantasy.

RAY: That's priestly. I have to genuflect, don't I?

JAMES: If he made you do something like that, we'd all go to hell as accessories.

RAY: I have the powers of the confessional. I'll absolve you all. Believe me—I can do that!

ANDY: Boy, that's cool. A person could sin all they want around you.

RAY: See—he understands how it works. Come on. What depraved act of debauchery are you going to give me?

KEVIN: Ray, I can't give you a wild fantasy. I know you'll probably hate me forever, but I can't.

RAY: You're right, I will hate you.

JAMES: I think you should make him stand up and cluck like a chicken.

RAY: If you do that, I'll never speak to you again.

KEVIN: Hey, now, there's a thought.

JAMES: No fair bribing!

RAY (*lunging for James*): Kill the leather queen! (*The guys pull him away*)

KEVIN: Okay, I've got it. Pick somebody and give him a full back massage. Starting at the top and going *all* the way down.

RAY (*smiling*): Oh, I like that one. (*Delightedly shows everyone he has a Fantasy card*)

PHILIP: Very good, Kevin. Sensuous without crossing any lines. Very inventive.

KEVIN: Thank you.

JAMES: Well? Who are you going to pick?

PHILIP: Brian has great buns.

JAMES: Kevin's been under a lot of stress lately—probably all knotted up.

RAY: Hold on, don't rush me. These things must be done *delicately*. (*If he does Margaret Hamilton at all, it should only be on the last word*)

KEVIN: Well, don't take all night or I'll give you the chicken clucking one instead.

RAY: Okay, okay. Peter.

PETER: But I'm naked. What if I get a boner? (*Ray makes a big "Oh, well" gesture*)

JAMES: It's only a back massage.

PHILIP: If you pop a woody just put a pillow on your lap till it goes away.

RAY: Well, that's settled. Come on, lie down on the floor.

PETER: How come people always involve me in their fantasies?

PHILIP (*sweetly*): Because you're so damn cute. (*An order*) Now, get down on the floor.

(*Peter gets up and lies down on the floor, face down, facing toward the audience*)

BRIAN: I coulda used a massage myself. If someone else gets this one, pick me, okay?

PHILIP (*with a smile*): You got it.

(*Ray gets on top of Peter and starts to massage his shoulders*)

RAY: "Years from now—when you talk about this—and you will—be kind." (*Tea and Sympathy*)

PETER: I will—believe me. (*Ray begins*) Oh, that feels good. Ray, you're really good at this.

RAY: Shut up—you're tensing your muscles.

PETER: Sorry.

JAMES (*to Peter*): What would your mother say if she saw you now?

PETER: Oh, nothing would surprise her. She's pretty cool. Ever since I came out . . .

RAY (*smacking Peter on the butt*): Stop talking!

PETER: Sorry, sorry.

KEVIN (*to Andy*): What about you? Are you out to your family?

ANDY: Not really. I mean, I think they know, I *was* Nancy Drew for Halloween in the third grade . . .

RAY (*looking up—to Andy*): Sweetie . . . they know.

ANDY: But we've never really talked about it. What about you?

KEVIN: Oh, yeah. For years now. I think my family always knew, but it took me a while to come out because I was sure it would kill my mother.

ANDY (*to Kevin*): How did she find out? Did you tell her?

KEVIN: No. Actually she's the one who asked me. I was nineteen and home from college for the weekend. I couldn't believe she brought it up— I have no idea where it came from. But, I figured, what the hell, now is as good a time as any. So, I admitted it.

ANDY: How did she react?

KEVIN: Not that bad, really. I was surprised.

RAY: Mary Lou is fabulous!

KEVIN: After about a year or so, she'd call me up to say "Hey, turn on the TV—the Chippendales are on." That was when I knew she was okay about it. My sister was great too. The years that Matt and I were together, my family treated him just like they would a daughter-in-law. It was great.

(*Ray is now working on Peter's buns—with great enthusiasm*)

PHILIP: Oh, it's getting good down there. How do you feel, Peter?

PETER: Great.

PHILIP: And you, Ray?

RAY: It's a dirty job, but somebody's got to do it.

ANDY (*to Kevin*): So, Kevin, how'd your Mom feel when you and Matt broke up?

KEVIN: She was upset. I think it hit her as hard as it hit me. But she was great at helping me through it. (*Ray smiles at Kevin*) After seven years, your life kind of falls apart.

BRIAN: I can't imagine being with anyone for that long. Seven years.

RAY: Yeah, it's kind of like twenty in straight people years.

ANDY: What happened? If you don't mind me asking.

KEVIN: No, it's okay. I'm not sure really. It just stopped working, I guess. Relationships change. The sex had gotten boring for one thing. It's hard to keep that exciting over so many years. But, it also became less and less important—to me, anyway. And we both had a lot of pressures in our careers. But it was pretty amazing for most of our time together. I had never cared about someone that much before—like we thought about each other first, you know? But, our last year or so it was obvious that I wasn't the first person he was thinking about anymore. In fact, I was most often the last person.

(*Ray is doing Peter's legs now*)

ANDY: Do you still love him?

KEVIN: Yeah. I'll always love him, I think. Not the same way—I mean, not to be married to him. But, I don't think there's any way we won't always be important parts of each other's lives. At least I hope we can reach that point someday. I still miss him sometimes. It's funny, but the thing I miss most is . . . sleeping with him. I don't mean sex. But, every night, when we'd go to bed, I'd lie on my left side, and he'd lie on his left side right behind me—you know, like two spoons? And, he'd put his arm around me and hold me and we'd just lie like that till we fell asleep. It was the best feeling in the world—like, no matter what was wrong in my life, no matter how bad my day had been—everything was all right when he'd hold me like that. It was just so, I don't know, safe I guess. Whenever I think of Matt, I think of falling asleep like that. Maybe it isn't so much that I still miss him but that I miss that. I don't know.

(*Peter has been listening intently to this last speech. Ray is now finished*)

RAY (*with a quick slap to Peter's butt*): Done. How was that?

PETER: Great. You can keep going if you want.

RAY: You see—give 'em an inch and they want six or seven more. My turn, right? Brian—draw.

BRIAN: Okay. Fantasy.

RAY: Oh, goody, goody. I get to give someone a Fantasy. Hmmmmmmmm. What should it be?

JAMES: Come on, come on.

RAY: Patience—you have no comprehension of the creative process. *(His eyes light up)* I think I've got it. Kevin, do you have any porn magazines?

KEVIN: I beg your pardon! Of course I do.

RAY: Can we use one or two?

PHILIP: What are you cooking up?

BRIAN: I don't know, but I think I'm gonna like it.

KEVIN: Seriously? You want them?

RAY: Yeah.

KEVIN: Be right back (*He goes off to bedroom*)

ANDY: What are you going to make him do?

RAY: You'll see.

PHILIP: Make him do a dramatic reading of the dirty stories?

RAY: You'll all see in a minute. Keep calm, keep calm.

BRIAN: I want to know what it is!

PETER: Don't be in such a rush. You might wish you'd drawn a question.

BRIAN: There is nothing he could tell me to do that would bother me.

RAY: Hussy!

(*Kevin re-enters with a short stack of magazines, which he hands to Ray*)

KEVIN: Here you go.

PHILIP: Kevin, I'm surprised at you—having magazines like that around.

KEVIN: Oh, they aren't mine. My grandmother came to visit last month and she left them here.

BRIAN: Hello!—what's my fantasy?

RAY (*flipping through magazines*): Hold on a second, I'm looking.

KEVIN: Be afraid—be really afraid.

BRIAN: Hell, I'm excited.

PETER: I'm glad this one isn't mine.

RAY: Okay. (*He has opened a magazine to a specific page*) Pick somebody here and recreate with him (*reveals the open magazine to them*) this pose. (*Hands magazines to Brian*)

BRIAN: Oh, cool. Let's see. (*Takes magazines*)

KEVIN: What was your card?

BRIAN: Oh, it's a Fantasy. (*Shows card*)

RAY: Now, remember—you have to try to recreate the positions *exactly*—facial expressions and all.

BRIAN: And I get to pick my partner?

RAY: Yes. You get to pick your partner.

BRIAN: Okay. I choose Philip.

RAY: I would never have guessed.

PHILIP: How did I know I wasn't going to escape this? (*He takes his underwear off*)

KEVIN: Ray, this is very creative of you.

RAY: Thank you, darling.

ANDY: Can I see one of those?

RAY (*handing Andy a magazine*): Now, be careful—you'll go blind.

BRIAN (*to Philip*): Okay, come here. (*Refers to magazine*) You be the one on top, and I'll be the one on bottom.

JAMES: Surprise!

PETER: I am so glad I didn't get this one!

(*Brian and Philip start to get into position—feel free to ad lib throughout this section based upon the actual photo you choose to recreate. The feel of this scene should be funny—the pose should be ludicrous when taken out of context—it should not be sleazy, pornographic, or seriously sexy and certainly not involve any act of penetration. It is intentional that there is not more specific dialogue here—it really depends upon the photo—the guys can help and offer suggestions— "No, your left hand," "Lift your head a little higher,"—that sort of thing*)

PETER (*Brian and Philip try to figure out what they're doing while trying* *to also look at the magazine in their hands):* Here. I can help. I was an altar boy. (*He takes magazine and holds it up altar boy style for Brian and Philip to be able to see it. The image of a naked altar boy makes everyone look at Ray, who is scandalized by the implication*)

RAY: You are all going to hell.

BRIAN: Okay, what do you think? Are we close?

RAY: Lovely—now hit it on "go"—okay—on your marks, get set, go! (*On "go," they strike the complete pose*)

(*Cheers, applauding, ad libbing*)

RAY: Excellent, excellent. I'd buy the video.

BRIAN (*Brian and Philip join hands and bow*): Philip, thank you.

PHILIP: My pleasure, believe me.

JAMES: Your turn, Brian.

BRIAN (*going back to couch with Philip to sit down*): Here, we'll do this one together. Who should we pick? (*Brian and Philip whisper*)

BRIAN: Andy. You haven't gone in a while. Draw. (*Andy is absorbed in the magazine and is oblivious*)

RAY: Wake up, little Susie! It's your turn.

ANDY (*coming to*): Huh?

BRIAN: We're picking you. Draw a card.

ANDY: Oh. (*He does*) Fantasy.

PHILIP: All right. What should you do? We gotta think of something fun.

RAY: Kevin, ya got any livestock in the apartment?

KEVIN (*thinks for a second*): Fresh out. You killed that last sheep last time you were over.

RAY: Well, it wouldn't have died if it had cooperated.

PETER: Gross, you guys. Knock it off.

PHILIP (*Brian and Philip have been whispering back and forth*): Got it. Okay, Andy, first you have to get naked—we have to include that—and then pick someone and act out a fantasy of yours with them. Nothing sexual, like a real sex act, but something *sensual*. Something you've always wanted to do with someone.

ANDY: Like what? (*They all stare in disbelief—he can't think of anything?*)

PHILIP: Anything. As long as it's not directly sexual. Use your imagination.

ANDY: I can't think of anything like that.

BRIAN: Sure you can.

ANDY: Okay, let me think.

BRIAN: I know what I'd do.

JAMES: What?

BRIAN: I'm not gonna tell you—I might get this same one later.

RAY: Oh, Brian, honestly. There's only seven of us here. We couldn't possibly fulfill your fantasies.

PHILIP: Speak for yourself—maybe it only takes one.

BRIAN (*with a smile*): Maybe it does.

RAY: Yeah. And I'm the only gay priest in the archdiocese.

ANDY: Okay, I think I've got it. (*Grabbing Kevin*) Kevin, come with me for a second. Oh, and would you guys do me a favor? Would you mind moving the table out of the way?

RAY (*the guys don't know what this will be, but having to move furniture around to make room gets them excited*): We'd be delighted! (*The guys* *move the coffee table away, clearing floor space down center while Andy and Kevin start off towards the kitchen)*

KEVIN: Okay. We'll be back in a minute. (*Intended to be "Coffee Talk" from* Saturday Night Live. *However, if the actor can't do Linda Richmond, the section works with no reference at all)* Talk amongst yourselves. I'll give you a topic—"Men and what they do in bed that I hate most"—discuss. (*They exit)*

PHILIP: Oh, that's easy. It's the talkers I hate.

PETER: Talkers?

PHILIP: Yeah, the ones who've watched too many porn movies. You're really into it, and they start with this really bad porn dialogue—"Yeah, suck that dick. You like big dick, don't you? Yeah, take that big dick." *Instant* turn-off. Especially when they're like directing you to do something you're already doing. You're going down on them, and they say "Suck that dick." It's like, what the fuck do you think I'm doing, asshole? Changing a flat?

PETER: Okay, okay . . . the thing I hate most are the ones who scrape you with their teeth when they give you a blowjob. Ouch!

RAY: Oh, the worst. I agree. You just want to scream "watch the teeth, sister!" (*They all look at him incredulously. Once Ray sees their looks and it dawns on him what they are thinking, he is scandalized once again)* I didn't mean it like *that!!*

KEVIN: Andy'll be out in a minute. He's getting ready.

PHILIP: Getting ready? For what?

RAY: What does he have up his sleeve?

KEVIN: I can't tell you that.

RAY: Is it something terrible or embarrassing he's going to do to someone?

KEVIN: No. You'll see. He'll be out in a second.

RAY: Well, I for one am on the edge of my seat.

BRIAN: Well, if kissing is his favorite sexual act, how bad can it be? What, is he flossing and rinsing?

KEVIN: No comment.

(*Andy calls from offstage*)

ANDY: Okay, I'm ready. Can you turn the lights down a little?

BRIAN: Oh, come on, Andy. You've seen us undressed.

KEVIN: I think he wants a little atmosphere. (*Turns lights down just a bit to create mood*)

KEVIN: Okay. We're ready.

(*Andy enters—naked—carrying a few things wrapped in a towel. The guys cheer him*)

ANDY: Okay, Philip, lie down.

PHILIP: Me? You're going to do something to me?

RAY: My, aren't we popular, Miss America?

PHILIP (*getting up*): I hope this isn't going to be too kinky.

RAY: I hope it is!

PHILIP (*he has laid down*): Okay, do with me what you will.

(*Andy unwraps towel and takes out a can of whipped cream. The guys all react to this*)

PETER: Why, you little tramp.

(*Andy puts a dollop of whipped cream on each nipple, then a thin stripe down Philip's chest to just below the waistline. Just enough to make the point, not so much that it gets messy or is too much to lick off*)

RAY: My Lord, I think I am going to have a stroke.

PHILIP: That's cold.

JAMES: Looks good enough to eat.

RAY: I think that's the point.

(*Andy then takes out a bag of M & M's and places one brightly colored one—not brown ones—on each nipple*)

BRIAN: M & M's!

PETER: They melt in your mouth but not on your nipples.

(*Andy then puts a few more M & Ms down the stripe of whipped cream*)

RAY: Well! My goodness, it's like a little Philip Sundae! Try getting *that* at Baskin-Robbins! Well, maybe the one in the Village.

PETER: I think we need to add a banana and nuts.

RAY: I wouldn't touch that one with a ten foot pole.

BRIAN: Hell, I would.

RAY: Is it warm in here, or is it just me?

PHILIP: Right now, I'm pretty chilly.

(*Andy presents his Philip creation with a Ta-Da*)

KEVIN: Bravo, a masterpiece, Andy.

ANDY: Oh, I'm not done yet. (*He puts the candy and whipped cream aside—he kneels down and begins to lick and eat the whipped cream off of Philip's downstage nipple—very sensually*)

RAY: My heart can't take any more.

PHILIP: God. That's incredible.

ANDY (*between licks*): Tastes good too.

PETER: It's making me hungry.

RAY: I could never do that. Jenny Craig would never allow it.

PHILIP: It's sticky.

RAY: What's sticky, honey?

(*Andy goes to the upstage nipple*)

PHILIP: God, that feels so good.

BRIAN: I did something like this once with ice cream.

PHILIP: Ice cream? This is cold enough! How did you stand ice cream?

BRIAN: Your mouth warms it up pretty fast. Besides, it was the sugar cone that really caused problems.

RAY (*to Brian*): I don't want to know. (*To Andy, who has begun to eat the whipped cream running down Philip's chest*) You keep this up much longer, you're going to get zits.

JAMES: I don't think he's worried about that right now.

RAY: Sure, not now. But wait till he has to get a chemical peel. He'll regret it.

ANDY: No, I won't.

PHILIP: Don't you listen to them, they're just jealous.

PETER: Damn right, we are. I want to do a butterscotch one.

RAY: Do you want to be the butterscotchee or the butterscotcher?

PETER: Either one, I don't care.

(*Andy gives Philip's stomach one last long swipe down to the end of the stripe. Try to make this as neat looking as possible and not have Andy come up with a face full of whipped cream, looking like a bad 70s porn film)*

ANDY: Finished.

RAY (*approaches them with imaginary pen poised to take their order*)**:** Can I get you anything else? Coffee? Cappuccino?

(*Kevin goes to restore the lights. The guys all move the table back, etc.*)

PHILIP: That felt great.

BRIAN: Looked good, too. I'd like to taste it sometime.

PHILIP: Any time you want. (*Feeling his chest*) I'm a little sticky. (*Andy has wiped his mouth off with the towel and tosses it to Philip—Philip cleans himself off*)

ANDY: Thanks, Philip. That was fun.

RAY: Believe me, we all enjoyed that one.

KEVIN: So, Andy, how are you liking your first party with the gang?

ANDY: It's great. I want to play this all the time.

BRIAN: Well, maybe we need to start having parties every week.

PETER: I'm game.

KEVIN: What should we do for our next one?

ANDY: How about naked Twister?

RAY: My Lord, we've corrupted him.

JAMES: Okay, Andy, it's your turn.

ANDY: Right. Kevin, pick a card. And don't worry, whatever it is, I'll be nice.

KEVIN (*drawing and looking*)**:** Fantasy.

ANDY: Okay. Do twenty jumping jacks naked.

(*The guys fall apart*)

KEVIN: What? You said you'd be nice!

RAY: So, he lied. (*Ray gets up, makes a sign of the cross on Andy to absolve him. Then a wink to above*) There, clear of sin. Now strip and get with the jumping, buster, we don't have all night.

KEVIN: Well, I'm glad you all find this fantasy so amusing, because I don't have to do it. (*Shows his card—a Flip card—the guys freak*)

PHILIP: Ooops.

RAY: Remember my heart, Kevin. My doctor says aerobics can kill me.

PETER: So, who are you flipping to?

KEVIN: Let's see . . . (*He looks around, then focuses in on Ray—Ray freaks. Philip starts chanting "Get the priest, get the priest" and everyone joins in until Ray silences them with a death-threatening look that shrinks them*)

RAY (*to Kevin*): You just remember one thing. I am your *oldest* friend. I know *EVERYTHING!*

KEVIN (*blackmail works every time—he flips around*): James!

JAMES: SHIT! I knew you were going to say me. Goddamnit! (*As he begins to undress, with the guys laughing hysterically*) I'll get you for this. All of you! If it's the last thing I do, I'll get you for this.

RAY: Testy, testy!

KEVIN (*clapping*): Good fantasy, Andy. (*The guys all applaud for Andy. Ray takes this applause as if it were his own*)

RAY: Thank you, thank you, and for my next number . . . a tribute to Nancy Reagan. (*To the tune of "Tomorrow"*) "Your sun'll come out tomorrow."

(*The guys are dying. James is not amused, but he is not angry in a lasting sort of way. For someone so always in control, he doesn't like the idea that he will look ridiculous*)

JAMES: Okay, assholes. Ready for your jollies?

PETER: Go for it!

JAMES: Twenty?

RAY: Twenty.

JAMES: You guys are sick.

RAY: We know! Now make with the Jane Fonda, cupcakes!

JAMES: Christ! (*Starts doing jumping jacks—counting off*) One . . . Two . . .

(*This becomes a free-for-all with lots of movement. They break down in fits of hysteria at the site of James' dick bobbing up and down. They fall on the floor or over each other, get up and point, etc.*)

JAMES (*finishing*): Twenty! You guys are NUTS!

(*They are still laughing—the kind of laughter that makes your side hurt—then recover themselves*)

PETER: God, that was funny! You should have seen it bouncing up and down.

KEVIN: It looked like a bungee cord in search of a jumper!

JAMES: Very funny. Very, very funny.

PHILIP: James, where's your sense of humor? It *was* funny.

JAMES: Oh, yeah—I'm hysterical.

RAY: Yes, you are. (*Puts on a serious face*) I'm sorry. Really. We meant to laugh with you not at you. (*Pause—cracks up again*) But that was before we saw your wanger auditioning for a Pop-Tarts commercial! (*They all fall apart again, but James remains unamused*)

KEVIN: Come on, James. We're only kidding. Hey, how 'bout a shot?

ALL: SHOTS!

(*They all scamper to pour the shots*)

RAY: God, Mama's gonna need her beauty sleep tonight.

BRIAN: I could go all night. Let's go out dancing later.

PHILIP (*to Brian*)**:** Or, you and I could just continue at my place.

BRIAN: Is this a proposal?

PHILIP: Only an indecent one.

BRIAN: Is there any other kind? You're on.

RAY: Okay, you two. This isn't *The Love Connection*.

(*The shots are ready and passed out*)

ANDY: What are we toasting to?

BRIAN: To a bunch of naked boys sitting around talking.

PHILIP: No. (*Very pointedly*) To *five* naked boys sitting around talking and *two big clothed drips*.

(*They all turn to Kevin and Ray. The guys start tugging at them—yanking at their clothes, trying to get them to join in. Kevin and Ray fight for their lives against the guys' attack. Andy finally loosens Ray's belt and yanks it off, which stops them all cold*)

RAY: Hey! Where'd you learn how to do that?

PHILIP (*to Kevin and Ray*)**:** Well?

PETER: Yeah, well??

RAY (*Mary Richards*)**:** Oh, Mr. Grant! (*Kevin and Ray look at each other, make the decision, then shrug*)

KEVIN: Oh, what the hell. (*Kevin and Ray start to undress—the guys cheer them on*)

RAY: I'm so *sick* of being treated like I'm just a piece of meat around here!

BRIAN: Well, this is a religious experience.

PHILIP: Ray, I always knew you had it in you.

RAY: Honey, I haven't had it in me in so long I forgot what it feels like.

JAMES: Well, bend over and I'll refresh your memory.

RAY: I'd rather chew glass.

PHILIP: I wish I had a video camera right now.

BRIAN: I wish we'd had one all night. We could have sent a copy to the Cardinal.

RAY: Yeah, and you could have used it as an audition tape. That is how you get most of your work, isn't it?

(*Ray and Kevin are now naked and join the guys at the couch*)

PETER: Okay, we still have to think of a toast.

PHILIP: Why don't you give the toast, *Father*?

RAY: So you're like, kind of a bitch, right? (*He thinks*) Okay. I've got it. To friendship and to the knowledge that no matter what, we know we'll always be here for each other. I mean that. You guys are my family. You're very important to me.

PHILIP: Ditto.

BRIAN: Same here. I've lost enough friends already in my life to know how much you guys mean to me.

JAMES: I'll second that.

KEVIN: So, to all our friendships—old (*this for Andy*) and new.

PHILIP: And to all the men in our lives who've treated us like shit—may they rot in hell.

BRIAN: Men are pigs!

ALL: Yeah! Cheers!, etc. (*They clink and drink*)

JAMES: Well, is this game almost over or what?

ANDY: NO! I don't want to quit yet.

BRIAN: Well, there's only (*counting the deck*) two cards left anyway.

KEVIN: Okay. Who's turn was it?

RAY: Our bungee cord jumper!

JAMES: Peter—draw a card.

PETER: I hope it's a question. I'm in no mood for aerobics right now. (*Draws*) Good. Fact.

JAMES: Do you want to sleep with Kevin tonight?

PETER (*looking at Kevin—very sincerely*) Yes.

JAMES: Good. I believe him. You guys?

RAY: Well, duuhh, I'm not sure.

BRIAN: He's telling the truth. Show us your card. (*Peter reveals a Fact card, of course*) Okay. Your turn.

PETER (*without looking at Kevin*): Kevin—pick a card.

KEVIN (*picks a card—he knows what's coming, but he can't avoid it*): Fact.

PETER (*looking at Kevin*): Will you sleep with me tonight? I don't mean sex. Just sleep. I can do great spoons.

KEVIN (*with as much sincerity as he can muster, and with great gentleness*): I'm sorry, Peter, I can't. It's way too soon for me. This just scares me. And, besides, we still have to live together. What if it was a disaster? I like you a lot, and I feel lucky to have you as a friend. I just don't think it can be any more than that right now. I'm sorry.

(*There is a long, uncomfortable silence. Peter can't look at anyone, and they all feel for him. No one knows what to say. Only James sits there smugly*)

JAMES (*finally, after a pause—to Kevin*): You fucking liar.

(*It all of a sudden dawns on them*)

KEVIN (*showing his card—Fiction—and saying sheepishly*): Gotcha!

(*Peter is relieved, but it takes him a minute to compose himself*)

RAY: You asshole. You huge asshole!

KEVIN: What? I was playing the game. That's what I was supposed to do. Right?

(*A note here on Kevin's lie. Since his card said "Fiction" and since his honest answer to the question would be "Yes," the easy way for him to have answered this question would have been to say "No." But, afraid of that sounding too harsh, he chooses to soften it by letting him down easy with a sense of affection. So, rather than be the mean thing the guys perceive it as, he meant it as a loving thing*)

BRIAN: So, that's it? We wasted the last two turns on finding out what everyone already knew?

RAY (*to Kevin*): You are going straight to hell for that one.

KEVIN: What? It said Fiction—I *had* to lie.

RAY: Did you see that poor child's face?

KEVIN (*to Peter*): I'm sorry. (*Pause*) Look, some of what I said, though is true. I don't know if I'm ready for anything like this, so let's just take it slow and see what happens. Okay?

PETER (*with a smile*): Okay.

(*Kevin goes to hold Peter*)

RAY: I expect full details—with Polaroids if possible. (*To all*) Well, this has been an eventful little evening, hasn't it? So warmy feeling—like an episode of *The Brady Bunch* on Fire Island.

BRIAN: What's our plan for next month? We never decided.

KEVIN: We can talk about it later. Let's all just call each other.

PHILIP: Sounds good.

(*Pause. No one seems to know how to really wrap things up*)

RAY: I think we need a finale, don't you?

PHILIP (*with an "Oh, no" sense*): What kind of finale?

RAY: Oh, you know . . . something festive to tie the evening up in a little ribbon.

PHILIP (*suspiciously*): Like what?

RAY: Give Mama a minute. (*He thinks, then gets an idea*) I know! (*Ray gets up from sofa and runs excitedly toward the stereo*)

PHILIP (*At the sight of Ray flitting behind him*): It's the Flying Nun! (*Ray stops dead in his tracks—turns to Philip*)

RAY (Mommie Dearest—*this section works best when really imitating Faye Dunaway and Diana Scarwid's inflections*): Why can't you give me the respect that I'm entitled to? Why can't you treat me like I would be treated by any stranger on the street?

PHILIP: Because I am not (*the guys all join in*) one of your FANS!!! (*Ray goes for Philip's throat, then they all laugh and Ray breaks away to look through Kevin's tapes or CDs*)

RAY: Oh, goody—he's got it.

PHILIP: What is it?

RAY: Oh, just something from a wonderful bygone era.

JAMES: Oh, you aren't going to play Judy Garland, are you?

RAY: No, I'm not going to play Judy. Although she is our patron saint. (*He crosses himself and takes a long, thoughtful pause*)

BRIAN (*to Ray*): What are you doing?

RAY: I was having a moment for Judy!!! (*Pushing the start button*) Okay— here it is!

JAMES: What is it?

RAY: Patience. Patience.

(*The first chords of the music plays—it is "Close to You" by The Carpenters—as soon as the intro begins, various reactions from the guys*)

JAMES: NO! Not this!

RAY (*No one is going to say a word against Karen—Ray won't allow it*): She had the voice of an angel. An *angel!!*

JAMES: Oh, I hate this kind of stuff!

KEVIN: She was a goddess!

BRIAN: Oh, I love her. I used to sit home on rainy Saturday afternoons and just listen to her.

ANDY (*finally recognizing it*): Oh, my grandmother used to play this all the time when I was a kid. (*Ray leaps to his feet to attack him, but James intercedes*)

(*They pair up and slow dance. Ray and James, Philip and Brian, Kevin and Peter. Andy is without a partner. Peter tosses him the teddy bear. Ray sees this and relinquishes James to dance with him. Ray ducks off stage. NOTE: See the Production Notes regarding this song. On the bridge— "That is why, all the girls in town . . .", Ray re-enters with his turtleneck*) *capped over his head flowing down like long hair, and begins to lip sync as Karen. The guys fall apart. Brian, Peter, and Andy do a back-up routine behind him as the others crack up. The energy here is like the jumping jacks—it is very animated with a lot of movement and lots of joking around. After the "Whaa, whaa, close to you's" begin, the guys all fall out onto the sofa, and as they hug and laugh, leaving the audience with this brief tableau, the lights fade out . . .)*

(Curtain)

DANCING IN THE MIRROR

by John M. Clum

Dancing in the Mirror was first produced at the 1999 Duke University Festival of New Works for the Stage. The production was directed by Kevin Low with original music by Masanao Sato and Jason Fagg. Jeffery West and Kevin Poole played Philip and Steven.

An earlier version of the play was performed as part of the *Pieces of the Quilt Project* of the Alma Defina Group, San Francisco, in July and December, 1998. Sean San Jose directed.

Dedication

For its muses: Greg Scott and Erin Cressida Wilson

Characters

Steven is twenty-five. He is dressed in the usual caterwaiter getup. Tux shirt, tie, cummerbund.

Philip is in his forties. He wears a tux. He walks with a cane.

Setting

A bare stage except for a bonsai tree and a case of wine on the floor.

AUTHOR'S INTRODUCTION

Dancing in the Mirror was inspired by a couple of parties thrown by one of the most charismatic people I know. HIV-positive for seventeen years, this man lives life to the fullest. On his fiftieth birthday, at which all hundred guests had to wear fancy hats of their choosing, our friend was celebrating survival and he did it with a vengeance. A few months later he was hit by lymphoma and a crushed thighbone. He made his recuperation a party Auntie Mame would have envied. We'd go to his bedside to laugh with him. At an Easter dinner at our friend's house, I met a handsome young man, waiter by profession, who our friend had met in the hospital. They had lived through the same gruesome infection together.

When I got the opportunity to write a short work for the Pieces of the Quilt project, I was asked to write a monologue for an older, flamboyant queen (now there was type casting!). So I imagined and wrote the meeting of a fifty-year-old man and a caterwaiter in a pantry during a large birthday party. The first version, *Across a Crowded Room*, was a fifteen-minute monologue from the point of view of the middle-aged birthday boy. My Duke colleague, playwright Erin Cressida Wilson, encouraged me to turn it into a two-character play.

Though the *Pieces of the Quilt* series is meant to be a memorial to those we have lost to HIV-related infections, I wanted to write a play about those who live with HIV. In the course of the half hour of *Dancing in the Mirror*, Philip and Steven come to regain their erotic spark, their ability to revel in the pleasures their own bodies can offer them.

I have never had the opportunity to see the performances of my work in San Francisco, but was lucky enough to see a perfect production as part of the annual Duke Festival of New Works for the Stage, a showcase for the work of faculty and student writers and visiting professionals. The Festival has introduced works by Nilo Cruz, Dakota Powell, Jose Rivera, Ariel Dorfman, Tina Landau, and Reynolds Price. A brilliant young Singaporean director, Kevin Low, gave the script just the right tone. Two student composer-performers created a lovely score that was both unobtrusive and powerful. Jeffery West, an actor with loads of stage and screen credentials, gave Philip just the right sort of wistfulness and Kevin Poole, who had just finished playing the lead in a remake of *Ode to Billy Joe*, was a touching Steven, appropriately ironic and angry. It's a writer's dream to have such an ideal performance of his work.

JOHN CLUM
Baltimore, 2000

When the audience enters, Steven and Philip are at opposite sides of the stage looking at each other.

STEVEN (*to audience*): I am turning into a tree.
I want to turn into a tree.

When I was human,
I loved my body more than anything in the world.
Since the moment it stopped being a pudgy boy's body
and became magical.
Then I loved watching other boys' bodies grow.
Their backs turning into that inverted triangle as shoulders broadened.
The thrilling line of hair from the navel
Pointing to the nest for those growing treasures.

I loved watching that happen to me.
Loved my new body.
I would lock myself in the bathroom, take off my clothes, a striptease,
And dance for myself.
Through the mirror I was also the adoring audience,
watching this new body dance.
Two people. The adoring eyes. The adored body.

Later I loved skin, beautiful skin. The textures, the colors, the smells.
I loved the feel of my skin against the skin of others. Electric.
But I kept my distance. Usually.
I wanted to be like I saw myself in the mirror; beautiful, but unreachable.
People who looked could imagine whatever they wanted,
but they'd never get too close.
People could want me, but I would wait to bed the one I wanted,
Another unattainable, mysterious image.
Oh, I knew that his mystery was the same as mine—
There was no mystery at all.
Nothing but eyes and a body.

The worst thing that could happen, I thought, was age, which was like
falling off the face of the earth.

Little did I know.

I was careful.
Careful to stay in shape.

Careful not to get emotional.
Who wanted to get emotional?
Careful about precautions when I got physical.
But sometimes I got carried away,
When I occasionally found my match,
Mirror images caressing, kissing, licking, sucking, penetrating.

Was I superficial to love surfaces? Skin? Hell, no! Realistic.

Then I started turning into a tree.
A blight—purple spots.
A band of radioactive bark across my torso burning fiercely.
Unwanted fruit—lumps.
Oh, everything can be controlled now.
I won't die.
Mad doctors saw to that.
They hit me with invisible bolts of lightning,
Bored into me and filled me with acid that burned.
The insides I never thought about now hurt.
Now I'll be okay for a long time, they say.
They say I may not have any more lesions or radioactive bands
or lumps,
But I'm not me anymore.
This isn't the body I loved to watch dance.

Until my skin turned against me, I never felt anything intensely but the
pleasure of my skin.
Now that the insides have been scorched, I wonder what else
they can feel.
Can I stir something in there to glow the way my skin glowed?
Can it feel as wonderful as the ravishment I know I'll never enjoy again?
Can it hurt more than the burning of my torso?

Now I need to believe there's something under the rough bark.
But I don't believe there is.

I'm working again, tending bar at this party
Serving champagne to the A list.
A hundred or so of the Guest of Honor's closest friends.
The gay guys all know each other.
The straights are trying to act cool.

The guest of honor looks.
He's been looking at me all night.
What does he see?
This one frightens me.
He's another kind of mirror.
And I avoid mirrors now.

I head toward the pantry to get more wine.
The guest of honor is following me.
He's turning into something too.
You can see he's fighting like hell to stay human, but he knows
his skin isn't flesh anymore.
It's bark. Like mine.

PHILIP (*to audience*): I used to be a party doll.
Not the prettiest guy around but the most fun
When in doubt I surrounded myself with people.
Let them feed whatever hunger I have.
Now crowds make me feel lonely.

For seventeen years I have survived the plague.
My friends died, my lovers died, but I lived.
Like the Flying Dutchman, I'm cursed,
Outliving everyone, half living.

(*Philip sings Wagner's* Flying Dutchman *theme. Laughs*)

That's what this party is about.
It's not just a birthday party.
It's a survival party.
I should consider myself lucky. I have survived.

(*Sings first lines of* I'm Still Here *from Follies*)

But these are not the terms I bargained for.
I'm tired of survival.
After this performance, I'm going to end it.
That was the plan. Until . . .

That bartender with the beautiful, haunted eyes,
I've been watching him all night.

I'm fascinated, hooked,
And, like a dog on a scent, I follow that young man
into the kitchen pantry.
How seventies.
Except this number was barely alive in the seventies.
What the fuck am I doing?
Pretending everything's all right,
Time hasn't passed.
Or maybe I am a ghost, haunting him,
He's certainly acting like he doesn't see me.

Now that I've followed him in here with him, what do I do?
I know what I'd have done in the seventies.
But it's the nineties and I'm old—er, and coupled, and—"compromised."
(*To Steven*) Hi. Thought maybe I could give you a hand carrying
in the wine.
I know. How the hell am I going to carry in the wine with this cane?
I haven't seen you around. Are you new in town?
Oh, God! That was bad.
Don't worry. I won't compromise your virtue.

STEVEN (*to audience*): What do I do with this old queen?
Blow him off or flirt with him?
Well, it's his party.
(*To Philip*) Virtue? What's that?
(*Steven bends down to get the wine, showing off his ass*)

PHILIP: Oh! I'm not invisible.
(*Steven looks baffled*) What's your name?

STEVEN: Steven. And you're Philip, right?

PHILIP: Right.

STEVEN: Happy Birthday!

PHILIP: Thanks. I'm forty today.

STEVEN: Did they make a mistake with the candles?

PHILIP: You counted the candles? You know the ugly truth.

I'm really middle-aged now. Whoopee! A triumph of sorts.
I'm a living irony. I've made a fortune in antiques while living
in terror of age.
Like many of us, I wanted to be Dorian Gray.
Instead, I'm the picture.
Don't tell me I don't look it.
I look like Margaret Hamilton on a bad day.
"I'm melting."
I'm sorry to lay all this on you. I had to be honest with someone tonight.
It's my birthday, after all.
Tonight, for the last time, I'm youth and beauty.
Like you.

STEVEN (*to audience*): He's good! I haven't heard a line like that in years.
It bounces off, though, and lands on the ground.
(*to Philip*) Thank you.

PHILIP: I've watched you from across the room, Steven.
Zillions of people between me and you.
Faces of well-wishers thrust before mine, small talk flying
everywhere,
but I haven't been able to take my eyes off of you.

(*Sings first line of* Some Enchanted Evening *from* South Pacific)

God, I'm singing Rodgers and Hammerstein to a caterwaiter
in a pantry! I am losing it.

STEVEN: I think it's very flattering.

PHILIP: Really? Thank you!
I thought it was just corny—as Kansas in August.
Sorry. Once I start . . .
Too much of the Turning Leaf, I'm afraid.
Turning Leaf.
I don't know what it has to do with grapes, but, well, for this event . . .
A burst of brilliant color, then you pick them off the ground.

STEVEN (*to Philip*): We'd better get back to the party.

PHILIP: Ah, the party.

Dear Martin planned this fete to celebrate my survival.
To make my triumph over It palpable.
But it's not working.
Tonight—all these nice people—are just a diversion.
I'm still hungry.
For? I don't know exactly. *Someone.*
You, I think.

STEVEN (*to audience*): I'm picking up on his cues, giving the right responses—I was always good at that.
I'm remaining mysterious.
Until strips of my skin start peeling off.
(*Steven starts to leave*)

PHILIP: Please. Stay just a minute more.

STEVEN: Look—I've got to get back.

PHILIP: Who's going to fire you? Me? It's my party, darling.
I know I don't look like the sort of guy you want to spend
time in a pantry with.
And I absolutely understand.
Humor me just a moment more. Please. (*Beat*)

Do you know when I first saw you, I fantasized you, naked,
popping out of my birthday cake.
Pure old fashioned lust I was grateful to be able to feel.
Am I scaring you, Steven?
I'm harmless, really.
I'm not going to rip your clothes off.
However much I'd like to

STEVEN (*to audience*): If he ripped them off now, he'd be in for a big surprise.
Bark.

PHILIP: I'm supposed to go back into the hospital Monday.
The alien has spawned new monsters. Young, nasty ones.
Monday they inject me with poison to fight my other poison—again.
More puking and aching and—worst of all—hair loss.

They say it will keep me alive.
But I swore I wouldn't let them do that to me again.
I was going to finish the job tonight.
I've been saving up the pills.
At midnight, like Cinderella, I would disappear.
No more Night of the Living Dead.
Then I saw you and realized that blood still courses through these veins.
It's not just attraction. We're joined somehow.
Aren't we?

STEVEN (*to audience*): Flayed! That's the word, isn't it?
His words are ripping off strips of my wounded skin,
That hadn't finished hardening into bark.
He's living through what I lived through.
He sees me.
No fair!
When he finishes with the skin, what will he see?
Something is spurting out!

(*Stephen holds onto himself frantically to avoid bursting or physically falling apart*)

PHILIP: Steven! What are you doing?

STEVEN: They did it to *me!*
They kept me alive, but they changed me.
I'm something else now.
You want to see! Look!
(*Stephen takes off his shirt*)
This one I'm unwrapping for you, you think is so beautiful.
I hate it.
My skin is gone.
Something else is growing in its place.
A tree. Wood, not flesh.

PHILIP: Trees don't feel.

STEVEN: I feel nothing.

(*Steven is sobbing. Philip holds him*)

PHILIP: You're feeling something now, aren't you?

STEVEN: I don't want to.

PHILIP: But you are, aren't you?
                              As I am.

STEVEN: A new burn,
                  Like the chemo, but further inside.

PHILIP: That will keep you alive,
                  Till you feel your skin again.
                  Till you see it's still beautiful.
                  I've decided to survive. You did that.
                  You're obligated now.

STEVEN: To what?

PHILIP: To me. To live. To fight.

STEVEN: What the fuck are you talking about?

PHILIP: Listen! You know what I mean.
                  A beautiful warrior. Noble.
                  You're fighting your horrors beautifully.
         The dragon can't be slain, but you tried and survived.
   Beautiful warriors carry battle scars outside and in but stay radiant.

STEVEN: You can't see . . .

PHILIP: Yes I can.
                  Do you still think battles are easy?
   I'm so glad the fates—or the Psychic Friends Network—or Martin—
                  hired you to be behind that bar tonight.
                  So we can help each other.

STEVEN: I can't help you.

PHILIP: I need a kindred spirit. So do you.
                  Feel my skin. Put your hands under my shirt.
                  We can share heat.

Please.
(*Steven puts his hand under Philip's shirt*)
You're shuddering.

STEVEN: Warmth. Inside.

PHILIP: What about the outside?

STEVEN: Oh, yes!

(*For a long moment Steven and Philip silently hold each other. They look into each other's eyes. They come close to kissing, but don't*)

PHILIP: Bark, my ass!

STEVEN: Your boyfriend might think this is a little weird.

PHILIP: Dear Martin.
I'm not forgetting him.
Martin fights for me, loves me. I love him.
But he's scared of my body too.
I need a comrade. Someone who knows.
We can make the fight beautiful.

STEVEN: What can we give each other?

PHILIP: Such a pragmatist.
We've already given a lot.
See what happens.

STEVEN: This is eerie. Tonight's my first job since I got out of the hospital

PHILIP: No kidding?
And you get trapped in the pantry by a crazy person.
I'm sure that's happened to you before.

STEVEN: Not this way.

PHILIP: Well, I've had some encounters in confined spaces with humpy young men in my time, but none quite like this.

STEVEN: You want to see the rest?

PHILIP: Not necessary.
>> We've seen each other inside to inside.
>> Where beauty lies.
>> Will you help me?

STEVEN: What?

PHILIP: Live! I'll help you.

STEVEN: I'm not sure I know how to do this. I was better with the body stuff.

PHILIP: No reason to stop that. There will be gentlemen callers, I'm sure.
>> We have something else.
>> Now you'd better put your shirt back on.
>> We'd both better get back to the party.
>> The guests will be wondering what happened to the bartender—
>> and the wine.

STEVEN: And the birthday boy.

PHILIP: Oh, I'll be across the room.
>> Watching.
>> Knowing.

STEVEN: I might love being watched again.

PHILIP: That's a start.

STEVEN: I'll be watching you too.
>> I love you.
>> I don't know what that means.

PHILIP: No one does.
>> Thank you.
>> We'll help each other survive.
>> Ghosts and trees no more.

STEVEN: I wasn't kidding about the tree.

PHILIP: I know, but, sometimes, darlin', you've just got to laugh!
>> You're still beautiful.

Believe it!
Now how the fuck are we going to make a graceful exit from here?

STEVEN (*to audience*): And he was gone.

PHILIP (*to audience*): How times change.
When I was his age, I would have had him in that pantry, and maybe never
seen him again.
Now we make connections that are more fraught but lovely in their way.

STEVEN (*to audience*): They've always gone for the body before. What
else was there?
Is there more now?
I felt . . . something . . . inside.
I picked up a case of wine and went back to the bar.
My fellow bartender was pissed off and ever so curious.
Philip was standing on the other side of the room by the fireplace
with his back to me
Talking to Martin and some friends,
A couple I had seen before, a tall guy and his partner.
I could see his face in the mirror over the fireplace.
Our eyes met through the mirror. He winked.
I excused myself again, much to the dismay of my fellow bartender,
And went into the small bathroom off the kitchen.
I took my clothes off. My old striptease.
I looked into the mirror at the guy in there. Not bad.
I danced a little, just a few steps, just enough to show we liked
each other again,
The dancer and the watcher.
I put my clothes back on and went back to work.
The other bartender was really curious and pissed off.
I took him home later.
This body had to touch someone.
Skin to skin.
It felt good, but there are other connections now.
Inside to inside.

PHILIP (*to audience*): That night Martin and I had sex.
Bo, was he surprised!
So was I.
Monday Steven and Martin were at my bedside.

Martin brought flowers.
Steven brought a tree, one of those bonsai things.

Steven and Martin, beauty and truth.
What can I say?
"Fools give you reasons,
Wise men never try."

BORDERS

DEPORTING THE DIVAS

by Guillermo Reyes

Deporting the Divas was originally directed by Jorge Huerta and produced at the Celebration Theatre of Los Angeles with the following cast:

Michael/Sergeant	Julian Vicente
	Robert Adanto
	(alternate leads)
Marge/Dean/Leonel/Sirena/	
Groom 2	Christopher Liam Moore
Sedicio/Miss Fresno/The Fan/	
Groom 1/Silvano	Rene Moreno
Teacher/Lucy	Rush Gomez

The play was further developed and produced at Borderlands Theatre of Tucson; in a co-production between Theatre Rhinoceros and Teatro de la Esperanza in San Francisco; Miracle Theatre of Portland, OR; In Mixed Company of Phoenix; and The Sixth at Penn Studio of San Diego.

POSSIBLE CHARACTER BREAKDOWN

Other combinations are possible, can also be done with four actors.
ACTOR 1—Michael/Sergeant
ACTOR 2—Marge/Dean McMurphy/Leonel/Groom 2
ACTOR 3—Sedicio/The Fan
ACTOR 4—The Teacher/Lucy/Groom 1
ACTOR 5—Miss Fresno/Sirena/Silvano

AUTHOR'S INTRODUCTION

In 1994, California Governor Pete Wilson jumped onto the bandwagon of immigrant-bashing by endorsing the notorious Proposition 187, ensuring his re-election. This hotly debated and dubious proposition sought to legislate immigration policy usually reserved for the federal government by expelling the children of illegal immigrants from school and denying all sorts of government aid, including prenatal care to immigrants. But the political winds were foreboding for legal immigrants as well. The California electorate was convinced that the ills of the state could be blamed on all foreigners, and the Republican Congress elected that year went to work to deny legal immigrants all sorts of public funding.

At that time, I had recently (and for the first time ever) written a play that had met with positive reviews and popular appeal. *Men on the Verge of a His-panic Breakdown* started at the Celebration Theatre as an off-night event on Mondays and Tuesdays, was transferred to the mainstage and played for several months. Actor Felix Pire, expertly directed by Joseph Megel, had pulled off a phenomenon of laughter and pathos that I didn't myself understand. They would eventually recreate the same magic for off-Broadway in the spring of 1997 where the play won the Outer Critics Circle Award for best solo performance. That play was an anthology of monologues delving into the lives of immigrants who happened to be either gay or "ambiguous." Their sexuality influenced the world's view of them as "outsiders" but their immigrant status, especially in California, put them at odds with the prevailing political winds that sought to scapegoat all immigrants. Something in the play hit a chord with both the gay and the Latino community and sympathetic viewers who were neither Latino nor gay.

I hadn't set out to write an epic on the lives of the gay immigrants, but there was enough material that could justify a "sequel." *Deporting the Divas* became a follow-up and was initially written as a sketch-monologue play on various aspects of the various controversies over immigration and sexual identity that California society was contending with. Yes, it was written to be timely and contemporary, with an eye out for all sorts of current trends. Four years later, I'm convinced that it's a mirror of its time and there's no need to update it.

Professor Jorge Huerta at UC San Diego, a Chicano theater scholar and director, saw *Men on the Verge* in L.A. and expressed an interest in directing my next play (in fact demanded to do so), and he arranged the various readings and development workshops needed to get "Divas" off the ground. "Divas" went through several successful readings and became a four-man play which specifically told the story of a Mexican-American (supposedly straight and married) officer and his relationship to an undocumented young man. Duty to one's country and one's wife became challenged by the alternative lifestyles that young Sedicio represented. The world premiere of "Divas" in 1996 brought me back to Celebration in L.A., but was met with mixed notices. The love story and the "issue-oriented" monologues were suddenly at odds. Even trusted friends complained of a lack of structural unity. I was lucky that Borderlands Theatre of Tucson was committed to doing the play and they accepted a major rewrite in which the central love story became the main focus and the monologues a secondary issue. By the time the play opened at Theatre Rhinoceros in San Francisco, the love story had completely taken over the text, and the side issues, the fantasies and secondary monologue, de-emphasized. For better or for worse, the play had become a love story. This time the Bay Area Critics nominated it for Best Original Play and the play won the Drama-Logue Award in the same category. Readers of this version will see, more or less, the version that emerged in San Francisco and was subsequently produced in other cities such as Portland (Miracle Theatre) and Phoenix (In Mixed Company), and New York (Here Space).

Thus far, as of this writing, a production in San Diego itself has eluded me. The issues hit too close to home, the theater scene is homophobic, who knows? The play needs to go home, in my opinion. Inspired by the borderland culture I experienced as a graduate student at UC San Diego, I tried to capture the lively bustle and hustle of a busy city on the move by coming to grips with one of its primary issues, its status as a border city where the two nationalities, so crucial to Mexican-Americans, come face to face, even more so in relationship to the ambiguities of sexual preference.

I wanted to face up to my personal issues as a Chilean-born American citizen of tainted sexuality and to do so with the style and wit of the many fabulous "divas" who haunt the main characters' imagination and who provide him with an imaginative escape from a challenging world. I wanted to tackle sex and politics with the alacrity of song and dance, mystery and fantasy, and emerge the better man (and diva) for it.

GUILLERMO REYES
Tempe, Arizona, 2000

ACT I

Introduction

Marge emerges from the audience. She is a real woman played by a man, not a drag queen, a "Church Lady" type.

MARGE: Excuse me. This won't take long . . . I just wanted to make sure to welcome you all, on behalf of my very own Ladies of the Club. I'm, of course, Marge McCarthy, your Chairwoman-for-Life. So welcome to tonight's little *divertissement* entitled *Deporting the Divas* by Mr.—oh, heaven help me—(*mispronouncing*) Gooey-llar-moe Rees.

The name may sound foreign and illegal, but the author is, I understand, a U.S. citizen. We'll take him at his word and won't check his papers. Now, girls, girls, I know I got you all to come out here without even telling you what this play was about. Tricky of me, I know, but I hope you do stay regardless of the homosexual propaganda you'll see here tonight—I better choose my words carefully: those people are all around us as we speak, isn't this fun? But, don't worry, the artistic management promises no fellatio or cunning-aningulus on stage—now don't look too disappointed, girls. (*Laughs*) Oh, I'm so naughty tonight!

Anyway, I figured the gay issue would be no problem. We all have sons in the military—and daughters, especially daughters. That issue, I figured, is covered. I think, however, frankly, you ladies would be a lot more intimidated tonight by the immigrant issue. Having a gay son these days is not as tragic as having an immigrant in the family. It's bad enough that some of you haven't spoken to me since I voted against Proposition 187 and I'm not a liberal, God help me, but I tell you this much, ladies, nobody's about to deport my hired help!

It's not fair that some of you are even threatening to revoke my chairwomanhood just because of this one li' issue and all I can tell you, ladies, is . . . I have files!

Yes, employment files on all the illegals you ladies have hired through the years. As my cousin Joseph McCarthy might have said: If I go, ladies, you're coming down with me!

Like you, Mrs. McGillicutty whose children speak more Spanish than Linda Ronstadt. All those illegal nannies and gardeners brought them up humming the lyrics to "Canciones de Mi Padre." Well, I've got your file, lady!

And you, Mrs. Tanner whose husband gambled Orange County's money on the Merril Lynch lottery! You talk impeachment, I'm talking stud service—Salvadoran illegal window washer—possible illegitimate children—husband can't tell the difference? Get the message, sugar?

You women don't know how lucky you are that I'm mostly discreet and lovable and at peace with my demons, so don't fuck with me, ladies! You leave my chairwomanhood alone and next year, when I run for mayor of San Diego, I expect you to campaign for me door to door! Or else.

Well . . . (*very sweetly now*) do enjoy *Romancing*—err—*Deporting the Divas*, and look for me: I make an appearance as a character somewhere in Act 2. I'm being played by a man. I don't know if he's gay, Mrs. Hillerby. You should know, you married one. Ooops! I told you—I'm just so naughty tonight, I better stop—Okay, I've stopped, so thank you again for being here, my very own, my brave, indomitable Ladies of the Club!

Prologue

San Diego, the border. In the background, we hear "The Wedding Samba," sung by Carmen Miranda.

Michael enters, carrying a flashlight. He's a young, late 20s, INS officer, Mexican-American. With his flashlight, he lights up the stage, looking longingly at the place surrounding him. We don't know what this place is, or where he is. We do know he's searching for something there. He's not searching for illegal aliens, that's for sure, and we realize this place holds some sort of memory for him.

He turns to the audience. He has to share this moment with us. He's in a frenzied, maniacal mood, better know as a "His-panic breakdown."

MICHAEL: This is where it happened. 1995. San Diego, California. The borderland. The desert. In this very barn. I saw it here: the two grooms dancing the "quebradita" to the beat of "The Wedding Samba" . . . yes, it was a gay wedding—a Mexican—make that a Mexican-American gay wedding—female priest, multi-layered cake, no-host bar, practical gifts: toaster ovens and Mary Kay products—

Oh, they say I've had it. I'm seeing things, talking to myself, to an imaginary audience as if I were an actor or make that a character in a B-movie. My wife's leaving—no, I think she left already—but I saw it— And I was only coming in here to round them up, deport a few "illegals" which is my job so don't judge me, but instead this happened, the same-sex wedding with a Southwestern motif . . . since then, I've seen a lot more and I'm often scared that what I will see next brings me closer to madness—either that or personal fulfillment, whichever comes first, and at this point, let it all come at once, let it roll over me like the voices of singing. Sirens luring me to a voyage of no return. (*Hears something*) Who's there? (*We hear someone hiding*) Hello?

(*With his flashlight, he suddenly see the spooky, ghostly look of the luscious Miss Fresno, played by a man*)

MISS FRESNO: Help me!

(*Lights down as we proceed to "Office Politics"*)

Scene One: Office Politics

Dean is on the phone behind his desk at the Border Patrol Office. It's a frenzied place in a busy department.

DEAN (*on phone*): Marge, Marge, we're going through a major crackdown, it's the busiest border on Earth so I don't have time to go see *Deporting the Divas*. (*Michael comes in*) Look, I got my future brother-in-law here. Files? I don't give a damn about your files any longer, Marge McCarthy—I fired my illegal babysitter long ago, you can't touch me now! (*He hangs up. To Michael*) There you are. Well, I got you an assignment. (*Phone rings*) Take a message, Suze!

MICHAEL (*sounds affected, as if he believes he's some superspy or something*): Hey. Where to this time, chief?

DEAN: I'm not your "chief," I'm your patrol commander! I don't have time for your Sam Spade impersonations! Now, says here . . . Salvadoran guy. Private AIDS Hospice of La Jolla. Go get him, don't botch this one up.

MICHAEL: Why do I get stuck with HIV immigrants?

DEAN: I don't know. Shit happens.

MICHAEL: You're making me some sorta specialist in HIV immigra . . .

DEAN: I promise only one newscamera this time.

MICHAEL: A newscamera? No, no publicity.

DEAN: Well, the press got hold of this story already: "Illegal Aliens with AIDS!: Taxpayers Get Stuck with the Bill."

MICHAEL: Oh, great.

DEAN: We gotta show the tabloids we're doing our job. I got Washington on my back, Mr. President wants to get re-elected, the Attorney General— WACO slut—wants a smooth crackdown without incidents—and I'm stuck here with border patrolmen who get too much sun like you. What is wrong with you these days anyway? A raid on a gay wedding in the middle of the desert? People are saying we're homophobic.

MICHAEL: Well, aren't we?

DEAN: Xenophobic maybe, but that's our job! Besides, I'm trying to find the right moment to declare my candidacy, all right? Do you mind?

MICHAEL: Your candidacy?

DEAN: For Mayor, Mike. If I can run a border, I can run a city—hey, that's my slogan right there. I bring stability and moral guidance . . .

MICHAEL: Tell that to your ex-wife—

DEAN: Well, I'm in love with your sister now—

MICHAEL: No! Not my sist . . .

DEAN: Thanks for introducing us by the way. I'm marrying Mex'can like Jeb Bush.

MICHAEL: Great, you're marrying my sister as a political move.

DEAN: No, she's got great legs, like you do, Mikey.

MICHAEL: Spare me.

(*There is a loud fuss outside, we hear the Clerk and the Teacher*)

CLERK (*off stage*): You can't go in there, sir.

DEAN: What the hell is . . . ? (*Sees the Teacher*) You again!

TEACHER: Five minutes! That's all I need.

DEAN: I told you already I don't need any of your workshops around here.

TEACHER: This one's different, a new concept for the nineties: "Self-Esteem for Immigrants."

DEAN: What?

MICHAEL: I like the ring of it, chief.

DEAN: Who asked you? Self-esteem for who?

TEACHER (*correcting*)**:** Whom!

DEAN: Look here, mister!

TEACHER: Sorry. Now, look, look, look, I'm sure you got a lot of depressed, resentful immigrants being kicked back across the border. But that's where I come in—the friendly Puerto Rican! Mainland Puerto Rican. A Nuyorican. While they wait to get deported, I give my lecture. It'll boost their self-esteem, and these people can then leave the country with a renewed confidence and vigor that'll make them contribute to the society where they came from, and they may no longer need to migrate illegally to this country because a new life-enhancing attitude will give them the focus, the energy, and yes the self-esteem needed to make it in their own country. It's good for you, good for the country, the taxpayers will love it.

(*Dean looks impressed all of a sudden, surprising himself*)

DEAN: Well, mister . . . you got something there. "Self-Esteem for Immigrants."

TEACHER: So I get the contract?

DEAN: I don't know . . . give me a second here . . .

TEACHER: It's my most innovative workshop since "Reempowerment for

Liberals," "Celebrating your Celibacy," "Embracing your Inner Foreigner," and "Joan Crawford for Beginners," very popular in San Francisco. But this time I think I've really done it. This is it! My claim to fame: "Self-Esteem for Immigrants." (*To Michael*) Waddy you think, mister?

MICHAEL: Well, I—

DEAN: Leave him out of this. Mister, I don't know whether to hire you or call security.

TEACHER: Please, I need to supplement my income. I teach Spanish for Assimilated Latinos at the City College, never enough enrollments though.

MICHAEL: Come on, boss.

DEAN: What the heck. (*To Clerk*) Form 1-A. Basic contact for a coupla seminars and that's it.

TEACHER: You won't be sorry, mister. You won't be. Thank you, thank you.

(*Teacher shakes Dean's hand exuberantly, almost hugs him and kisses him. Dean gets him off of him*)

DEAN: That way. (*Teacher exits*) And you. You oughta go to night school, get your mind off of things . . .

MICHAEL: I know that, it's true, since Teresita left, I've been alone, I miss the kids. I talk to myself, I watch old movies, I break out in song, I see the strangest things—oh, like Miss Fresno—

DEAN: Miss Fresno?

MICHAEL: My latest encounter in the barn.

DEAN: Another one? After that gay wedding, I'm not sure I want to hear another one of your fanta . . .

MICHAEL: Why, she is not a fantasy, now listen—(*Lights change*)

DEAN: No, no more flashbacks! Damn! I hate those.

(*We go back to the image we saw in the prologue. Miss Fresno stands there. Dean stands frozen in the background*)

MISS FRESNO: Help me.

MICHAEL: Are you all right, miss?

FRESNO: No, I'm not. I just can't face them, all of them, the crowds, the cameras, the endless admirers. I've had it with this life of hiding.

MICHAEL: Hiding? Hiding what? And please tell me I'm not seeing things. People already wonder about me.

FRESNO: What you see is what you get, handsome.

MICHAEL: Really?

FRESNO: Well, not really . . . I'm actually a . . . I'm a . . .

MICHAEL: A what?

FRESNO: I'm . . . I'm an illegal alien, okay?

MICHAEL: But you can't be. You're Miss Fresno, the favorite to win Miss California.

FRESNO: I'm a Guatemalan of German descent, so I pass as they say. I've got no papers, so it's your job to—.

MICHAEL: I know my job, miss, but you're not a—you're not! You can't be.

FRESNO: And move over—I prefer this light. (*Light sparkles above her*) That feels good. Reminds me of my days in the sun watching Mommy pick lettuce.

MICHAEL: Really?

FRESNO: Mommy's the one who discovered my unusual talents. On her deathbed, she held my hand and whispered in my ear: "You look like a white woman, mija, use it."

MICHAEL: And you have obviously.

FRESNO: Except the Mayor of Fresno now thinks he owns me. He's the one who appointed all the judges, and lo and behold, I became queen overnight, but during the coronation, some peach picker/activist breaks into the crowd and shouts "Miss Fresno is an illegal alien!" And he says my mother died of pesticide poisoning for which the mayor, owner of the orchard, should be held responsible along with the system itself. What a radical! But of course they don't listen to him, and they deport him even though he's a Chicano because most people in the U.S. don't know Chicanos are, like, U.S. citizens—who can keep up, you know? So they let me stay and here I am, a candidate for Miss California. I'm headed for Omaha for the Miss USA contest, and then Miss Universe, this year to be held in (*scared*) oh, my God, Guatemala City, my birth place!

MICHAEL: Great. (*As a headline*) "Local Girl Does Good."

FRESNO: But won't they be able to tell in my native country that I'm one of them passing for us, us passing for them? My life's out of control! I am a fraud so no, no, I can't go through with this.

MICHAEL: You have to!

FRESNO: No, I'm all yours now, you people put me on a plane to Guatemala and I'll gladly join my aunt Chuchi Immstrausser back in Guatemala City! I surrender! Well?

MICHAEL (*not quite believing her*): The guys back at the fraternity put you up to this, didn't they?

FRESNO: What? No, I—

MICHAEL: Go back to the suburbs, Deb! (*Laughs*)

FRESNO (*deeper voice*): Look, *pendejo*, I'm hiding a lot more than my legal status, okay?

MICHAEL: Like what?

FRESNO: What I really am is a . . . a . . . well, let me show you. (*Starts unbuttoning her dress*)

MICHAEL (*more intimidated by this*): Wait! Maybe I don't want to know!

FRESNO: Nobody does! Nobody cares! (*She cries and hugs him*)

MICHAEL: Oh, please . . . don't do that, Miss, you really should pursue your big dream at any cost. I mean it!

FRESNO: But do you really think I could go all the way to Miss Universe?

MICHAEL: I think you could.

FRESNO: Even though I'm a . . . a foreigner? And if I went back to my country, would I really be welcomed there?

MICHAEL: Why worry about it? We all learn to show the face that's most convenient.

FRESNO: Really? Do you speak from experience, border boy?

MICHAEL: I say, if they see you as Miss Fresno, why disappoint them? If they see me as Michael, average, beer-guzzling guy with the remote in my hand, mortgage, kids, basketball hoop in the driveway, let them have him.

FRESNO: I see. Okay, fine, if the Border Patrol thinks I'm Deb from the suburbs, who am I to question you? Then take me back to the pageant, hon', I should be in time for the swimsuit competition.

MICHAEL: I'd be honored to. (*He takes her in his arms and carries her to the exit*)

FRESNO: I will remember you. You've been gentle and considerate and—

MICHAEL: Masculine.

FRESNO: Very. Rest assured. You've given me a *firm* shoulder to cry on. What should I give you? (*Melodramatically, "old movie" style*) . . . a memory.

MICHAEL: A memory? But is that ever enough, Miss Fresno?

(*Lights have turned more mystical, more glowing and celestial*)

FRESNO: That is the purpose of us queens—beauty queens, I mean. To let our memory guide you in times of crisis, all of us, in so many shapes and disguises, and wigs. We are heavenly creatures. In the more devout times, I would have come dressed as the Virgin of Guadalupe, but nowadays, you'll have to settle for Miss Fresno.

MICHAEL: Okay. I'm settled.

FRESNO: We will be there for you, my Miguel Angel—

MICHAEL: That's my childhood name—

FRESNO: Miguel Angel, my little angel with clipped wings. I won't forget you. (*She kisses him gently, then pulls away, he's left looking mesmerized*)

(*She walks away to bathe in her glorious spotlight as if back to her pageant*)

FRESNO: Hi, I'm Debbie from Fresno, California and I want peace on Earth and free body waxing for all.

(*She exits. Office lights are restored. Dean looks mesmerized, there's a moment of silence between them until finally Dean has to say something*)

DEAN: Have you thought about taking more Spanish?

MICHAEL: What has that got to do with anything?

DEAN: You need it for the promotion, Mikey.

MICHAEL: Promotion, is that all you ever think about?

DEAN: Besides, Jesuschrist, you're alone in the mountains reading detective novels and hallucinating about weird shit—

MICHAEL: But Miss Fresno is real.

DEAN: Just do something, give up espresso, take up yoga or something—get Teresita back as soon as possible and apologize to her—

MICHAEL: You don't understand, she left me.

DEAN: And can you blame her?

MICHAEL: She doesn't understand my need for . . . for a love affair.

DEAN: She's your wife!

MICHAEL: I don't mean adultery. I mean I need something grand, and magnificent, almost unreal in my life—even if it just happens in my head.

DEAN: You just need more Spanish—roll those r's. And now go do your job, it's the law.

MICHAEL: Fine, excuse me, I have an HIV immigrant from El Salvador to deport—thanks to you! (*Exits*)

DEAN: Man! You . . . you just be careful out in the desert. Wear a hat!

(*Dean looks around, looking shaken. He looks up at the light where Miss Fresno bathed in her magic glow and wonders how that happened? The phone rings. He hesitates, but then finally answers*)

DEAN: Hello? Lucita! Yeh, your brother's fine, just going through a phase—the film noir phase, baby, don't ask me to expl . . . we're all concerned for him, honey. I don't know what's happening to him. Well, I need him, too, I'm feeling all alone in this border. (*Howl of a coyote in the background, a cry of solitude or a mating call; whatever it is, it sounds funky*) We need our Mikey, we need him back the way he used to be, all there, all normal! What ever happened to Mikey?

(*Lights down*)

Scene Two: First Lesson

MICHAEL (*to audience*): San Diego . . . City College . . . Beginning Spanish for Pochos.

(*The teacher approaches*)

TEACHER: Roll those R's, damnit.

(*Teacher exits as poor Michael struggles to roll those r's*)

MICHAEL (*doing the "r" exercise*): "Que rapido corren los ferrocarriles en los rieles. . . ."

TEACHER: You are an embarrassment to your people, Miguel.

(*Teacher exits*)

MICHAEL (*to audience*): And that night, I met him—

(*Sedicio comes in. A light shines on him. It's a very important attitudinal entrance, very diva-like as he wears sunglasses, a dark sports coat, black pants, and a Tt-shirt. He approaches Michael*)

MICHAEL: There he was, ready to utter the words that would forever change my life!

SEDICIO: Is that seat taken?

MICHAEL: Ah, no.

SEDICIO: Let me through then, move it. (*Squeezes past him, then settles down on his seat*) Am I late? Did I miss something?

MICHAEL: Only the whole first week.

SEDICIO: What? You mean the class started last week—Oh, well, who can keep track of the time? Now wait a minute, haven't I met you before?

MICHAEL: I don't think so.

SEDICIO: Sure . . . you're that INS officer. You deported my cousin Javier and his wife last year.

MICHAEL: Nothing personal.

SEDICIO: That's all right. I can't stand them either—especially Javier who's such a homophobe.

MICHAEL: Excuse me?

SEDICIO: Oh, I'm openly gay and he doesn't approve, but I'll have you know they slipped in a few weeks afterwards just by driving through the border.

MICHAEL: They drove through just like that?

SEDICIO: My mom brought them in for a family funeral. Old aunt died of heartbreak and spinsterhood. They stayed to help with the farm. We exploit them, but they're family.

MICHAEL: Right.

SEDICIO: That was a joke.

MICHAEL: Oh?

SEDICIO: I'm actually a fiery advocate of immigrant rights myself but a joke is an attempt to find a comfortable middle ground with someone like you who represents the Enemy.

MICHAEL: I am no one's "enemy."

SEDICIO: And don't tell me you're here to learn Spanish, too, border man.

MICHAEL: Just don't make fun of me please, that teacher's been hounding me.

SEDICIO (*meaning teacher*): Here he comes.

TEACHER: Para los estudianates nuevos . . . yo soy el profesor Serrat, yo soy de Barcelona.

SEDICIO: Good, a real Spaniard!

TEACHER: Excuse me, I'm not a Spaniard, I'm a Catalonian! (*Teacher withdraws, insulted*)

SEDICIO: Ooops! Sorry.

MICHAEL: Last week he was a Puerto Rican from New York.

SEDICIO: I don't get it.

(*Sedicio's left looking confused, and self-conscious*)

MICHAEL (*to audience*): The next couple of weeks, we sit next to each other, not saying much, staring at each other until one night, he thanks me. (*To Sedicio*) Thank me for what?

SEDICIO: For not laughing at me that first day like the rest of the class did.

MICHAEL: Were they laughing? I don't think they—

SEDICIO (*very spazzy, paranoid and cute*): Mocking me, all of them. I was feeling very, very Richie Valenz that day, sensing the turbulence in my private life, the aftermath of a bad one-night stand with a Marine, but you don't need to hear all that—and that teacher, I insulted him without meaning to. You're a real doll, thanks, I owe you.

MICHAEL: Okay, you do. (*To audience*) After class, I ask him out for . . . (*To Sedicio*) Coffee?

SEDICIO: Coffee?

MICHAEL: No?

SEDICIO: Yes! . . . Ah . . . Quel Fromage Coffee House on Fifth and University. Separate cars, street parking should be *doable*.

MICHAEL: No, why take two cars? Let's ride together, you show me the way. I drive an Isuzu Hombre, of course.

SEDICIO: But of course.

MICHAEL (*transition*): Coffee house. Hillcrest. He seems to know everyone. (*Jazz music plays, lending ambience to the place*)

SEDICIO (*acting bohemian and talking Italian to other customers*): Francesca, come va? Ciao, Rinaldi. Tutto bene, caro, tutto bene! This here's Michele. (*Pronounced Mee–kay–lay*)

MICHAEL: Ciao.

SEDICIO: Rinaldi and I go way back. He and I still get together occasionally to—you know—

MICHAEL (*a little titillated*): To what?

SEDICIO: To discuss Derrida's theory on poetic discourse, of course.

MICHAEL: Of course.

SEDICIO: Not that he knows anything about it. He's way too Susan Sontag.

MICHAEL: I read Ayn Rand once.

SEDICIO: Don't even try it. Well, what should I get? Everything's so tempting.

MICHAEL (*to audience*): I order. (*Ordering*) Just regular coffee of the day, please.

SEDICIO: For me, double cappuccino with nonfat milk, cinnamon on top, twist of lemon on the side, two packs of Nutrasweet, one of those long spoons for mixing, and a job application. Thanks, doll.

MICHAEL: Espresso goes to his head. He gets to the point.

SEDICIO: Are you a top or a bottom?

MICHAEL: What? (*To audience*) What the hell was he talking about?

SEDICIO: Do you take it or do you give it? (*To audience*) He'd either punch me or take me.

MICHAEL (*to audience*): He couldn't have been this gay—

SEDICIO (*to audience*): He couldn't have been this straight.

MICHAEL (*breaking reality*): Now wait a second—

SEDICIO: What?

MICHAEL: Don't think I haven't noticed how you break the fourth wall, and start talking to the audience. But you can't do that—

SEDICIO: You do it, too, doesn't he?

MICHAEL: Because this is my story, I am the narrator here!

SEDICIO: The first person narrative can be very patriarchal and oppressive!

MICHAEL: What is that supposed to mean?

SEDICIO: Share your narrative, Michael.

MICHAEL: I will not! This is my space, my struggle, my moment to shine!

SEDICIO: I will not sleep with you then.

MICHAEL: Who says I want to?

SEDICIO: Isn't that what this is building up to? Can you deny it? Huh? (*Michael sits down like a kid who's been scolded by his mother*) Now, let's get something straight right now! I don't have time for closeted men. I want to marry a man by the time I'm twenty-five, and I think I'm already past that, but who's counting. Either you're interested or you're not. I need an answer and I need it now! (*To audience*) I am getting good at this! So . . . Michael? Miguel? Michele?

(*Michael looks a little troubled, "tuned out"*)

SEDICIO (*bragging*): Some revelation had dawned upon him, I have that effect on men.

MICHAEL: I'm just a little . . .

SEDICIO: Married?

MICHAEL: What?

SEDICIO: You're wearing the ring.

MICHAEL: Oh. And that didn't stop you from flirting, did it?

SEDICIO: You asked me out. I figured don't ask, don't tell.

MICHAEL: Yes . . . as you can see, I'm going through some personal . . . changes.

SEDICIO: And you work for the INS—you're a real mess, aren't you?

MICHAEL (*a little upset*): Excuse me?

SEDICIO: I'm sorry. I wasn't passing judgment, I was just observing: Mexican-American Border patrolman who doesn't speak Spanish and is also in the closet. You've got a lot of "issues" and I like that in a man. I'm issue-laden myself, I just got a BA in Italian Literature, and what am I doing with my life? I'm filling out job applications to dole out cappuccino to a bunch of Failed Poets—and look, look, there goes my UC professor: Signora Sabatini! She sold me on the humanities. Fuck the Humanities, lady! Vaffanculo! Vaffanculo!

MICHAEL: Calm down.

SEDICIO: Sorry. How has your week been?

MICHAEL: Like you wouldn't believe—especially that damn wedding—

SEDICIO: Breeder concepts!

MICHAEL: No, this was a gay wedding.

SEDICIO: Oooh, do tell.

MICHAEL: Two Mexican boys. No, one was Mexican-American . . . out in the desert, dancing the "quebradita," it was a very strange sight, never seen nothing like that. At first, I just thought they were a buncha illegals—or undocumented workers, excuse me—so I raided the place and, well, it wasn't what I thought—they were just "getting married" and I disturbed their wedding, and I'm the laughing stock of the department now, we're not supposed to go after weddings, no matter how different. Since then, I . . .

SEDICIO: You were left traumatized by a gay wedding?

MICHAEL: No, it just left me wondering, I guess.

SEDICIO: Wondering what?

MICHAEL: Let's just say, I had to get out of the house and enroll in a Spanish class.

SEDICIO: Really? I'm taking it only because I need to meet a husband.

MICHAEL: In class?

SEDICIO: I'm attracted to Latino men who speak lousy Spanish.

MICHAEL (*to audience*): That would be me!

SEDICIO: My grammar always needs reviewing anyway and it's so lovable for a Latin boy to speak such awful Spanish as you do. I mean it's cute, it's actually macho.

MICHAEL: Then I'm "macho." So, ah . . . ah . . . when—when do we cut to the chase and do what you gay men do?

SEDICIO: What?

MICHAEL: I don't know how you folks—proceed—in mating rituals and all—but I read it in *Newsweek*, about how promiscuous you all are, let's get to that.

SEDICIO: Whatever happened to candlelights, music, and a substantial dinner?

MICHAEL: Don't you back down now. You wanted an answer and you wanted it now so here you are. My wife left me for a reason, to test me perhaps, to see how far I'd go, and now here I am with you. I need to know what I feel and why I feel it, whether this is the right thing for me or not and you've practically volunteered, so you can't take it back. You flirted with me and now you're stuck. So when do we get to it? Give me a time and a place 'cause I need some big changes in my life and I need them soon, preferably now!

SEDICIO (*intimidated*): But . . . I'm into dating.

MICHAEL: What about that Marine?

SEDICIO: That was a very sordid one-night stand!

MICHAEL: That's what I need then!

SEDICIO: I won't do that again.

MICHAEL: Great, now you say that!

SEDICIO: I have rules about all this, I'm gonna be a teacher one day, and I believe in establishing the rules right upfront. Three dates might get you a hickey.

MICHAEL: Does this count as a date?

SEDICIO: I should say not!

MICHAEL: I think it does. We'll go out tomorrow, and the day after and that's it. You live close, don't you?

SEDICIO: Near the Gay Center on Normal Street.

MICHAEL: Within walking distance?

SEDICIO: Yes, why?

MICHAEL: Well, because—(*backing down a bit*) look, I have a lot of studying—my promotion actually depends on me learning better Spanish. How would you like to tutor me? I'll come over.

SEDICIO: I'm not comfortable with this, Michael! It borders on sleaze.

MICHAEL: Then here's my card. Need a ride?

SEDICIO: Not right now.

MICHAEL: Suit yourself. But now at least you know where to find me. (*Michael exits*)

SEDICIO: Goodness! (*To audience*) What have I done? A Marine, a border patrolman, I'm being used by the sexually repressed right-wing of this country. (*Transition to apartment*) But leave it to my roommate Leonel, the only Costa Rican in San Diego, to encourage sexual compulsion—

LEONEL (*cynically, deep voice*): Oye—There are no knights in shining armor, so suck the frogs while you can.

SEDICIO: Just because you choose to be unattached and promiscuous.

LEONEL: Lifestyle judgment alert!

SEDICIO: I'm sorry, comadre, but some of us prefer the nurturing qualities of a long-term relationship. That's called civilized behavior.

LEONEL: That's called reading too much Jane Austen. (*Shows him the wig*) Now—*oye tu, mira*—you like this?

SEDICIO: What? You look like—

LEONEL: Marge McCarthy, *la politician esa!* I'm gonna win first prize this time, I know I am. *Y tu?* Why don't you come?

SEDICIO: No. I can't. People will proposition me, and a boy can get tired of that—I am just a romantic lost in the banality of San Diego! Help!

(*Enter Michael*)

MICHAEL: So I end up on his doorstep. (*Knocks or says*) Knock, knock, knock.

LEONEL: It's past midnight! The zoo is closed!

SEDICIO: Oh, my God, it's him—

LEONEL (*looking through window*): Ay papacito!

SEDICIO: : Shhhh!

LEONEL: How did he find you?

SEDICIO: I've let him give me rides the last couple of weeks.

LEONEL: A ride on his what?

SEDICIO: Quiet! (*As he pantomimes opening door*) Michael?

MICHAEL (*nervous as he sees Leonel*): Hi. Is that . . . Marge?

LEONEL: I better leave before somebody gets aroused.

MICHAEL: Nice to mee . . .

LEONEL: We haven't met, chico, and I don't ask for names. (*Exits*)

SEDICIO: Don't mind him. Leonel is wanted in Costa Rica for indecent acts with iguanas.

MICHAEL: Okay. Well, I could have sworn he looks so much like Marge McCarthy.

SEDICIO: So, what brings you here, border man? Tutoring?

MICHAEL: No. I was on my way home.

SEDICIO: Right, near Julian.

MICHAEL: Yes . . . I'd like to start staying in the city, less driving that way—

SEDICIO: Look. I made you a list.

MICHAEL: A list?

SEDICIO: I was going to give it to you in class, but fine—here's what I will do before a meaningful relationship, and here's what I won't do until after the commitment ceremony, and here's the gray area, a very generous gray area. Take it or leave it.

MICHAEL: I don't need this.

SEDICIO: Look here, I won't go out with you unless you agree to fol-low—

MICHAEL: Listen to me! I've been thinking about what you said and maybe you're right.

SEDICIO: I am? I'm usually known for rigorous equivocations.

MICHAEL: Please. Maybe we should be cautious and take it slowly this day and age: I'm willing to explore a relationship with another man what-ever that means—it's new territory for me but I'm open to it—So here it goes: I want to make love to you—

SEDICIO: A little louder so the neighbors can hear.

MICHAEL: Let me finish. I want to make love to you only within the boundaries that you have so wisely set up.

SEDICIO: To hell with my boundaries, baby, come to mamma.

MICHAEL: Yes.

SEDICIO: Wait! One more thing!

MICHAEL: What?

SEDICIO: Just so you know, just so it's out there and let the chips fall where they may: I . . . I'm undocumented and proud!

(*Beat*)

MICHAEL: Well . . . ah . . . (*To audience*) Would a man compromise all his values and duties for one moment of satisfaction? (*He checks him out again, then back to audience*) Oh, yeah! (*He grabs Sedicio, they kiss, tri-umphant music plays, the lovers dance*)

(*There's a switch of lights, as this scene follows a progression of imagery choreographed to sensual movements. They do a dip. Sedicio ends up on top, which horrifies Michael who breaks out of this*)

MICHAEL: I'm on top.

SEDICIO: Whatever. (*They correct the dip, Michael's on top*)

SEDICIO: We both failed class that semester!

(*Teacher enters quickly, crossing stage*)

TEACHER: Latino Students Fail Spanish! Shame, shame, shame! (*Teacher exits quickly*)

(*Out in the desert, in the car*)

SEDICIO (*romantic*): I demand long walks along the border fence.

MICHAEL: Tight embraces in the night as more aliens are apprehended and loaded onto trucks.

SEDICIO: Romance flourishes as politicians whip up hysteria and disdain.

MICHAEL: We take endless drives into the desert.

SEDICIO: The car radio blares out a "bolero" from a radio in Tijuana.

(*Actor sings or radio blares out "La Historia de Un Amor" or other romantic song, possibly "Mi Mundo" by Camilo Sesto, they dance romantically like Leslie Caron and Gene Kelly in* American in Paris *very briefly but enough to set a tone of romantic excess. which should also be comic*)

MICHAEL: We dance by the sunset.

SEDICIO: Wet kisses resonate into the night as the snakes rattle around us, savoring the drool of hot saliva on the sand.

MICHAEL: But suddenly—INS helicopters invade the night as we embrace beneath the starlit sky.

SEDICIO: Let's go before they think we're committing shocking, immoral acts that will destroy Western Civilization.

MICHAEL: Like sodomy?

SEDICIO: No, immigrating!

(*Michael grabs him as helicopters fade away*)

MICHAEL: I keep him safe in my arms, and my mind begins to imagine creative ways to bend . . . his rules.

SEDICIO: He likes to talk dirty!

MICHAEL (*to Sed*): Dirty? I'm just trying to share "fantasies."

SEDICIO: I'm tired of fantasy. I demand reality.

MICHAEL: Listen . . . You might think it's odd but sometimes, I fantasize that I'm a detective—

SEDICIO: What? Why?

MICHAEL: I'm a police detective and one day while I'm investigating a crime, I meet her—

SEDICIO (*jealous*): Her? Who?

MICHAEL: She's an Argentinian tango temptress.

SEDICIO: A real woman?

MICHAEL: You never know. That's the mystery of Sirena.

SEDICIO: She has a name and everything?

MICHAEL: As long as she's dressed as a woman. Do you ever—?

SEDICIO: I'm not about to dress up as a woman.

MICHAEL: I thought all gay men—

SEDICIO: Get with the program, border man. Not everyone's a drag artist, not that there's anything wrong with it. I mean, I'm not against these gay icons, the obligatory Streisand album, preferably the first, but that's about it. I think people should get out of the house a lot more, leave alone the old movies, organize politically, and just seize power from the pigs—

MICHAEL: We're a free country, there's no need to be so militant.

SEDICIO: Oh, yeah? I think gays and lesbians should take over the military and impose a reign of obligatory same-gender sex.

MICHAEL: Well, it sounds unpatriotic, but what the heck, why don't we work on it, you train me.

SEDICIO: No don't you get started. I'm not ready for that type of sex—

MICHAEL: You want me to "come out," don't you?

SEDICIO: Politically first.

MICHAEL: I just don't understand your rules and ideas and politics.

SEDICIO: You're still with me after all these weeks, aren't you?

MICHAEL: Yes.

SEDICIO: Because you like me, my kisses, my soft-core approach to eroticism.

MICHAEL: I think you're a prude. And I thought I was repressed!

SEDICIO: You either believe in a relationship or you believe in a series of quick insertions. I've already made that mistake before without lubricants and without emotional attachments and I don't know which one is more painful. But I'll grant you one fantasy.

MICHAEL: Really? What?

SEDICIO: Something no gay man should do without.

MICHAEL: Like what?

SEDICIO: I can't, it's too personal.

MICHAEL: Say it.

SEDICIO: No, you'll just laugh—

MICHAEL: Come on!

SEDICIO: A finale.

MICHAEL: A what?

SEDICIO: Out of *Funny Girl* preferably, the song where the heroine of the story pours out her heart in gut-wrenching pathos . . . she was a struggling chorus girl once, now she's a star but her man's no longer with her. He returns from jail one day, but he's no longer the man he used to be, they're not meant to be together any longer, but she tells him, "you've made me feel beautiful." "You are beautiful," he says. To a gawky young woman, that means everything. He leaves, but she's ready to face her public, a curtain goes up, she faces the lights and she begins her song . . . her voice takes flight . . . she is a star! (*"My Man" sung by Barbra Streisand plays softly*)

MICHAEL: That's what you fantasize about?

SEDICIO: Look, *pendeho*. One day, if you're a real homo, you'll understand the importance of a good finale to get you through the day. I mean, can you even sing?

MICHAEL: Not in public.

SEDICIO: Case in point. One day, you'll sing "My Man" in public.

MICHAEL: No way!

SEDICIO: It's a rite of passage.

MICHAEL: Look, that's enough. Shut up, Barbra. (*Sound cue goes off*)

SEDICIO: How dare you shut Barbra up!

MICHAEL: Don't take it so personally . . . And don't worry, you don't have to dress up as Sirena. It's better to leave her where she belongs, in the imagination.

(*In the background, we see the silhouette of the sensual, tango temptress Sirena, dressed as a nightclub singer, all sinuous and shapely, then exits as the lovers kiss.*

We segue into "Nostalgias" as Michael returns with his trenchcoat and private dick hat and "Nostalgias—the Tango Fantasy" can begin)

Scene Three: Nostalgias—The Tango Fantasy

CHARACTERS:
Sirena Angustias—Tango singer and femme fatale
The Sergeant—from Santa Monica Police Department, Michael's alter ego.
A Fan (*at Nightclub*)/Shadow of Hans/Lucy the Secretary

Enter the Sergeant, Michael's alter ego, played by the same actor, leaning against a light post as the Santa Monica fog rolls into the night.

SERGEANT: She came into my life, as the dames usually do, in the line of duty. Investigating a crime. Homicide. A series of homicides. Involving some fairies—excuse me, I mean, gay males. That's sensitivity training for you, something new at the Santa Monica Police Department. I had to follow this one lead. They gave me her work address, a joint on Santa Monica Beach, the Tango Gulch where suspicious-looking people for various genders gathered to engage in illicit activities such as indoor smoking. I coulda busted them—damn smokers!—but instead I decided to indulge in the tobacco vice myself. It turned out, the late-night crowd was also summoned to witness and experience her . . . her . . .

(*Sergeant sits by a table. A voice comes on*)

VOICE: Ladies and gentlemen, please welcome back, after her third divorce and six months of rehab followed by liposuction, it's that spitfire of Buenos Aires . . . Sirena Angustias.

(*Enter Sirena, dressed up as a chanteuse, starts singing a spirited tango in the Libertad Lamarque tradition, a melodramatic 40s tune about broken hearts, death, vengeance, redemption such as, perhaps, "Uno," with its revealing lyrics about the singer's loss of her heart due to a destructive affair:*

> *"Si yo tuviera un corazon,*
> *el mismo que perdi*
> *Si yo pudiera como ayer*
> *querer sin presentir. . . ."*

Sirena is of course played by a man, but she is not just a camp impersonation of womanhood, she is womanhood, at least in its 1940s incarnation of a masochistic suffering heroine with a hidden past and tremendous destructive passion)

SERGEANT: Sirena . . . deep down, I understood she was a travesty of womanhood, but my body responded to the illusion.

(Sirena sings towards him, he is entranced and withdraws)

SERGEANT: So . . . *(Clears his throat as he composes himself)* She joined me after the show.

(She approaches, hand outstretched demanding to be kissed. He shakes it instead)

SIRENA: Good evening, Sergeant.

SERGEANT: At last we meet, Sirena.

SIRENA: What can I do for you? I don't normally speak to the cops.

(A fan interrupts)

FAN: Excuse me, Miss Angustias—

SIRENA: Yes, I know, dear, you'd like my autograph.

FAN: No, would you carve your name with a knife deep in my heart?

SIRENA: I'll have to work on it, asshole. Get! *(The fan leaves, all scared)* They get worse every day. What about you, what do you demand from Sirena?

SERGEANT: I notice you haven't returned my phone calls.

SIRENA: I don't return phone calls, I just don't do that.

SERGEANT: I can't work that way. Now . . . See this picture? (*Shows her picture of young blonde boy*)

SIRENA: Looks familiar.

SERGEANT: More than familiar. He's been seen here with you for the past coupla months, you and he been keeping each other company.

SIRENA: What of it?

SERGEANT: He's wanted in several states.

SIRENA: He's a German tourist, an endangered species. You have him confused with someone else.

SERGEANT: I think you're a little brighter than that, senorita.

SIRENA: That's "senora" to you.

SERGEANT: Your little German tourist is an agent of DEFANG.

SIRENA: Defang? You mean—

SERGEANT: Yes, the notorious militia that kidnaps gay men and tries to turn them straight with 24-hour videos of exotic animals mating and re-producing in National Geographic documentaries.

SIRENA: Such cruelty!

SERGEANT: And he's no German, he's a Puerto Rican.

SIRENA: Mainland or native?

SERGEANT: Don't matter!

SIRENA: No, you can't trick me! I will never cooperate with the cops!

SERGEANT: I have contacts with the INS.

SIRENA: Oh? What of it?

SERGEANT: Come on, Sirena, you married the owner of the nightclub and showed up at the INS as a citizen's wife to straighten out your legal status—

SIRENA: How did you—?

SERGEANT: You were able to fool the INS that you were a woman, but you can't fool the Santa Monica Police Department. Your marriage is invalid! Honestly, I'm shocked—it's not even a marriage based on love.

SIRENA: A woman is entitled to her adventure!

SERGEANT: Come on now, I could have you deported overnight, especially since you're wanted in Argentina for crimes committed there—

SIRENA: Como te atreves, pibe?!? (*How dare you!*)

SERGEANT: Every man you have loved ends up a cadaver.

SIRENA: A girl's bad luck.

SERGEANT: There was the American ambassador, gunned down by terrorists one night in the streets of Buenos Aires.

SIRENA: His crime was loving me too much.

SERGEANT: Oh? There was Martin de la Grazia, Tango czar of Patagonia, found with an icicle piercing his heart as it melted.

SIRENA: Any jealous lover would have done that, I have many of them.

SERGEANT: There was General Bencaduto, infamous, deadly, but cute, head of the secret police during the dark 70s. He was found naked, his body bitten all over by probing, serrated teeth.

SIRENA: The teeth of a beast, not a woman.

SERGEANT: I can see why you've settled into your rent-controlled apartment in West Hollywood. . . . I have done my homework, Sirena, you cooperate with me or I'll have you deported.

SIRENA: You drive a tough bargain. . . . (*Seductively*) I like that in a man.

SERGEANT: Just the facts, little lady.

SIRENA: I . . . I met him at . . . (*Stops*) no, I can't, I won't cooperate, my German boy is not a criminal, for once in my life I am involved with someone who loves me for what I am, he wouldn't dare "defang" me. Deport me, do with me what you'd like, but I will not betray the man who loves me, adores me, and worships me as I deserve to be worshipped! For I am a pagan goddess! (*Sirena exits, hissing the line "goddesssssss"*)

SERGEANT: I left it at that. That's what I usually do, plant the seeds of doubt. Meanwhile, I went home that night to open up a can of sardines and lulled myself to sleep with an oversized bottle of Sapporo. The Santa Monica fog had started to creep into the place . . . I slept with the gun neatly placed near my heart, it's a comfort of sorts.

A few days passed, and life at the department continued as it usually does. . . I arrived that morning. Lucy behind the desk, drinking her tenth cup of espresso.

(*A wired Lucy, also played by a man, sits behind a desk. She's a stern-looking spinster who dresses like a jail warden and is not so secretly in love with the Sergeant*)

LUCY: Your coffee, Sergeant. And, ah, there's some glamorous tango transvestite here to see you. (*She takes his coat*)

SERGEANT: Really?

LUCY: Yes, I made her wait with the prostitutes.

SERGEANT: Lucy, for goddsake!

LUCY: I don't like her! She's more feminine than I'll ever be! Sergeant?

(*He's been trying to comb himself and get himself ready to impress Sirena*)

SERGEANT (*distracted*): Ah, yes, coffee's a little cold.

LUCY: But it can't be! Gosh-darn it! I just made it—

SERGEANT: It's only coffee, Lucy.

LUCY: It's not just coffee, it's my failure to provide for you in every possible way! How can I ever make you happy, Sergeant?

SERGEANT: You poor woman, have a raise, buy new shoes with it.

LUCY: Why, Sergeant!

SERGEANT: Later, sweetie. (*Lucy exits smiling. He motions towards Sirena*) There she was overlooking the window, rays of the sun behind her, as they reflected on the Venetian blinds, furs neatly in place, she looked like Eva Peron's illegitimate daughter. Why, Sirena . . .

SIRENA: Que tal, che? (*She starts to cry*)

SERGEANT: What happened? You pissed off that Lucy sent you here with the hookers?

SIRENA: Nonsense, we all practice a trade or other. (*To one of the hookers, quick aside*) Catch ya later, Heidi. No . . . I was crying because . . . The signs are all there, you were right.

SERGEANT: From the top.

SIRENA: Just go get him.

SERGEANT: How did you meet? Are there more of them around? Where do they gather?

SIRENA: Just get him, I'll be your main witness, I have the outfit for it.

SERGEANT: Sit down . . . from the top. Talk, you tango troll!

SIRENA: All right. How did we meet? Like you and I. At the club . . . It was one A.M., the fog had rolled in as I sat down to relax by the bar, late night cappuccino in hand, and eager to read by the dim light, the collected works of Manuel Puig.

SERGEANT: Who?

SIRENA: Never mind. There in my early A.M. solitude, he approached me. I looked up and saw the blue eyes blinding me like searchlights, the blonde Nordic hair like lustrous gold shining in the dark of night, and his voice the delicate purr of a kitten.

I was in love already. Or rather, Sirena was in love, for love should be handled in the third-person tense, as an emotion too distant to be reconciled with the reality of first-person grammar.

SERGEANT: I hate grammar, go on.

SIRENA: Oh, I can't! I'm betraying the man I treasure, he'll be put away for good, and yet what becomes of me, Sergeant, all alone, me, a woman of many needs.

SERGEANT: Some other swell guy will come along!

SIRENA: Not quite like him. I admire the blatant carnality of his lips.

SERGEANT: I know, I know, Sirena—

SIRENA: No, you don't. People like you never understand!

SERGEANT: From the moment I saw ya, don't you think I realized it, you need to be kissed and kissed hard by someone who knows how on all your lips!

SIRENA: Sergeant, I'm surprised!

SERGEANT: I'm surprised, too. Let's face it, from day one, since we met, I've felt it.

SIRENA: Felt what?

SERGEANT: This sense of destiny. Haven't you?

SIRENA (*not convincing*): Ah, sure . . . I've felt it.

SERGEANT: I feel a tango coming on.

SIRENA: What? Don't even kid about such things.

(*Music plays. He seizes her and makes her do the tango*)

SIRENA: Sergeant, please! oh!

(*She finally relents and takes on that grand attitudinal posture that the tango requires, with all its twists and turns, and facial gestures that betray grand diva-dom. He finally lets her drop, and they're both out of breath*)

SIRENA: You throw a pretty mean tango there, Sergeant.

SERGEANT: As long as you're dressed as a woman, of course. I'm no queer.

SIRENA: Of course not.

SERGEANT: I'm a boy from the barrio, East L.A., we don't do sexual ambivalence there, but as a woman, you are a creature who deserves to be worshipped, Sirena. (*He kisses her. She allows it, but then she pulls away*)

SIRENA: Why, Sergeant . . . What should we do next?

SERGEANT (*passionately*): The inevitable.

SIRENA (*with sadistic connotation*): Arrest the boy and have him flogged naked?

SERGEANT: No, I mean . . . we've had a few bachelor parties in this room.

SIRENA: Sergeant . . . please. (*She slaps him*) We have an emergency on our hands, we must find the Defanguer—we must put an end to him, otherwise, you said it, he'll be a threat to the community.

SERGEANT: Of course . . . ah, after the show tonight, he'll come by, I assume—

SIRENA: I have plans to meet him by the pier.

SERGEANT: No, not the damn pier, Sirena.

SIRENA: I think it's romantic. And if we're going to work together in destroying the only relationship in my life that's come close to absolute passion, then we'll do it my way!

SERGEANT: All right . . . we'll be there. Meanwhile, behave naturally—

SIRENA: As naturally as I can. And Sergeant?

SERGEANT: What?

SIRENA: You're a swell type of guy.

(*Sirena blows a kiss, he's left entranced*)

SERGEANT: My life was in shambles, never thought I'd fall for some tango transvestite . . . I was in love—or rather, the Sergeant was in love, in the third-person tense as a passion disembodied and detached from my real self. That night . . .

(*Sedicio enters and interrupts. They're in Leonel/Sedicio's apartment*)

SEDICIO: Excuse me? Over here—Michael—could we get some light, management, thank you.

MICHAEL: My big bust-up is coming up.

SEDICIO: There are just a couple of things I don't understand.

MICHAEL: What? It's a pretty simple tale of mystery and suspense—

SEDICIO: I mean her.

MICHAEL: What? You don't like her? You're jealous?

SEDICIO: Not even! I mean she's so full of attitude—

MICHAEL: Oh, and you're not?

SEDICIO: Like . . . I mean, are you attracted to men or not?

MICHAEL: This isn't the time for—

SEDICIO: For instance, I know quite well I'm attracted to men, and I don't see myself falling for transvestites. Face it. This tango fantasy is a perfect example of the socio-political repression that you, as a man, have absorbed into your psyche.

MICHAEL: You got it all wrong.

SEDICIO: Yes, you're really attracted to men, but somehow it's more acceptable that he'd be dressed up as a woman. It's a mask, it's a closet, get over it.

MICHAEL: You're reading too much into it.

SEDICIO: I have an expensive college education behind all my theories.

MICHAEL: And what good has it done you? Let me finish—

SEDICIO: Look . . . I just need to know. Do I have a chance?

MICHAEL: What?

SEDICIO: I need to know if I'm wasting my time.

MICHAEL: No, you're not but . . . look, maybe this mystery is just a bisexual fantasy.

SEDICIO: I don't believe in bisexuals, I'm opposed to them, and since when do you call yourself that?

MICHAEL: Isn't there room for a little ambiguity here?

SEDICIO: I think it's time for you to leave behind your repressed fantasies no matter how glamorous, and embrace the "open border" lifestyle that I represent.

(*Sirena comes out*)

SIRENA (*to Sedicio*): Excuse me, a-hem, your politics are truly admirable, *my dear, and in many ways correct, but you're fucking up my act, kid! Michael, get back into my fantasy at once! (Sirena exists with grand flair)*

MICHAEL: I warned you.

SEDICIO: Just wait till the Commitment Scenes in Act Two.

MICHAEL: Beat it!

SEDICIO (*sexual connotation*): I intend to.

(*Michael gets back into the Sergeant's role and continues. Lights off on Sedicio who watches from now on, skeptically*)

SERGEANT: That night, I'm not sure what happened. We arrived on time at the pier. One A.M. The show should have ended by then. I had the place surrounded. Everything was ready for my big bust up—I knew I had Defang in my left hand!

But something went wrong—we heard the screams from a distance, a dark corner of the pier we hadn't been vigilant enough to light—

SIRENA: Help me! He's got a gun.

(*We see Sirena being held by a man in the shadows*)

SERGEANT: She tried to negotiate.

SIRENA: He wants a hundred thousand fliers posted all over West Hollywood, maybe Silver Lake, too—a few places in Malibu. Malibu? There aren't that many queers in Mal—he's serious! He wants the world to know the benefits of Defang, the organization that will bust the entire gay movement and put everyone back in the closet by the next presidential election!

SERGEANT: Nothin' doing. I'm as straight as any man, but I won't do this to my queer brothers and sisters—sensitivity training has paid off!

SIRENA: In that case . . .

SERGEANT: We heard the scream—and then the splash. We ran to the water, and then we saw the ocean turning red. At first, we thought it was

Sirena's makeup running, but no it was blood, there were sharks in the ocean. I thought I had lost her. Sirena! Instead, Sirena washed up against the Santa Monica shore, padded shoulders firmly in place. She looked like a creature of the ocean landing on my private beach. Venus emerging from her shell.

SIRENA (*coughing up water*): Cough-cough—where is he? The Boy from Stuttgart?

SERGEANT: Still thinking of him? Damn! And then she saw it, wash up on the sand—it was the toupee of blonde golden hair—

SIRENA: And his contact lenses! His dentures—he used dentures?

SERGEANT: Even his pecs washed up at the shore.

SIRENA: Why is it that every time I love a man, the best parts of him turn out to be false?

SERGEANT: So he's dead. (*Not very sensitive transition*) How about a drink?

SIRENA: I'm sorry, Sergeant, it's best that we part as friends. That is what we are, isn't it?

SERGEANT: Yes, of course, but what the hell, I love you, Sirena, in the first-person singular, damnit! I know it's not reciprocal—but that's the thing about you divas, always falling for the guy who'll do the most damage. I love you and reserve the right to! Just don't let the guys in the soccer club know. You'll keep my secret, I'll keep yours.

SIRENA: Oh, Sarge. You're gentle, considerate, upright, decent, not my type at all. (*She kisses him lightly on the cheeks and then they separate*) I won't forget you. Call on me when you need some fashion tips—just where did you get that godawful tie! I shall miss you.

(*They part. Sirena exits. Lucy enters, looking awkward in new dress and shoes*)

LUCY: Sergeant.

SERGEANT: Why, Lucy, what are you doing at the pier at 2 A.M.? You look terrific.

LUCY: New shoes, new hairdo, Sergeant, I got a new attitude!

SERGEANT: That's nice. Why don't we get a squad car to take you home, okay?

LUCY: She's gone, isn't she? For good.

SERGEANT: Yes.

LUCY: Isn't it time for you to indulge in more normal passions, Sergeant?

SERGEANT: Maybe it is. But I need time.

LUCY: Time for mourning, I understand. Will I see you at the office?

SERGEANT: I'll be there.

LUCY: Look around you, Sarge. I think you'll find some swell gal around the corner when you least expect it.

SERGEANT: Yes, thank you, Lucy.

(*Lucy exits, looking rejected, but still hopeful*)

SERGEANT: Poor Lucy, she was so damn hairy.
    From then on, instead of going home at night to eat from my sardine can, I would show up at the Tango Gulch, have a drink with the boys and the girls and the "others" . . . and there she would be . . . (*Sirena enters. She sings "Nostalgias": "Nostalgias, de escuchar su risa loca y sentir junto a mi boca . . . "*)
    Sirena, spitfire of Buenos Aires, shady dame from the Pampas who loves to sing the tango. . . . she was my woman. I was her sergeant. And from a distance, our lives were swell, just swell together.

(*She ends on Nostalgias' sweetly bitter ending:*

> *"Desde mi triste soledad,*
> *vere caer las rosas*
> *muertas*
> *de mi juventud."*)

(*Lights go off*)

ACT II

Scene One: *Carmen Miranda for Beginners*

Teacher/Lecturer, a nervous, lonesome, desperate little man who's eager to be heard as if for the first time in his life. He addresses the audience. He's wearing a robe that hides his Carmen Miranda outfit beneath.

TEACHER: All right, settle down, people. Act Two is about to begin. I'm not going to say it again. Thank you.

I know most of you are eager to get back and explore the romance and passion of Act One, but I just had to get this off my chest. I'm a little angry that the playwright doesn't give me any quality time with Michael. Mikey? Miguel. Michele. What's with that guy, Sedicio? Says he's not ready for that type of sex? What the hell's that supposed to mean? Little Miss Prude! I would have put out a long time ago, baby! Shown Mikey a thing or two, taught him the ropes if you get my drift, heh, heh.

But that's all right, my self-esteem does not suffer. Although my image does: I'm just comic relief around here. (*A hand reaches out, grabs him, trying to pull him off stage. Teacher struggles with him*)

Hey, dickhead! Go do some rewrites!

The playwright depicts me as some ridiculous seminar instructor when actually, I'm a serious scholar, and I'll take a few minutes now to address a very pressing matter—this is the cause of my life, mind you—and I've got petitions for you folks to sign outside—so I'm here to protest the shameful exclusion from the university curriculum of an ignored, cultural minority—no, I'm not talking about Chicano poets. Forget literature, honey. I'm talking about the grand culturally advanced aesthetics of . . . Carmen Miranda.

Who? How dare you? Who, she says. Well, I guess I'll have to do my "Carmen Miranda for Beginners" lecture then, won't I? I'm tired of how the film schools of this nation have taken it upon themselves to exclude Carmen—such a shame, such a scandal, it's discrimination against Brazilians, it's plainly Eurocentric. Is it because of the hat? The hat! I think I've got one lying around. Here! (*Pulls out Carmen Miranda hat from suitcase, and exhibits it*) Carmen . . . Oh, Carmen, where is she now? Carmen Miranda. Brazilian bombshell, samba dancer, and singer. Big star in the 1940s. Most people don't know this but . . . she was a woman. Yes, she was. No drag queen could have done what she did, awaken the inner goddess in me, well, (*self-conscious*), in all of us, I mean. All that energy released upon a simple hat. (*Wipes away tear of emotion*)

You see, for her it wasn't just a hat. For her, this was an extension or shall we say a craneal appendage much more powerful than any phallus. As you see here, the hat came adorned with rich, ripe, juicy tropical fruits which were, in my opinion, a precursor to the Stonewall riots. The Stonewall riots? As in New York City—queens riot after Judy Garland's death—you see, that bar at Stonewall was well-represented by Puerto Rican drag queens well versed in the Carmen Miranda tradition of fruity hats. So let's give credit where credit is due, shall we?

Through the years, the fruit hat has become a symbol of a pagan ritual of sexual ambivalence. A Carmen Miranda song such as "Mama—Eu Quero Mamar" translates roughly into "Mama, I want to suck your dick." My Portuguese is rough and I like it that way, okay? Of course, this theory of sexual ambivalence in Carmen Miranda songs did get me into trouble with my thesis committee at Stanford and my enemies did finally succeed in locking me up at the Rancho Santa Fe Mental Ward in California. Part of the conspiracy, yes, *the* Conspiracy, which goes up to the highest reaches of the federal government! An attempt to deny us the rich cultural heritage embodied in the gay immigrant! . . . Anyway, let's not forget the shoes. The shoes! (*Pulls out these platform shoes*) She designed them herself. She was a tiny little thing so . . . I can't resist . . . (*He puts them on*)

You see, I'm convinced Carmen is the key to finding the answer. Yes, the answer to one of the great mysteries of sexual identity: what's the connection between the gay male and the female Diva? Carmen, Madonna, Eartha, Diana, Evita, Barbra, Judy, especially Judy! My theory is: the Diva has been battered, trashed around, used, and spat out like a queer or like an illegal alien, or combinations thereof, and yet she has fought back with sweat, guts, and tears and continues to occupy a space in our collective imagination. She's tough, she's grand . . . (*The robe comes off and he's wearing a wonderful Carmen Miranda outfit*)

She's fabulous! Occasionally, she falls from grace, but only to blast from a stereo yet again! She deserves to be worshipped as the spiritual androgynous force of nature that she is! She is there to redeem our genders and to bless and coalesce them and, at last, we are free to love and dance and taste forbidden fruit. (*Wipes a tear*) Well, I'm so inspired today for some inexplicable reason. It's my tenth anniversary of celibacy. Shall we celebrate it? (*Looks in the direction of theater entrance again*) Oh, the theater management has chosen to call out their hunky security guards. Sometimes, one has to look at male authority in the face and say, take me! All right, all right. Let me just leave you all with one of Carmen's favorites. . . . (*He claps and the music magically comes on*) I say let the weddings begin!

(*He plays "The Wedding Samba" which segues perfectly into the next playlet,* Why Gay Weddings Make Me Cry, *as the two grooms dance a mishmash of the "quebradita" and the "samba."*)

Scene Two: Why Gay Weddings Make Me Cry

The two grooms dance the "quebradita" as Carmen Miranda song "The Wedding Samba" plays in the background. It's a lively spirited dance and it should be obvious that this is no ordinary gay couple. These are newlyweds. One puts a ring over the other's finger. They kiss. Michael comes out, addresses the audience.

MICHAEL (*to audience*): San Ysidro, the border. An informant calls in with a tip, says they gather in an old shack in the desert, dozens of them, clustering there and making their getaway at midnight in caravans. We surround the place. We come in, knocking down the door. But these are no ordinary immigrants and by the look of things no ordinary grooms.

GROOM 1: Our papers are in order.

GROOM 2: Here's our wedding certificate—

MICHAEL: Not quite the papers I had in mind.

GROOM 2: I'm a U.S. citizen.

MICHAEL: How about the other "groom?"

GROOM 1: Ah, student visa, of course.

GROOM 2: You can't deport my, ah, husband at a time like this. It's all perfectly legal.

MICHAEL: Not the wedding.

GROOM 2: But it's symbolic!

GROOM 1: Would you like to kiss the bride?

(*They laugh, Michael feels humiliated, the grooms exit*)

MICHAEL: A laugh at my expense . . . why not? I smiled, gave them a break, didn't check papers—And so the grooms danced the "quebradita" that night. When I got back home, Teresita had left a note . . . she was taking the kids to stay with her mother in Arizona—permanently! My lips were cold, she said, my arms failed to embrace and hold. I drank a beer overlooking the glowing mountain sunset. It's a comfort of sorts . . . (*Transition to office*) A couple of months later.

(*Dean enters quickly, hands him an invitation*)

DEAN: Time to do it.

MICHAEL: What? What is this?

DEAN: The wedding invitation, your sister's finally agreed to go ahead with it. This spring.

MICHAEL: Congratulations, I guess.

DEAN: No cheap gifts, if you don't mind.

MICHAEL: Dean . . .

DEAN: Yes? Anything going on, big guy? You got out of the house, huh? Learning better Spanish?

MICHAEL: Yeah, and some of the lyrics from "My Man."

DEAN: What?

MICHAEL: I mean, Barbra Streisand sang that in *Funny Girl*. It was the finale, very moving. I rented it. I was just curious.

DEAN: Well, don't get too curious.

MICHAEL: I'm learning lots of new things, Dean.

DEAN: Right. Well, gotta go—and, oh, don't forget your report on that HIV immigrant, need it tomorrow morning—

MICHAEL: But Dean—

DEAN: Gotta go. (*Dean exits*)

(*Transition to Tijuana*)

SEDICIO: Border Town, Mexico. Tijuana.

MICHAEL: Not real Mexico.

SEDICIO: Our Mexican friends are embarrassed by Tijuana.

MICHAEL: Not real Mexico, they say.

SEDICIO: Does that mean San Diego is not real USA? Think about it.

MICHAEL: We have our pictures taken on the little horsey.

SEDICIO: We explore the Curio Shop.

MICHAEL: Masks, puppets, wigs! The Divas can't be far behind.

SEDICIO: Can people tell we're in love?

MICHAEL: Can people tell I'm an INS officer?

SEDICIO: There's still too much that's left unsaid.

MICHAEL: Nothing needs to be said—except (*To Sedicio*) I got a letter from my five-year-old in Flagstaff. Crayon letter.

SEDICIO: How quaint. I think it's time for the little ones to meet me.

MICHAEL: What?

SEDICIO: Shouldn't they get used to me?

MICHAEL: I'm not used to you.

SEDICIO: Let's drive out to Arizona and meet them.

MICHAEL: The type of things you like to do are illegal in Arizona.

SEDICIO: Come on, I'm serious, I think the kids should meet their father's boyfriend. It is what I am after all, isn't it?

MICHAEL: You'll meet the kids when and if I'm ready.

SEDICIO: It's been almost three months. So let's try this . . . (*to audience*) and this is called a major relationship test—watch closely and don't try this at home—(*to Michael*) when are you planning to move in and kick Leonel out?

MICHAEL: Move in?

SEDICIO: Yes, as my lover should.

MICHAEL: I wouldn't want to kick out anybody.

SEDICIO: We'll move out on our own then. How about one of those condos out here in Rosarito?

MICHAEL: An INS officer living in Mexico, how would that look?

SEDICIO: There's plenty of Americans living in Rosarito, the whole border is a joke anyway. I mean look at us.

MICHAEL: The border is still the law. You break it, you pay for it.

SEDICIO: It's more complex than that, you oughta know, you're bisexual.

MICHAEL: You don't need to call me that in public!

SEDICIO: You're a Chicano at least. Can you say that in public?

MICHAEL: Mexican-American. (*Louder for public to hear*) I'm also a married man here!

SEDICIO: We'll work on that.

MICHAEL: I'll be the one to "work on that."

SEDICIO: I've sent out the invitations.

MICHAEL: What type of invitations?

SEDICIO: To the housewarming party. Both our names are on it.

MICHAEL: Hold on—

SEDICIO: I also invited a priest.

MICHAEL: A priest?

SEDICIO: A priestess actually—New Age church, very nondenominational. She might be a witch actually.

MICHAEL: A witch?

SEDICIO: Trust me, you don't want a Catholic priest.

MICHAEL: And you expect me to—

SEDICIO: You don't have to be there. I'll commit to a relationship, and one day you'll show up to fulfill your side of it.

MICHAEL: You're actually holding a gay wedding without me.

SEDICIO: I'm inviting you now, wear a tux. Bring the kids.

MICHAEL: Marriage is overrated. If I were a gay activist, I'd put my energy elsewhere.

SEDICIO: Okay, I'm feeling a little rejected right now.

MICHAEL: Good! You should.

SEDICIO: Michael, I'm in love with you and I want to spend the rest of my life with you.

MICHAEL: Oh? Oh . . . No kiddin'! Damn!

SEDICIO: And one day, you'll give up your stupid job—

MICHAEL: I like my job, thank you very much!

SEDICIO: —which requires you to sell out your own people—

MICHAEL: That's not—

SEDICIO: —not to mention your soul, and you'll go traveling the world with me. We'll be free.

MICHAEL: Oh, yeah? Who's gonna pay for it? I think my job serves a purpose—

SEDICIO: What purpose, Michael? Michael?

(*Suddenly, out of the Curio shop's Masks and Wigs area emerges the ghostly-looking Silvano. Sedicio freezes. Michael briefly enters another reality*)

SILVANO: What took you so long?

MICHAEL: What? You were in intensive care, we had to wait—

SILVANO: The world doesn't wait. The job must get done. Do yours! Now look at me, I'm dressed for my deportation! I've waited for you all this time, my Miguel Angel!

MICHAEL: How did you know my name?

(*Sedicio snaps him out of it. Lights are restored. Silvano exits*)

SEDICIO: Michael . . . I'm talking to you.

MICHAEL: Yes, my job . . . Has it ever occurred to you that people need jobs, that not everyone can hang out at the coffee house reading whatever you read?

SEDICIO: Nietszche, Kerouac, Sor Juana and Jacqueline Susann.

MICHAEL: See what I mean? Not everyone can be idle—

SEDICIO: Idle? I—I make occasional pocket money—

MICHAEL: How?

SEDICIO: Oh, smuggling drugs.

MICHAEL: What? What?

SEDICIO: Oh, I don't mean coke or pot. I mean, occasionally people with AIDS ask me to go down to Tijuana and buy them medication not approved by the FDA. I figure it's a service to people while maintaining my well-known "edge."

MICHAEL: Edge? This isn't about "edge." You're gonna get in trouble with your edge! Hell, I'm gonna get in tr . . .

SEDICIO: Oh, Michael, the rules were made up by people who believe God is a straight man who runs a college somewhere in South Carolina where interracial dating is still banned.

MICHAEL: To you nothing is sacred.

SEDICIO: That's not true. I think love between two responsible adults is sacred—in the pagan sense of the word.

MICHAEL: I don't see myself going to family get-togethers talking about my male partner.

SEDICIO: Oh, you mean those family get-togethers when all the men are in patio drinking their Tecate talking about the world cup and all the women are in the kitchen making little tortillas.

MICHAEL: Right, you've obviously been there, you know what I mean. I don't see Uncle Ramon drinking his tenth beer and then leaning over to ask how Little Sedicio is putting out.

SEDICIO: Assuming our lovemaking can be reduced to such a vulgar expression as "putting out."

MICHAEL: You know what I mean, and Uncle Ramon's become a Mormon, too.

SEDICIO: I slept with a gay Mormon once—

MICHAEL: That's enough out of you!

SEDICIO: Cute missionary boy this big.

MICHAEL: Stop!

SEDICIO: Are you blushing?

MICHAEL: You're pushing it!

SEDICIO: All the way inside, baby, till it hurts!

MICHAEL: No, you forget—you don't do that on the first date!

(*Marge McCarthy enters*)

MARGE: Mike, is that you?

MICHAEL: Oh, my God.

MARGE: Michael, I know that face anywhere. (*To Sedicio*) Oh, yo soy Marge—

SEDICIO: You speak better Spanish than I do, girlfriend.

MARGE: Oh, well, thank you! He's so cute. You too, Mike. Is this your new . . . ?

MICHAEL: Classmate.

MARGE: I see. So when is Teresita coming back from Arizona? She's a gem, that girl, such a gem. We have group tickets to see "Deporting the Divas" by Googallamoe Reeves, and sorry, no hubbys allowed, no kids, either, just us girls. I hope she can make it. So when are you two getting back together again, huh? Huh?

MICHAEL: Marge, do we have to talk about this now?

SEDICIO: I think you should, Mike.

MARGE: If I may say so, the future of this country depends on couples like you and Teresita getting back together again. It's good for the kids, it's—

MICHAEL: Yes, I know.

MARGE: You know me, I'm still not over Ronald Reagan divorcing Jane Wyman. Some of those Reagan kids are still messed up. Oh, and that boss of yours stood me up at "El Conquistador."

MICHAEL: He's engaged to my sister, Marge.

MARGE: Oh. I didn't know this. I see. I'm tired of how little respect I get. There's even some homosexual running around in San Diego dressing up as me and he won first prize in a contest. I'm just the butt of all jokes because I believe that America is for Americans only—you two count, I guess! Anyway, I'm sorry. I have new candelabra to buy, and then me and the girls are gonna get ourselves some of those birdbath margaritas, and we're gonna learn to do the macarena! We just love TJ, maybe you'd like to join us—

MICHAEL: No, Marge, but thank you.

MARGE: I see. I've got files, you know! And I'm going to use them. I will strike soon, very soon, at the Miss USA pageant.

MICHAEL: What?

MARGE: Ooops, gotta go. Wait for me, girls! Arianna, I love that ceramic burro. (*She exits*)

SEDICIO: You didn't introduce me as your boyfriend.

MICHAEL: Not to Marge McCarthy. We should go.

SEDICIO: Michael, a few seconds ago, I declared my love for you—very naive of me, I've never done that before, but . . . React, Michael—

MICHAEL: Maybe I'm not ready to react, all right? And maybe I won't be driving into the city as much any more.

SEDICIO: Sure, run away from it, Mike.

MICHAEL: Have fun crossing the border!

SEDICIO: Like my relatives, you mean?

MICHAEL: You know, a man can get tired of your little comeback lines. You sound so—so gay when you do that.

SEDICIO: Excuse me! What is that supposed to . . . ? Michael!

(*Michael exits. Transition back to Sedicio's apartment*)

SEDICIO: Back to my apartment on Normal Street. (*Calling out*) Leonel? Somebody? Hello?

(*Leonel enters carrying a suitcase*)

SEDICIO: What's wrong? Where are you going?

LEONEL: Back to Costa Rica, that's all.

SEDICIO: Why? You can't leave—

LEONEL: Mira. Mira esto. (*Look*)

(*Leonel shows him a letter*)

SEDICIO: What is this?

LEONEL: Marge McCarthy's lawyer wants me to "cease and desist" from dressing up as her. *Vieja loca, chingona.* She calls it defamation, and if I don't stop, she'll send the INS after me.

SEDICIO: What? She can't do that, you've got a student visa, don't you? (*Leonel doesn't answer*) *Ay cabrona*, Leonel, you're not undocumented? Are you?

LEONEL: My visa lapsed. Like yours. I used to think I would apply for citizenship—*pero ahora*, I'm disgusted with everything that's going on here. Maybe I can go back to Costa Rica and harass Americans living there.

SEDICIO: No. What about your fabulous Marge number?

LEONEL: Maybe I don't want to be a part of a country where people like Marge McCarthy can get power.

SEDICIO: Every country has extremists.

LEONEL: Well, Costa Rica doesn't even have an Army, we're free, and no matter what Steven Spielberg says, we don't have dinosaurs.

SEDICIO: All right then, leave! Abandon me, go ahead.

LEONEL: I'm not abandoning you, honey.

SEDICIO: Yes, you are. This whole immigration thing will blow over soon enough, it always does. I want you to stay. I'll miss you, comadre—I love you.

LEONEL: You play rough . . . Why can't you come with me?

SEDICIO: What?

LEONEL: Come stay with me and my parents. Very supportive. My dad is probably repressed, and my mom's a dyke for sure. You'll love the iguana burgers. They taste just like chicken.

SEDICIO: I can't—

LEONEL: We'll start our own nightclub: Las Locas del Cha-Cha-Cha.

SEDICIO: I have to stay here, and you know why.

LEONEL: Lover boy?

SEDICIO: Of course. I go where he goes.

LEONEL: You're a romantic, chico, better leave now before reality sinks in.

SEDICIO: I just believe in a long-term relationship or, better yet, a marriage. Why is that too much to ask for?

LEONEL: You're an idealist. I say leave this country before they start calling you a wetback. You came as a student, and leave it at that, don't give them the satisfaction of calling you anything else.

SEDICIO: No, I'm stuck on him. I'm in love.

LEONEL: My poor cow. I mean . . . I'll miss you, my baby! The doors are always open to you in San Jose—my San Jose, not the Silicon Valley version. We will be waiting for you, me and the iguanas.

(*Leonel hugs him, then goes to get his suitcases. Sedicio watches him go, looking lonely*)

Scene Three: Deporting the Fabulous

Michael reminisces. Sounds of hospital. In Silvano's room, at AIDS ward. Silvano, who appeared to him in that vision earlier in Tijuano, is dressed in classy, white suit, looking pale, ashen, ghostly. As if he were Sirena without the drag. We pick up where they left off.

SILVANO: What took you so long, my Miguel Angel?

MICHAEL: How did you know—?

SILVANO: Why shouldn't I know your name? I have my sources. I asked for the brown butt.

MICHAEL: Excuse me?

SILVANO: If anybody's going to deport me, I want him to be Latin, brown, and hunky. So take me.

MICHAEL: I'll give you a few minutes.

SILVANO: It's all a trick, you know.

MICHAEL: Huh? What is?

SILVANO: You people get to pay for my deportation.

MICHAEL: So be it.

SILVANO: It's not as if my family couldn't afford the price of a plane ticket. My father owns San Salvador!

MICHAEL: That's nice.

SILVANO: All of it—including the army, especially the army. When we want people to disappear, we make sure they do. Are you intimidated yet?

MICHAEL: I notice you're not packing.

SILVANO: I have everything I need back home! You thought I was just one of these Indian-looking peasants you're used to deporting, didn't you? You didn't count on me speaking English and Spanish better than you, or French or Esperanto, or residing in the most expensive, exclusive AIDS hospital in all of San Diego County. If I cared enough, I could have gotten my papers straightened out by marrying a senator's daughter. Yes, I have those types of connections. But I let the tourist visa lapse, and at this point it doesn't matter, does it? The joke's on you: you're doing me a favor. And by the way, in case you were wondering, I'm not demented, I'm just fabulous.

MICHAEL: I believe you, now please . . .

SILVANO: Wait. Let me look at you. Turn around.

MICHAEL: Why?

SILVANO: You remind me of someone I loved once, or lusted after, who knows the difference? (*Takes a look*) No, it looks like virgin ass to me. I forget faces, but not asses.

MICHAEL: Interesting skill.

SILVANO: Why aren't you wearing gloves?

MICHAEL: Should I be?

SILVANO: Some of the cops did at that last ACT UP rally I went to, buncha sissies. Speak to me or I'll have my guards punish you.

MICHAEL: I don't see no guards here.

SILVANO: Oh . . . they must have been deported, too, or father must have withdrawn them. Father is like that—if I'd only married the right upper class woman, I would have inherited El Salvador, all of it! I'm not entitled to any privileges at all any more, am I?

MICHAEL: I'm sure you'll be all right.

SILVANO: Don't reassure me, you have no right to! Why can't you be more of an asshole about it? What type of straight man are you?

MICHAEL: This isn't about me, is it?

SILVANO: Every second you breathe is about you! You may hug me if you'd like.

MICHAEL: What?

SILVANO: Am I embarrassing you?

MICHAEL: No.

SILVANO: Well, I mean to! I don't know what your sexuality is, but you look disgustingly repressed to me. Here, you may kiss my hand.

MICHAEL: Please . . .

SILVANO (*very serious, as if starved for the lightest of touch*)**:** Or shake it at the very least. I beg of you.

(*Michael smiles timidly. He barely touches Silvano's hand when Silvano draws him close for a tight embrace. Michael is left all shocked, his arms limp on the side. Silvano pulls back feeling good, all smiling*)

SILVANO: Cigarette?

MICHAEL: It's as if . . . I recognized you.

SILVANO: Wrong glory hole.

MICHAEL: No, I mean . . . You might think its weird but you remind me of someone, perhaps Miss Fresno?

SILVANO: That low class bimbo!

MICHAEL: Sorry. Then has anybody every written a detective novel about you?

SILVANO: Well . . . I suppose I am a tragic heroine of many novels.

MICHAEL (*like a new discovery, an eccentric one*)**:** You are then Sirena.

SILVANO: What's her attitude like?

MICHAEL: Major attitude.

SILVANO: Would you call her a diva?

MICHAEL: I think so.

SILVANO: Then she deserves to be deported!

MICHAEL: Well, she lives in the imagination.

SILVANO: Why live anywhere else? Sirena—illegal alien and diva! I like that. We have connected then.

MICHAEL: We have?

SILVANO: In ten minutes, we have consummated an affair that will endure the test of time. You are a romantic, Miguel. Don't ever lose that.

MICHAEL: I shouldn't—I won't.

SILVANO: And when you do fall in love, don't forget to break his/her heart.

MICHAEL: What?

SILVANO: Let her experience the heartbreak due to every single diva in the universe. Make up afterwards, but first the pain, the struggle, the essence of all diva-dom. She'll survive. She has the music and the lyrics for it—

MICHAEL: Lyrics?

SILVANO: To die to the finale of *La Traviata*.

MICHAEL: What about *Funny Girl*?

SILVANO: Why! You've been initiated!

MICHAEL: So there's more than one finale?

SILVANO: Dozens! And *Funny Girl* is mere Broadway, vulgar, very vulgar. La Traviata is class! Avoid Puccini's *Butterfly*. Self-destructive, politically incorrect.

MICHAEL: Okay. I will remember that.

SILVANO: You must remember that. It is my only gift to you, my own finale. Take me now.

(*There's the glare of a news camera outside. Silvano stops, surprised, blinded by the lights*)

MICHAEL: Oh . . . I hope you don't mind the news camera.

SILVANO (*recovers quickly*)**:** Not at all. I've been waiting for cameras all my life! (*Straightens out his hair*) I go first. I lead, Miguel, you follow!Ladies and gentlemen of the press, I'm ready for your questions. (*Exits*)

(*Michael is left alone for a second. He looks around. He touches his face, senses some strange sensation about this room, something unfathomable having just occurred, not knowing what to make of it. But a sensation it was*)

Scene Four: Mid-Life Crisis

Back at the office. Michael waits for Dean who arrives talking on the cellular phone

DEAN: Look, Marge, I'm not gonna hold any debate right on the border. We're not gonna come together face to face, okay? What? You're coming over to confront me? Right here in the same room? I think that would be impossible, Marge. What? Come on, you know—Let's say we're too much alike, okay? Marge—we're played by the same actor, okay? (*To*

Michael as he hangs up) I'm up ten points in the polls and she can't accept that. Come on, what are you waiting for? You have a job to do.

MICHAEL: Well . . . this case you gave me—

DEAN: I didn't give you another HIV immigrant, did I? I went out of my way to—

MICHAEL: No. I just can't do this one. (*Gives the file back to him*)

DEAN: Why? And I don't want to hear it. I got a campaign, a wedding, a child custody hearing from my last marriage—don't give me any more headaches now.

MICHAEL: Assign it to somebody else, then.

DEAN (*looks at file*): But what's wrong with this?

MICHAEL: Well, he's . . .

DEAN: He's just Mexican—just average Mexican—

MICHAEL: I'm—

DEAN: . . . been here ten years, won't answer our letters asking him to show up for deportation hearings, he's an open and shut case—

MICHAEL: I'm sleeping with him, Dean!

DEAN (*as if his ulcer suddenly ripped through him*): Oh!

MICHAEL: Except we haven't, you know, all the way.

DEAN: OH!

MICHAEL: You all right?

DEAN: Yeah. How's your Spanish class?

MICHAEL: Dean, you're not gonna avoid this one—

DEAN: Yes, I am.

MICHAEL: You've known for a long time what I'm going through, haven't you?

DEAN: Look, I'm marrying into your family, so I don't need to know all the deep, dark secrets yet. I want to find out later, like my last marriage.

MICHAEL: Look at me—

DEAN: No, no, I'm gonna lose more hair that way. Look, you're the best man, Teresita's the bridesmaid—get that friend of yours to straighten out his papers, make him marry a lesbian or something, I don't care—either that, or get him out of your life. Deport him, that's easy. I wish I could do that to my ex-wife—and damnit, didn't you notice he was . . . ?

MICHAEL: I didn't check his papers before sleeping with him, if that's what you . . .

DEAN: I want a calm wedding and my ex-wife's already threatening to show up with an uzi, probably given to her by Marge McCarthy. It'll be another WACO out there—so please, please, let's not—

MICHAEL: You don't even care about what I might be feeling—

DEAN: No! You're going through some middle-aged crisis at twenty-eight. Snap out of it, that's all I can say. Do your job, and remember you've got kids. The family comes first. You're a fuckin' Latin, you oughta know that! Now I need some anti-diarrhea tablets—damn, I'm gonna shit in my pants—

MICHAEL: Hold on!

DEAN: I can't hold on.

MICHAEL: What if I don't do my job?

DEAN: What?

MICHAEL: What if I disobey?

DEAN: You've never done that—

MICHAEL: But what if I do? What if I can no longer do my job at all? I'm still haunted by dreams of that last HIV immigrant. I'm getting sick of all this. You'll have to fire me, Dean.

DEAN: No. Remember the bills, the child support, child support, say it a hundred times—there's no easy way. I should know, got my share of bills from my last marriage. I should know, trust me. I'm living proof that it's not that simple, Mikey. We're lifers, man, we're lifers. Here's the file, do your job. I really gotta go!

(*Dean exits in a real rush for the bathroom, Michael's left holding his file, not knowing what to do. The voice of a receptionist paging Michael comes on*)

VOICE: Michael Gonzalez . . . pick up line two.

MICHAEL (*he reaches for phone*): Yeah . . . Teresita? Is everything okay? The kids, are they . . . ? Good, that's good to hear. So why? Yeah, I plan to drive out there for Alfie's birthday, but . . . you're what? How many months?

(*Lights down*)

Scene Five: The Final Lesson

Transition to the class, the teacher enters.

TEACHER: Spanish class, the new semester begins. (*Looking desolate*) Such low enrollments again. (*He hears something*) I think I hear one!

(*Michael enters, looking worried*)

MICHAEL: Hiya, Teach.

TEACHER: Oh, Mr. Gonzalez! Welcome back to the language of your ancestors!

MICHAEL: My ancestors were Toltec Indians, *pendejo!*

TEACHER: Sorry.

MICHAEL: It's all right. So . . . how's your Self-Esteem class?

TEACHER: Oh, just fine, I've only lost half the class.

MICHAEL: To deportation?

TEACHER: No, to self-repatriation. They leave the country just to spite me. (*Sedicio enters*) Another student! (*On his knees*) Welcome back, oh, young Master!

SEDICIO: Get up, have some dignity. Michael, we have to talk.

MICHAEL: There's a class going on, sit down!

SEDICIO: But—

TEACHER: Sit down, kid! All right. So welcome you all back to another exciting semester of Spanish for Pochos. Some of you missed my lecture, "Carmen Miranda for Beginners." My picture's in the San Diego Union. I'm being carried away by security guards for interrupting a performance of *Deporting the Divas*, see? (*No response*) Okay. Let's do the roll! We have one . . . two students! Very good! While we wait for a few more, let me tell you, today I have brought you my new advanced technique: Karaoke for Spanish students. You follow the bouncing ball, and you learn the language by singing it.

SEDICIO: Michael doesn't sing in public.

MICHAEL: Sedicio doesn't have sex on the first date!

TEACHER: Okay. Well, well, well. . . look, today's song is very romantic. Shall we hold hands and sing it together? (*They look silent, Teacher looks defensive*) It's a nice Camilo Sesto song. "Algo de Mi." (*As the song plays, he translates and gets emotional*) It says, "A part of me is dying, I want to live, I want to know WHY? you leave, my love." You try it, Sedicio. (*Sedicio looks unamused*) Come on, Sedicio, don't be such a prissy fuck! (*Michael gets up as if enthralled by this idea*) Oh, Michael, very good. Look at the gleam in his eyes, Sedicio. What's wrong with him? What have I done? He's scaring me.

MICHAEL (*he recites or sings the text, which culminates in repressed emotion*): "Me acostumbro—"

TEACHER (*corrects*): Acostumbre.

(*Michael starts slowly, and is entranced and in himself at first*)

MICHAEL: "Me acostumbre . . . a tus besos . . .
       y a tu piel, color de miel,
       a la espiga de tu cuerpo
       a tu risa y a tu ser . . .

       Algo de mi, algo de mi
       algo de mi se va muriendo,
       quiero vivir, quiero vivir
       saber por que te vas, amor."

(*The music takes off, lights switch, there's sudden magic as if Michael's been transported to a world of illusion where he's suddenly singing for a hundred thousand fans, and his voice has taken flight—this could be lipsynched to the song. The music stops, he looks self-conscious, and he sits down quickly*)

TEACHER: Oh, my! Your Spanish *has* improved.

MICHAEL (*self conscious, back to his straight self*): Yes, well, a-hem.

TEACHER: This song brings out the inner Spaniard in you, don't you think so, Sedicio?

(*Michael's beeper goes off*)

MICHAEL: Oh, important page . . . excuse me.

SEDICIO: Michael?

(*Michael exits*)

TEACHER: What happened just now? It looks like one of my students actually *learned* something. That's never quite happened before!

SEDICIO: You're such a great teacher.

TEACHER: You think so? Oh! (*Starts to cry*)

SEDICIO: What's wrong?

TEACHER: I've never even been called a *fair* teacher, let alone a great one. They don't call me the "serial workshop leader" for nothing.

SEDICIO: But you're terrific. I'm going to be a teacher one day and I really like to borrow some of your weird techniques.

TEACHER: You don't know the last thing about me, kid, I've been all over the country trying to make a living teaching the most ridiculous seminars. "Spanish for Pochos" or "Spanish for Latinos Who Ought to Know Better"—is the most normal class I've ever taught—and I admit, I'm no Catalan—

SEDICIO: Really?

TEACHER: I'm no Puerto Rican either, oh, I won't get into it! It's shocking, so shocking. The things we do to survive in this world.

SEDICIO: No, tell me. Who are you really?

TEACHER (*sinister*): You don't need to know, kid.

(*Michael returns*)

MICHAEL: I'm sorry, it's work.

SEDICIO: Michael, we have to talk.

MICHAEL: I have to go—they caught Miss Fresno as she was about to be crowned Miss USA!

TEACHER: What?

MICHAEL: Marge McCarthy denounced her in front of the cameras—and now Marge is up twenty points in the polls. Since my boss is running against her, it's a job for the INS, excuse me.

SEDICIO: Michael . . . that song, I never heard you sing.

TEACHER: Repressed talents, we all got 'em.

MICHAEL: Later, Seth.

SEDICIO: Michael!

(Michael stops. But he can't quite say it, the weight of his job, Sedicio's file, the fact that he can't quite bring himself to even talk about it right now—all of this silences him. He prefers to leave)

MICHAEL: Later. *(Michael exits)*

TEACHER: The truth is, Sedicio, I'm an illegal alien trapped in a citizen's body.

(Sedicio gives him a funny look. Lights off. We hear the break of thunder)

MICHAEL *(to audience)*: Well, it rained that weekend . . . a couple of weeks had passed—couple of weeks was a long time to be alone in the middle of a mountain downpour, stuck inside with 150 channels on a satellite dish, and yet so far away from civilization. That night, she made a grand return into my life—not Teresita: her!

(Sirena enters carrying a book)

SIRENA: *Que tal, pibe.*

MICHAEL: Sirena! Come here, gal, and let's do the tango thing.

SIRENA: Sergeant please, the midnight cappuccino awaits me as I try to read the collected works of Manuel Puig.

MICHAEL: You're still reading that shit?

SIRENA: I'm in the middle of *Betrayed by Rita Hayworth*. She was a fiery Latina, you know.

MICHAEL: Come here, let's dance to "La Cumparsita."

SIRENA: No, not "La Cumparsita." Lives have been destroyed over "La Cumparsita."

MICHAEL: Please.

SIRENA: Not this time, Miguel.

MICHAEL: Huh? You didn't call me Sergeant.

SIRENA: That is your name, Miguel Angel. You're not a Sergeant with the Santa Monica Police Department. You're a border patrol man in Pete Wilson's hometown, you'll have to live with that.

MICHAEL: I only want to dance one more time.

SIRENA: A girl can only live with so much heartache.

MICHAEL: What heartache? Men are at your feet.

SIRENA: They seem to die there, don't they? No, this time I mean you, my Miguel Angel. For so many years, I've kept my feelings for you strictly closeted.

MICHAEL: Really? You never said anything.

SIRENA: This outfit doesn't allow for a full range of emotions.

MICHAEL: So you do love me?

SIRENA: I adore you as the raw, brave, barrio boy that you are.

MICHAEL: Don't call me that.

SIRENA: Your low-class demeanor, your peasant outlook on life, you come from the finest line of grape pickers. You are a man of the earth, color of the soil. So you see, I'm not your fantasy, you are mine, Miguel.

MICHAEL: I have that much control over you.

SIRENA: And you don't even realize it. It's better that I leave you now.

MICHAEL: No, we haven't danced in so long.

SIRENA: One day you will find somebody more appropriate to your needs.

MICHAEL: Actually, I think I've found somebody.

SIRENA (*jealous*): Who is the bitch?

MICHAEL: His name is . . . Sedicio.

SIRENA: He has a name? And he's a man? Oh-oh! (*Cries*)

MICHAEL: You didn't know?

SIRENA: Fucking stay away from me, I'm feeling like Medea right now, okay? I'm no longer necessary.

MICHAEL: Don't say that.

SIRENA: You'll have to suffer the consequences. You . . . you have carved your name deep into the femme fatale's heart! Let the storms rage! Sirena seethes with disdain! You are in danger! The waters will crush the pier, they'll wash away the Coronado Brigge, and you can forget the La Jolla Playhouse! You're all history! My gender has spoken! (*Thunder breaks with an array of lights. Even Sirena's impressed by the effects*) Nice! (*Doors open magically for her grand exit*)

MICHAEL: Sirena, don't leave . . . Sirena! (*Sees shadow of Sedicio outside*) What's he doing in the rain holding a damn cake box?

(*They face each other*)

SEDICIO: . . . Drove over to Julian for its world-famous apple pie. Would you like some?

MICHAEL: You don't always drive to Julian just for famous apple pie.

SEDICIO: May I come in? Are you alone?

MICHAEL: Yes, come in.

SEDICIO: The rain exasperates me.

MICHAEL: Just say what's really bothering you, Seth.

SEDICIO (*trying to remain playful and cheerful*): Sedicio, that's my name. Sedicio Manuel Inchaustegui-Linares. I prefer longer names that resonate—

MICHAEL: Look, Sedicio—

SEDICIO: And that was lovely singing. I mean you missed a few notes, but you did it charmingly. You have become a true member of the Tribe. I pronounce you a Diva.

MICHAEL: We don't belong together, Sedicio.

SEDICIO: I understand. I scare you, I'm a little maniacal—

MICHAEL: No, don't blame yourself, it's me actually. Only six months ago, I'd never been with a man. I'm twenty-eight years old. I'd never realized that I would want to be with a man.

SEDICIO: I'm flattered then, I brought you out.

MICHAEL: You're not listening! Teresita and I—we're thinking of getting back together.

SEDICIO: Well, you can't do that, that's all.

MICHAEL: It would be best for the kids. Look, I do like you—

SEDICIO: No, I don't need to be "liked."

MICHAEL: Hell, I'm attracted to you! You don't understand what it's been like for me.

SEDICIO: You must try this apple pie—very mom-like, very patriotic—

MICHAEL: Sedicio, I love my wife, I want to be with her. Maybe I am just bisexual, at most—

SEDICIO: At most!

MICHAEL: And I'm not that eager to pursue this "lifestyle."

SEDICIO: And you have an INS job because of the benefits, I understand!

MICHAEL: I actually like my job.

SEDICIO: Deporting relatives is very fulfilling.

MICHAEL: I'm sick and tired of your remarks about my job. If enforcing the law is not important to you, that's your problem. Legal immigrants are still welcome in this country.

SEDICIO: Are they?

MICHAEL: People like you should apply, stand in line, come legally, like all my relatives did. (*Shows pictures*) See? There they all are. La Familia!

SEDICIO: Fine, good for them! Why couldn't we form a family?

MICHAEL: You should go . . . the rain has slowed down. The drive should be safe.

SEDICIO: No, I brought you a gift—

MICHAEL: I know, thanks for the pie.

SEDICIO: No, not that stupid pie.

MICHAEL: What are you talking about now?

SEDICIO: I've been so naive. I realize now that what you needed was a lot more intimate—no, no, the word is carnal—

MICHAEL: What?

SEDICIO: That's the word. Carnal and immediate, for the here and now. It's all you really wanted, an experiment, something to satisfy your curiosity, and I thought I would change all that with my rules and regulations—so no, fine, this is it, this is all you want, no intimacy, nothing, you win!

MICHAEL: No, your rules made sense at the time.

SEDICIO: No, I have brought you what you needed. (*Shows him a single condom and holds it out to him*) This is what you needed, isn't it?

MICHAEL (*quite tempted, there's a second of silence, but he has to control himself*): Ah—look—how come we've never discussed your legal status?

SEDICIO: Don't change the subject. What's more important right now, Michael? What's the priority right now?

(*Michael struggles with temptation, Sedicio takes off his shirt, and, after a few seconds of hesitation, Michael approaches to touch him, but he can't quite go through with this. Sedicio tries kissing him, holding on to him with his instinct to play around, to laugh, to be a kid again, but Michael—as much as he may want to—can't quite let himself be seduced right now. He pulls back*)

MICHAEL: Maybe we can get you a lawyer and . . .

SEDICIO: Maybe I'm not interested in "legality." Not even in gay marriage any more, too respectable.

MICHAEL: Put your shirt back on! And how can you say things like that? How can you live the way you do?

SEDICIO: Maybe I don't mind passing for something I'm not. Yes, most of us learn how to hide it, learn English correctly, get the right false ID's, try to "look white." But I don't need to lecture you on the art of hiding, Miguel Angel, you're the expert. So where do you stand on all of this, Michael? Whose side are you on?

MICHAEL: Does it come to that, taking sides?

SEDICIO: These days maybe. Yes!

MICHAEL: I've only got one side, Sedicio: my family's. Why doesn't that matter to you? Why isn't that important?

SEDICIO: There are alternate families, there are other ways to live, and some of us don't belong anywhere other than the border. In Mexico, I'd end up joining the rebels of Chiapas, who knows where I belong—we're only "special citizens" of the borderland.

MICHAEL: Tell that to the INS. I'm just warning you—we've got your file.

SEDICIO: Don't threaten me!

MICHAEL: I'm just telling you—

SEDICIO: You know where to find me then. (*Starts to leave*)

MICHAEL: Teresita knows.

SEDICIO: What? She knows?

MICHAEL: It's as if she's known all along. Of course, now she's pregnant again, and that complicates things . . . The best I can do is . . . keep seeing you occasionally. Teresita understands.

SEDICIO: Oh, that's just great, she "understands."

MICHAEL: As long as I'm discreet, she says. So that's it: a discreet affair on the side is the best I can do right now, Sedicio. It's not ideal, but I've wanted you so much all this time, I've been scared of falling in love with you—

SEDICIO: And you have, of course? Madly and desperately?

MICHAEL: Ah . . .

SEDICIO: Say it!

MICHAEL: Yes. I suppose . . . I-I love you. But that won't be enough for you. A discreet—a very discreet affair on the side is all I can offer, with Teresita's understanding, take it or leave it.

SEDICIO: Well . . . I was determined to come here and give up all my silly rules—

MICHAEL: Yes, compromises do work.

SEDICIO: It's all so tempting but don't you see . . . I couldn't honestly call myself "the other person in your life" and live with it. I won't share you with anyone.

MICHAEL: Well . . . it's the best I can do.

(*Beat*)

SEDICIO: The rain stopped.

MICHAEL: Yes, it has. But you don't need to go.

SEDICIO: Yes, I do. One more thing. What is it about the desert "mirage" or whatever it was . . . that gay wedding, Michael?

MICHAEL: I don't know.

SEDICIO: What is it about that wedding that touched you?

MICHAEL: It didn't "touch" me.

SEDICIO: That left you looking so . . . alone.

MICHAEL: It bothered me, that's all. It shocked me. For one brief moment, I saw myself as one of the grooms. All right?

SEDICIO: One day you'll take me to that barn—

MICHAEL: It's probably not there any more. Summer fires, brush fires, it's probably gone. There's nothing there to see.

SEDICIO: Don't you wish, don't you just wish . . . that there were something there for you, waiting just for you, my Miguel Angel? One big party for the two of us to celebrate our union?

(*They stare at each other. Sedicio kisses him lightly on the cheek. Sedicio's about to walk out, but this time, it's not just any exit. The doors swing wide open for him as they might have done earlier for Miss Fresno and Sirena, and he exits in a grand, fabulous manner like any other of the Divas. Lights and music support him.*
Michael puts on his badge and INS jacket as he delivers final monologue)

MICHAEL: I run into him occasionally—on weekends when I drive into the city, he sees me, he spies on me all alone in a bar. I may flirt with a stranger, and I let him watch me do it . . . I don't have to say a word. That's how it is between us now. This distance. I only got to attend one wedding that year. My sister married my boss. We're one big INS family now.

But tonight I woke up—it wasn't too late for a drive. I went out to the desert, and here it is, the barn. Where the gay wedding took place. Yet, inside, there's nothing, a few old grain sacks, an abandoned dilapidated building in the middle of nowhere. How could a Mexican gay wedding have taken place here? Who knows? I hear the sound of "The Wedding Samba," and I sit around with my flashlight expecting to see the two grooms, the guests, the wedding cake, but night wears on . . . nothing happens . . . I am alone a few steps from the border, and I just sit there with the clear desert sky above me and I wait.

And suddenly I hear it in the background, that song that the crazy teacher taught me—my first love song in Spanish! The curtain goes up, he faces the lights, he's ready to face his adoring public.

(*If the actor can sing, he gets to do "Algo de Mi" or any other love song with the urgency of "My Man" in* Funny Girl. *If he can't sing, he can continue with these words; whichever way it's done, it's appropriate that Michael gets to stage his own grandiose finale*)

. . . . and my lips sing along in my own rendition of a grand finale worthy of any suffering, aching "heroine"—"Algo de Mi"—and my voice summons them to me. That's when the Divas surround me, standing tall, ready to transport me to that grand, fabulous world where I will arise, one day, ready and eager to face the music and sing along!

(*In the midst of all this, the other actors surround him dressed up as the appropriate Divas—Sirena, Miss Fresno, Lucy. The Divas will be there for him as he works this all out in his vivid, hopeful imagination. Lights down, end of play*)

SOMEWHERE IN THE PACIFIC

by Neal Bell

SOMEWHERE IN THE PACIFIC was originally produced by Manbites Dog Theatre in Durham, N.C. in February, 1999. The production was directed by Jody McAuliffe with the following cast:

Albers	David Ring
De Lucca	Mark Filiaci
Billy	Eamonn Farrell
Chotkowski	Derrick Ivey
Hobie	Adam Smith
Duane	Peter Gail
McGuiness	Adam Saunders

No performance or reading of this work in any medium may be given without express permission of the author. Inquiries regarding performance rights, publication, or duplication of any kind should be addressed to the author's agent: Joyce Ketay, 1501 Broadway, Suite 1908, New York, N.Y. 10036. Phone 212-354-6825.

Characters

Albers—A Navy Captain. 40s
De Lucca—A Navy lieutenant. Alber's aide.
Billy—A Navy seaman first class. 19
Chotkowski—Marine. Early 30s
Hobie—Marine. Early 20s
Duane—Marine. Early 20s
McGuiness—Marine. Early 20s
Two Enemy Soldiers
(can be doubled by the actors playing Albers and De Lucca)

Setting

A Liberty Ship, being used to transport troops.
Late July, 1945. Somewhere in the Pacific.

AUTHOR'S INTRODUCTION

When I read Allan Berube's *Coming Out Under Fire: Gay Men and Women in World War Two*, I was haunted by one passage describing how the Army (at one American camp) interrogated suspected homosexuals. The suspect was stripped naked and then had to face a board of (clothed) officers, who pummeled the humiliated subject with intimate questions. That seemed to capture—with ugly poetic precision—the cruelty/fear and the obsession/attraction that seem to entwine in homophobia. It also seemed like an image that could have great theatrical power.

So that was the germ of *Somewhere in the Pacific*—the image of a naked man in a pool of light being tormented for being. And that's the image that—as I tried to create a world for it, and a story that would build up to it—began to seem more and more problematic. That happened because, as the play developed, the focus seemed to shift from the individual, Billy (the openly gay character), to the group in which Billy finds an uneasy place. Homophobia in the military stayed at the heart of the story but I felt that the other characters were victims of it as much as Billy.

In the original draft, produced as a workshop at Playwrights Horizons, Billy's interrogation appeared as the next to last scene—a flash forward. Though the scene was bravely and well-acted by a terrific cast, it didn't work. The rest of the play was more indirect; this one scene felt like agit-prop. It also interrupted the flow of the story to its climax. I was trying to make the point that—after the horrors of war endured by *all* the men—for the gay man there was another, government-sanctioned horror to follow. Yet giving this point an entire scene was throwing the play out of balance. It suggested that Billy's postwar fate was more important, somehow, than that of the other men. And that contradicted my belief (as I said before) that *all* the men are connected, and affected, by the presence of the other, the stranger, the "enemy" among them.

So, reluctantly, I began to think about dropping the scene that had been my starting point. Luckily, I had the chance to see how that would work when *Somewhere in the Pacific* got a second production, at Manbites Dog Theater in Durham, North Carolina. The wonderful cast rehearsed the play both ways—with the interrogation scene and without—and the play simply made more sense without it. Thus confirming that writer's workshop adage I've always distrusted: "Never trust your best ideas."

I did a lot of reading on the war in the Pacific as I prepared to write this play. One memoir in particular stands out, *With the Old Breed* by Eugene B. Sledge. It's a compelling, harrowing story about the campaigns to capture

the islands of Peleliu and Okinawa, and it was invaluable in giving me a
nitty-gritty sense of what men living through that kind of combat endured.

NEAL BELL
Connecticut, 2000

Scene One

The foredeck of a battered Liberty Ship, being used to transport troops.
    Open water. The Central Pacific. Night.
    *Four marines have come topside in their underwear, unable to sleep in the
stifling heat below. The oldest—Chotkowski, 31—is standing at the rail,
looking out.*
    *The others—Duane, 19, and McGuiness and Hobie—both in their mid-
20s—lie on the deck in their skivvies, smoking.*
    Hobie looks at Chotkowski.

HOBIE: Anything? (*Chotkowski doesn't respond*) Chotkowski!

CHOTKOWSKI: Dark as an asshole.

McGUINESS: You should know . . .

DUANE (*of the ocean's immensity*): Lotta miles and miles . . .

McGUINESS: . . . spend enougha yer waking hours excavating.

DUANE: Miles and miles of miles and miles . . .

HOBIE: Where the *fuck* are we going *this* time?

DUANE: The orders said Okinawa.

HOBIE: They don't need us on Okinawa. They got the Tenth Army mop-
pin' up. We're going somewhere else.

CHOTKOWSKI: What else is left? The Mainland.

HOBIE: Right. They booked us into the Tokyo Hilton.

McGUINESS: That's the scuttlebutt.

HOBIE: That's what you heard? *I* heard my wife was faithful, still.

DUANE: You said your wife would spread for loose change.

HOBIE: So you get my drift.

DUANE: Your wife is a tramp?

HOBIE: The *other* drift.

DUANE: They *haven't* booked us into the Tokyo Hilton?

McGUINESS (*to Duane*): When your momma used to bounce you on her knee, did you land on your head?

(*Duane gets up, joining Chotkowski at the rail*)

DUANE: Miles and miles . . .

McGUINESS (*making the sound of a baby being bounced on its head*): Bonk—bonk—bonk—bonk—

DUANE: What my daddy'd always say, we'd be driving along, he sold vacuum cleaners, except no one could afford 'em, you know? "That's about all there is to this godforsaken, piss-poor state, just a lot of miles and miles of miles and miles . . ." My daddy thought that was funny.

McGUINESS: That's because I bet *his* momma dandled him badly, too. Like a family curse, musta been. It's sad: bonk, bonk, bonk, bonk . . .

(*Duane points at something above the horizon*)

DUANE: What the hell is that?

CHOTKOWSKI (*suddenly tenser*): Where?

DUANE: That glow out there . . . right over those waves . . . like a buncha falling stars . . .

CHOTKOWSKI (*relaxing*): Flying fish.

DUANE: Oh.

CHOTKOWSKI: You've seen 'em before. They always amaze you. Fucking flying fish.

DUANE (*peering out into the dark*): *Are* they fucking?

McGUINESS: Bonk. Bonk. Bonk. Bonk.

HOBIE (*bitter, almost under his breath*): The Mainland? (*Pause*) Why don't they just shoot us right now? Get it over with?

CHOTKOWSKI: Why don't you shut the fuck up? You fucking pussy. (*Pause*) I heard something about Korea. Maybe *that's* where we're going in.

DUANE: Korea?

McGUINESS: That's a country, Duane. Sticks out at the Nips—like this. (*He gives Duane the bird*)

CHOTKOWSKI: We grab up all the airfields—puts us right in Japan's backyard—

HOBIE: Nobody is going to Korea.

DUANE: The *Koreans* are.

(*McGuiness makes a final "bonk." The light changes, brighter. Chotkowski looks up*)

CHOTKOWSKI: Break in the clouds.

DUANE: God. Look at that moon.

HOBIE: Don't that make us a target?

CHOTKOWSKI (*clamping down on his own nerves*): If anyone was out there.

DUANE (*bravado*): All I see is fucking flying fish. And this band of light like a road on the water. All the way back to the States. We're alone.

McGUINESS: Except, Duh-*wayne*, it don't work like in the cartoons. You don't see a great big slanted eye looking out of a giant periscope.

(*Pause, as Hobie joins Duane and Chotkowski, staring out at the night*)

HOBIE: Shooting gallery. Moon right there and us in front of it. Picking our butts. Let the bucktooth bastards draw a bead on us. *Blam.* (*He turns to yell up at the bridge*) *Zig-Zag, You sons-of-bitches!* Jesus. Fucking Navy . . .

(*Pause. It gets darker*)

DUANE: It was just one sorry tear in the clouds. It's gone. See—dark as an asshole.

McGUINESS: You should know.

CHOTKOWSKI: And *now*, no Jap could make us out, we're starting to zig-zag. Figures.

(*A very young sailor, Seaman Billy DuPre, appears, taking a final bite of a banana*)

HOBIE: Fucking Navy . . . (*The Marines now notice the sailor*) No offense there, swabbie.

BILLY: You men wanta smoke? You should go below decks.

McGUINESS: You should suck my dick.

DUANE: It's an oven down there.

BILLY: There's a blackout, though.

McGUINESS: Like say there *was* a pig-boat fulla demented gooks out there, you think they could glaum the butt of this fucking Lucky?

BILLY: You aren't the only men on this ship.

CHOTKOWSKI: That's a fact. And that means . . .

BILLY: Maybe *you* guys don't die. But the rest of us do. (*Pause. Chotkowski, with elaborate disdain, flicks his cigarette over the side*) See, the rest of us—we forget where we are, for a second or two, we throw a candywrapper over the side, a banana peel— (*As he speaks, he tucks the banana peel away in a pocket of his dungarees*)

CHOTKOWSKI: *One cigarette butt*, Seaweed.

BILLY: Times how many men on this leaking tub? Three hundred and fifty cigarette butts. And how many 'Dear John' letters do you nautical bell-hops get? All of *them* in the drink. We leave a trail. The Japs find us. Down we go. But you guys don't die.

(*Pause. McGuiness stubs his cigarette out on the deck*)

McGUINESS: So Commodore, tell me—who do I ask for permission to take a dump? (*McGuiness, satisfied with his dig, gets up and signals for Duane to go with him*) Duane.

DUANE: I already took a dump, McGuiness. Let me finish my smoke.

McGUINESS (*pointing at Billy*): Okay. But some place where the air don't smell like a mackerel's heinder?

DUANE (*not getting it*): Don't believe I ever sniffed a mackerel up that close.

(*McGuiness, sighing, shakes his head and exits. With that heckler gone, Billy tries to explain himself*)

BILLY: A buddy of mine, he was on a ship . . . and they think it's because *they* were leaving a wake of crap, like a giant floating arrow: "Japs! Hit this!"

CHOTKOWSKI: Did your buddy make it? (*Pointing up*) Or is he up there?

HOBIE: "Hey you—with the wings and the harp! Put out that butt!"

BILLY: My buddy, I think, was dessert. For some well-fed shark.

(*Pause*)

CHOTKOWSKI: *You* seen any fighting?

BILLY: Not yet. Does that mean I can't have an opinion?

(*Chotkowski stares at Billy a moment, then starts to exit*)

CHOTKOWSKI: Pogies. Christ. (*Chotkowski is gone*)

DUANE (*in a reverie*): Three hundred and fifty cigarette butts . . .

HOBIE (*to Billy, answering his question*): It means you don't know enough shit to *concoct* an opinion. Fucking pogie . . . (*Hobie grinds his cigarette out and exits*)

(*Duane and Billy, left alone, look out at the dark*)

DUANE: I know you weren't talking 'bout all at once. But it *coulda* been all at once . . . shooting out in the dark, what a sight that'd be . . . three hundred and fifty falling stars . . . like a *school* of fucking flying fish.

BILLY: They *are* fucking, ya know. (*Duane looks at Billy, surprised*) How do you think they get up there? They start to hump way down, is what I heard. And they buck and they thrash all the way to the top, and their wings are pumping, faster and faster, and when they come—they come so hard—they go up. In the air. They just—take off . . . and it's like they were back in the ocean again—that dark, and deep—'till they fall back into the sky below 'em, ker-splunk, ker-splunk, ker-splunk, ker-splunk, ker-splunk: "What the *hell* was that?" But they can't figure out. So they shrug and they keep on fugging.

(*Pause. Duane—who's never had someone share one of his reveries—is unsettled*)

DUANE: You been at sea too long, Jack Tar. You're going Asiatic.

BILLY: Maybe I am.

DUANE (*moving away from Billy*): Well I need me another smoke. So I'm headin' below. Like you said.

BILLY: It's an oven. *You* said. (*Pause*) I won't tell. If you want to stay topside.

DUANE: Some other time.

BILLY: You bet. We can shoot the breeze . . . (*Duane shrugs, embarrassed, and exits. Hungry for contact, Billy watches him go*) We can shoot a few Nips. We can shoot ourselves. Fuck. *Fuck*. FUCK. (*Billy starts to exit, when Hobie re-enters, from the opposite side*)

HOBIE: Hey sailor. (*Billy stops*) What's your name?

BILLY: Billy.

HOBIE: Come here.

BILLY: What for? (*But Billy, before he can get an answer, approaches*)

HOBIE: I haven't seen my wife in a year and a half. She don't write, anymore. She useta . . .

BILLY: Why did she stop?

HOBIE: Something told her I was expendable. (*Pause. Hobie suddenly grabs the sailor, kissing him hard on the mouth. Billy pulls away, firm but not fighting. He stares at Hobie*)

BILLY: But you aren't. Marines are immortal. Right? (*Now Billy kisses Hobie—first tenderly, and then more and more ferociously*)

(*The lights fade*)

Scene Two

On the bridge. A few moments earlier. Captain Albers looks out at the night, through a pair of binoculars. Lieutenant De Lucca eyes him with concern. Both men are wearing life jackets.

DE LUCCA: Calm tonight.

ALBERS (*lowering the binoculars*): It's always calm.

DE LUCCA: Are you tight, sir?

(*Pause. The Captain thumps his chest*)

ALBERS: Calm in here. Where I *know* things. (*Pause*) Am I *what*?

DE LUCCA: I heard about your son.

ALBERS: My son.

DE LUCCA: I'm sorry, sir.

ALBERS: Did you two ever meet?

DE LUCCA: At the Officers' Club, one time. At Pearl. *I* was tight. I thought he was you.

ALBERS: I wish he was. I wish *he* was standing here . . . (*The light gets brighter*)

DE LUCCA: Sir?

ALBERS: Right here. Looking out at the night . . . feeling the breeze . . .

DE LUCCA: The moon's come out.

ALBERS: Smelling the air . . .

DE LUCCA: Do you think we should make a course-correction?

ALBERS: Rotten coconut smell . . . what a terrible stink . . . Must be a raggedy-ass little island out there. One pathetic palm tree. One dead Jap underneath it. Big buck-teeth in a grin . . . (*Albers takes a much-read letter out of his pocket, unfolds it*)

DE LUCCA: *Sir?* You did give us a standing order: if the weather changed— while you were asleep—

ALBERS: Am I sleeping? (*De Lucca, hearing the Captain's tone, looks away*) What's our speed?

DE LUCCA: About seventeen knots—

ALBERS: —which is fast enough to out-run a sub, don't you think? If a sub should spot us. If there *is* a sub out there. If we start to zig-zag, won't that slow us down?

DE LUCCA: Yes sir.

ALBERS: Do you want to slow down?

DE LUCCA: If the moon stays out—

ALBERS: I see one rip in the clouds. And it's mending . . . Look.

DE LUCCA: I'm looking, sir. We're a target.

(*Pause*)

ALBERS: My son would have broken, I think.

DE LUCCA: No sir.

ALBERS (*reads from the letter*)**:** "I'm afraid of the men." This is what he was writing—just before he died. "My own men. McGuiness thinks it's funny, whenever he finds a dead Jap, to stand over the wretched creature and piss in its mouth."

DE LUCCA: That got by the censors?

ALBERS: Didn't go through the mail. It was found on his body. (*He points at a stain on the letter*) This is his blood.

(*Pause*)

DE LUCCA: We *are* a target, sir.

ALBERS: I know. (*To himself*) Good. (*Pause*) Good.

DE LUCCA: No sir.

ALBERS: The moonlight's almost gone. (*De Lucca stares at his captain, refusing to flinch*) All right. Give the order to zig-zag.

DE LUCCA: Thank you, sir.

ALBERS: And fuck *you*, Mister De Lucca. (*Albers crumples up the letter*) Now tell me not to throw this over the side. (*De Lucca meets the captain's stare. Albers holds onto the crumpled-up letter*)

DE LUCCA: I don't think your boy would have broken, sir.

ALBERS: You thought he was *me*? At that club? My son was *hand-some*, goddamnit to hell. My son was at least a head taller. And he was young . . .

DE LUCCA: The light was bad. It was darker than this—

ALBERS: Give the order, Mister De Lucca.

DE LUCCA: Aye aye, sir.

(*De Lucca exits. The light changes, darker. Albers looks again through his binoculars. Through the P.A. system, Albers hears the voice of his son*)

VOICE ON THE P.A.: "I'm afraid of the men. My own men." (*Albers looks around, startled*) "McGuiness thinks it's funny, whenever he finds a dead Jap, to stand over the wretched creature and piss in its mouth. I was horrified, at first, and then ashamed. And now I'm not. I'm not anything. Now I just watch. Now it just seems like war. I'm afraid of *myself*."

ALBERS: David? (*Albers looks again through his binoculars, frantically searching the dark*)

VOICE ON P.A.: "Last night it rained till the water in the foxhole I was in was up to my knees, and one side of the trench gave way, and uncovered a young Jap soldier in the muck, who hadn't started to rot completely away, except for this hole in his skull where the brains had been . . ."

ALBERS: David, where are you?

VOICE ON THE P.A.: ". . . The hole filled up with water too, all the night we were there, pinned down by artillery fire . . . and I started to plunk little pieces of coral rock in the hole in his Nipponese head. I don't know why. To hear the sound: splish-splish-splish-splish . . ."

(*The voice fades out. The Captain suddenly stops, his binoculars trained on something*)

ALBERS: What in the name of God is that?

(*Lieutenant De Lucca re-enters, on edge*)

DE LUCCA: Something out there?

ALBERS (*pointing*): Against the moon. Two men. Can you see them? Floating in mid-air. Like fairies . . . Holding onto each other . . .

(*More concerned than ever, De Lucca watches his captain*)

DE LUCCA: You should try and get some rest, sir. I've squared away the watch.

ALBERS: The boy on radar say anything was around?

DE LUCCA: We're alone. All we have to do now is stay on course. Which I think even *I* can manage. (*Trying to make the captain smile*) Unless you agree with my father, sir—he used to say, "Kiddo, if brains were dynamite, you couldn't blow your nose."

(*The Captain* does *smile*)

ALBERS: All right. I don't think I can sleep, but all right. I'll pull a little blanket-duty. Call me any time—

DE LUCCA: Aye aye.

(*The Captain starts to walk off, pauses*)

ALBERS: I want you to understand, De Lucca.

DE LUCCA: Sir?

ALBERS: I'm glad my boy is dead. He's safe. I was always afraid . . .

(*De Lucca waits for the captain to finish. The Captain only stands there, looking out*)

DE LUCCA (*prompting*): Yes sir?

ALBERS: I was always afraid.

(*The Captain exits. De Lucca watches him go. The lights fade*)

Scene Three

High up in the air, above the ship. Near dawn. Billy and Hobie, breathing hard, hold onto each other, hanging in space.

HOBIE: I can't, jesus god, I can't breathe—

BILLY: You *are* breathing.

HOBIE: Am I?

(*Billy tries to soothe Hobie, rubbing his back. Hobie takes it in that he is, in fact, breathing. He starts to laugh*)

BILLY: Shh . . .

(*Hobie's laughter slowly fades*)

HOBIE: My old lady has this kind of . . . down on her lip, this golden fuzz, she hates it, says it's a goddamn moustache . . . but it's beautiful. *She's* beautiful. (*Pause*) I never knew—I must hurt her, with my beard.

BILLY: I don't think so.

HOBIE (*touching Billy's face*): Sandpaper.

BILLY: Wouldn't she tell you?

HOBIE: She doesn't say a lot. Hard to know what she's thinking. Women . . .

BILLY: Anybody.

HOBIE: What are *you* thinking?

BILLY: I'm cold.

HOBIE: So am I. (*They hold each other closer*) Do you have anybody?

BILLY: I did.

HOBIE (*getting it*)**:** Oh. Your buddy on that ship?

(*Billy nods*)

BILLY: He never knew he was the one—I mean, we were kids, we just said we were fooling around . . . but *I* wasn't fooling. He was the one.

HOBIE: Why didn't you tell him?

BILLY: I was going to . . .

HOBIE: Famous last words.

BILLY: No, I think my *actual* final words—he was getting on a train, I was seeing him off, pretending I could give a damn, he's leaning out a window, like an idiot, waving good-bye . . . "Don't take any wooden nickels!" At the top of my lungs—he's disappearing forever—"Don't do anything *I* wouldn't do!"

HOBIE: Like die.

BILLY: I guess.

(*Now Hobie comforts Billy, stroking his hair. Billy cries. Hobie nuzzles him*)

HOBIE: Fucking sandpaper.

BILLY: That's what I want.

HOBIE: No you don't. I could rub you raw.

BILLY: But that's what I want.

HOBIE: Shhh . . .

BILLY: Is it warmer?

HOBIE: Maybe. Sun's coming up.

BILLY: *Below* us? (*They both look down, realizing at last how high they are, way up in the air. Billy points down*) That's my ship?

HOBIE: Or all that blue is one *hell* of a bathtub. And that cattle boat down there is a toy.

BILLY: What the hell are we doing up *here*?

(*Hobie lets go of Billy, who takes a step back, in the empty air*)

HOBIE: My guess would be—unless you can flap your arms a lot harder than I can—falling.

(*Suddenly Hobie plunges out of sight, with a strangled cry. Billy, still floating, watches him fall, mesmerized*)

BILLY: Don't take any wooden nickels! Don't do anything I— (*Billy suddenly drops like a stone, disappearing with a drawn-out scream*)

(*The lights fade*)

Scene Four

The foredeck, a few moments earlier. Near dawn. Chotkowski, Duane, and McGuiness—still in their skivvies—are asleep on blankets scattered around the deck. Suddenly McGuiness sits up, waking out of a nightmare, with a cry.

CHOTKOWSKI (*half-asleep*): What the fuck—

McGUINESS (*whispering*): I heard something.

CHOTKOWSKI (*instantly awake*): Where?

McGUINESS (*wanting more company*): Duane!

DUANE: Mmmph . . .

McGUINESS: Duh-*wayne!*

(*Duane struggles awake*)

DUANE: What?

McGUINESS: Listen . . .

DUANE: To what? (*Pause. Duane hears nothing unusual*) Betty Grable was doing deep kneebends. On my *face*. Go back to sleep.

McGUINESS: No, listen—*listen!*

(*Far off, a couple of men are humming what sounds like the turn-of-the-century novelty-number, "Under The Bamboo Tree"*)

CHOTKOWSKI (*tense*): *What?*

DUANE: All I hear is water slapping the sides . . . and the engines groaning away . . . some pitiful s.o.b. singing one of those stupid songs he learned at his momma's knee, just to make himself even sadder than he already is . . . and that soft little 'fut-fut-fut,' hate to break the news, but that's you guys who ate too many beans, and now you're tooting away in your sleep, like a packa old dogs . . .

McGUINESS: Something *underneath* all that . . . like bamboo snapping . . .

DUANE: This bucket is old. It's just the deck creaking.

McGUINESS: Is it?

DUANE: Miss Grable better be waiting for me—wherever I was—

CHOTKOWSKI: Back home. In a barn. On top of some woebegone sheep. With fuzzy gams.

DUANE (*ignoring Chotkowski*): —if you wouldn't mind shutting the noise . . .

(*Duane quickly sinks back into sleep. Chotkowski stands and fakes a casual stretch*)

McGUINESS (*fighting panic*): Where the fuck are *you* going?

CHOTKOWSKI: To take a leak. You wanta help me aim?

McGUINESS: Go to hell.

CHOTKOWSKI (*starting to exit*): There is nobody out there, Mac.

McGUINESS: Then why are you running?

CHOTKOWSKI (*unexpectedly serious*): Because I'm scared. I'm shitless. I ran, before. Didn't you go with me? Over that hill? (*Pause*) See you in the movies, friend.

(*Chotkowski hurriedly exits, leaving McGuiness alone with the sleeping Duane. The offstage humming has turned into singing, nearer. The words are finally clear, and the voices seem to be two men who are substituting 'r's' for 'l's' in the song. Those substitutions are underlined*)

VOICES (*offstage, to the tune of "Under The Bamboo Tree"*): "If you <u>r</u>ak-a-me, <u>r</u>ike I <u>r</u>ak-a-you and we <u>r</u>ak-a both the same . . ."

McGUINESS (*whispering over the singing*): Someone *is* out there. "<u>R</u>ike I <u>r</u>ike-a you?" Oh Jesus—Duane?

(*But Duane sleeps on, and the voices continue singing, underneath McGuiness babbling on in his panic*)

VOICES (*offstage*): ". . . I <u>r</u>ak-a-say, this very day, I <u>r</u>ak-a-change your name . . ."

McGUINESS (*over the singing*): Duane? These bastards never learned this bull-fucking-shit at a *white* woman's knee—they can't say "l." They can't say "l"! *Duane!*

(*Duane doesn't stir, as two men stealthily enter, singing—dressed as Japanese soldiers, wearing cartoon-masks of the evil "yellow peril" of American propaganda—exaggerated slanted eyes, buck-teeth, and mustard-colored skin.*)

McGuiness watches, paralyzed with terror, as one of the soldiers—attaching his bayonet to his rifle—approaches him.

The other tiptoes up to Duane, brandishing a huge and gleaming machete.

The soldiers sing, as they stalk their prey)

SOLDIERS: ". . . 'Cause I rove-a you and rove-a you true and if you-a rove-a-me, one rive as two, two rive as one, under the bamboo tree."

(On the word "tree," the "Japanese" soldiers attack. One bayonets McGuiness in the chest. The other, with his machete, hacks away at something in Duane's boxer shorts.

Duane screams and then—in shock—passes out. The soldier, with his free hand, pulls a bloody peeled banana out of Duane's boxers. He holds the severed banana up to show his comrade, who nods at the trophy. McGuiness, mortally wounded, watches in horror)

McGUINESS *(to the soldier):* You cut it off? *(The soldier stuffs the bloody banana in Duane's open mouth) No! (Now both of the soldiers start to retreat, singing again)*

SOLDIERS: " 'Cause I rove-a you, and rove-a you true and if you-a rove-a me, one rive as two, two rive as one, under the bamboo tree."

(The soldiers are gone. The bloody banana still protrudes from Duane's mouth)

McGUINESS: Duane? *(McGuiness tries to crawl to his fallen comrade. But he's lost his strength and collapses, halfway there. Duane, on his back, not moving, starts to chew the banana stuck in his mouth. McGuiness, appalled, keeps watching as the banana disappears. When it's gone, Duane lies still again)* Duane? Are you dead? *(Duane doesn't respond)* Are you dead *now*? *(Duane seems to be)* That time in the valley? When Chotkowski and I were lost? Remember? I never told you this . . . I was going to, I swear to god . . . I ran away. I wasn't lost. I ran like hell. I thought we all had. I thought you were right behind me.

(McGuiness is chilled as Duane unsteadily starts to sit up)

The way all the leaves were shaking? You figured a wind had come up. Except it was shrapnel. Ripping through that wall of green and Chotkowski started stumbling back, like he'd heard something *I* didn't hear—maybe one goddamn C.O. with a brain in his head yelling, "Get the fuck out!" . . . So I ran . . . And I thought you were right behind me. You son-of-a-bitch.

(*Duane is now on all fours, staring balefully at McGuiness*)

I went back for you. I tried. And then I *did* get lost, I fell into a river, I cut myself to shit on that razor-grass, you remember what I looked like, when I finally stumbled into the camp? And you helped me burn the leeches off?

(*Duane, locking eyes with his buddy, vomits up the banana, all over his blanket. McGuiness has to look away*) You believed me then. Why can't you believe me now?

DUANE: Because I'm dead. And I know things. (*He thumps his chest*) Here. In my heart.

McGUINESS: I loved you, you son-of-a-bitch. Like my own brother.

DUANE: I'm *dead.*

(*Duane stands and exits, pulling behind him the vomit-covered blanket. McGuiness watches him go*)

McGUINESS: I left you behind! Duane! But I went back for you! I went back!

(*Chotkowski re-enters, casual, and lies back down on the deck, where he was sleeping. As he and McGuiness bicker, Duane re-enters, unnoticed—with an unsoiled blanket—and also settles down to sleep*)

CHOTKOWSKI (*looking up at the sky*)**:** The Southern Cross is gone—

McGUINESS: Where the fuck have *you* been?

CHOTKOWSKI: I was taking a leak. Did you want to help me aim?

McGUINESS: They were *here!*

CHOTKOWSKI: Who?

McGUINESS: Who the hell are we fighting? The Japs! They got Duane!

CHOTKOWSKI: You were dreaming, buddy. Duane is snoring his head off, right beside you. (*McGuiness looks over, stunned to see that Duane is back, intact*) And it looks to me, from the way his skivvies are standin' up and salutin'—Miss Grable musta renewed her labors. "*One-*two, *back* straight, *knees* bent . . ." (*McGuiness gives Duane a nudge*)

McGUINESS: Duane?

DUANE (*asleep*): Glumsh . . .

McGUINESS (*nudging harder*): *Duane!*

DUANE: *What?* What the sam-goddamn-hill do you want?

McGUINESS (*reassured, finally breathing again*): Nothing.

CHOTKOWSKI: Bucking for a Section Eight.

DUANE: Shoot a toe off, then. In the *morning.* Geez . . . (*Duane drifts off*)

McGUINESS: Henry?

CHOTKOWSKI: Would you stop beating your gums?

McGUINESS: In the valley . . .

CHOTKOWSKI: We aren't *in* the valley, now.

McGUINESS: But won't there be valleys in Japan? (*Chotkowski doesn't answer*) Why did you run?

CHOTKOWSKI: Are you writing a book? I just did. So did half the platoon. It don't keep me up nights.

McGUINESS: Then why aren't you asleep? (*Chotkowski rolls away from McGuiness. Offstage, nearby, we hear what sounds like a body falling onto the deck from a very great height. Then another*) Chotkowski!

What the fuck was that? (*Chotkowski snores. Duane does too. McGuiness, alone and upset, looks out at the night*) Somebody just came on board . . .

(*The lights fade*)

Scene Five

A moment earlier. Amidships. Dawn. The stage is empty. Suddenly Hobie drops from out of the sky, hitting the deck with a thud. Though he lands on his feet, and he isn't hurt, he's shaken up. He looks around him, trying to get his bearings.

HOBIE: What the . . . (*A second later, Billy hits the deck, a few feet away. He's rattled too, but also unhurt from the fall. Seeing Billy, everything comes back in a rush to Hobie*) Oh. (*He doesn't like what he remembers*) Oh Christ . . . (*Embarrassed, Hobie gets a cigarette out, lights up. Billy doesn't catch on to Hobie's mood*)

BILLY: Are you all right?

HOBIE: Extremely swell, I think. Yourself?

BILLY: Not bad.

HOBIE: Good enough. So I'll see you in Tokyo, maybe . . .

(*Now Billy gets it. He's hurt, but he tries not to show it*)

BILLY (*trying to kid*): Not if I see you first.

(*Hobie snorts and starts to exit, stops. Some leftover tenderness makes him want to leave Billy with* something)

HOBIE (*holding up his cigarette*): The only dirty joke my wife ever told me: "Do you smoke after sex?" "I don't know—I never looked."

(*Pause*)

BILLY: What color is her hair? Your wife.

HOBIE: How the hell should I know? (*As if he'd never said this before*) I haven't seen my wife in a year and a half. She don't write anymore. She useta . . .

BILLY: Why did she stop?

(*McGuiness—edgy, looking around for the source of the ominous thuds he heard in the previous scene—appears. He stops when he sees the two men talking. The tension between the two is so clear that McGuiness hides and listens in*)

HOBIE: I sent her a letter, I told her to stuff a piece of paper down her pants, let it stew all day, and then scribble a note on that. And she did. And it worked. I could smell her . . . a couple of days . . .

BILLY: And?

HOBIE: That's all she wrote.

BILLY: *Why?*

HOBIE: Because women know everything. Don't they? How far you'll ever get in your life, who you're screwing, who you'd *like* to screw but you never will, how much more you drank last night than you said, what you *really* think about the way her chin is starting to double up, how you hate the little sounds she makes when you're drilling her—"yip, yip, yip" . . . how to cut her losses . . .

BILLY: She hasn't lost you.

HOBIE: Yet. Fuck you.

BILLY: You just did.

HOBIE: What the hell are you talking about.

BILLY: I can smell you on my hands.

(*Pause. Hobie comes back to Billy, getting up into his face*)

HOBIE: Do I smell like a body?

BILLY: I like the way a man—

HOBIE (*shaking his head, interrupting*): Do I smell like a body washing up on a beach? I am going to die. Next week. Maybe sooner. My wife knows that. Why the hell don't you? You *also* yip like a goddamn dog when you come. But my wife is a lot better fuck. So you lose. (*Hobie grabs Billy*) If you *ever* try to buck me up again, you son-of-a-bitch . . . I will beat you to a bloody pulp. And nobody will stop me. No one. I'll say you put your hand on my dick.

BILLY: And you won't be lying. Will you?

(*Hobie pulls Billy so close, they could kiss. But they don't*)

HOBIE: You won't be recognizable. I'll heave you over. *You* can wash up on a beach.

BILLY: Beside you? How would that look? In the shallows . . . bumping against you . . . (*Making the sound of surf*) Poooosh . . . poooosh . . . I don't even like you. I don't even know your name. (*Pause. Hobie pushes Billy away and exits—trying not to run. Billy grabs a mop that's lying around, and starts—a little frantically—to mop the deck*) Rub it raw . . . rub it harder . . . *harder* . . . make it bleed . . .

(*McGuiness steps out of his hiding place*)

McGUINESS: Hey sailor . . .

(*Billy stares at McGuiness as the lights fade*)

Scene Six

The officers' wardroom—set up like a cop's investigation room, with a metal chair in a pool of light. Chotkowski sits in the glare, pissed off and holding a piece of paper. Behind him, in the shadows, are De Lucca and Captain Albers.

DE LUCCA (*offering*): Cuppa joe?

CHOTKOWSKI: The way you swab-jockies make it?

DE LUCCA: Okay. (*Reading from a list, to the Admiral*) This is Corporal Henry Chotkowski. Gunner. Fifth Division.

CHOTKOWSKI: Anybody care to tell me what the fuck this is all about?

ALBERS: Would you read the letter, Corporal?

CHOTKOWSKI (*of the paper in his hand*): This snivelling shit? I read it.

ALBERS: Out loud. In your normal tone of voice.

CHOTKOWSKI: Look, Captain, I don't want to be in the show—

ALBERS: This is not an audition.

CHOTKOWSKI: —wear a coconut bra, that crap—

ALBERS: Did you hear me, Corporal?

CHOTKOWSKI: Maybe it's good for morale, but myself, I would rather indulge in a little acey-deucy. Or take a big dump. Or jag off.

(*Pause*)

ALBERS (*steely*): Read the letter.

(*Pause. Chotkowski starts to read*)

CHOTKOWSKI: "Dear Dad—"

ALBERS: Skip down a few paragraphs. "The hole filled up . . ."

CHOTKOWSKI: I seen a lot worse than this—

ALBERS: So have I. Would you *read*.

CHOTKOWSKI (*reading*): "The hole filled up with water too, all the night we were there, pinned down by artillery fire . . . and I started to plunk little pieces of coral rock in the hole in his Nipponese head. I don't know why. To hear the sound: "splish . . ."

ALBERS (*interrupting*): That's enough. (*To De Lucca*) He's not the one. Bring the next man in. (*De Lucca exits. Pause. Chotkowski looks like there's more he'd like to say*) Thank you, Corporal. That'll be all.

(*Chotkowski starts to leave, then hesitates*)

CHOTKOWSKI: Sir . . .

ALBERS (*answering the unasked question*): If I knew, I couldn't tell you. We rendezvous with the fleet at Ie Shima, off Okinawa. You men get your orders there.

CHOTKOWSKI: They don't need us at Okinawa.

ALBERS: Then you go wherever they tell you to. So do I. Why, Corporal? Are you afraid?

(*Pause*)

CHOTKOWSKI: Aren't you?

ALBERS: No. Not anymore.

CHOTKOWSKI: Then you're a fool, sir.

ALBERS: Come again?

CHOTKOWSKI: You're a goddamn fool.

ALBERS: I see. Is that your ticket out? To get slapped in the brig? You can stand at a porthole, I'll give you my own fieldglasses? You can watch your buddies die on the beach . . . without you? (*Chotkowski trembles with fury*) Dismissed (*Chotkowski can't even move, he's so angry. Albers continues, yelling*) Mister De Lucca! Send the next one in. (*To Chotkowski, as he plucks the letter from the corporal's hand*) Somebody read this over the P.A. Trying to make me break. I would like to know who. I remember the voice. Would you get the hell out of my wardroom?

(*Speechless, Chotkowski spins around and thunders out, as the lights fade*)

Scene Seven

Amidships. A few moments earlier. Billy stares at McGuiness, who's grinning at him.

McGUINESS (*repeating his call*)**:** Hey *sailor* . . .

BILLY: What?

McGUINESS: Suck my dick. (*Pause*) Suck *my* dick. (*Pause*)

BILLY: Do you have one?

(*Billy starts swabbing the deck again. McGuiness' smile begins to congeal*)

DE LUCCA (*off, voice on P.A.*)**:** McGuiness! Front and center! Private McGuiness!

(*McGuiness, aggravated, looks off—not wanting to stop the game he's playing with Billy*)

McGUINESS: Does the Captain know you're a pansy?

(*Billy stops*)

BILLY: Tell him.

(*Pause*)

McGUINESS: Look: just suck my big fat dick.

DE LUCCA (*off, voice on P.A.*)**:** McGuiness! Private Brian McGuiness!

(*Pause*)

BILLY: I'm off-duty in a couple of hours. Come to the number-five turret. It's dark enough. Has a mattress somebody dragged in there a long time ago. It smells like a sacka dead rabbits. Like you. It smells like you. But it's safe. You can hear if anyone's coming. (*Pause*) I was always afraid I would meet a man like you. I used to have a dream . . .

McGUINESS: I read somewhere that dreams are wishes. *Readers' Digest.* How 'bout that? (*McGuiness exits*)

BILLY: In the dream, I kill the man. I beat him to a bloody pulp. And nobody stops me.

(*Billy keeps swabbing the deck. The lights fade*)

Scene Eight

The wardroom. A few moments earlier. Duane is in the chair, in the pool of light. Again De Lucca and Captain Albers stand in the shadows, listening. Duane is reading from the letter.

DUANE (*mid-way through*): ". . . except for this hole in his skull where the brains had been . . ." (*Duane starts to cry*)

DE LUCCA (*to Albers*): Is he the one you heard?

ALBERS (*shaking his head*): I don't know why he's crying. Son?

DUANE: I'm sorry, sir.

ALBERS: Want to talk about it?

DUANE: No, sir.

(*Pause. De Lucca exits to call the next man*)

ALBERS (*taking the letter from Duane*): Have you been here?

DUANE: . . . I was covered with maggots, once . . . This mortar hit a mass grave . . .

ALBERS: Go on . . .

DUANE: Well, we didn't *know* that's what it was—just ahead of where we had dug in, and it all went up—WHOOMP!—and then it was raining down on us for it seemed like hours, and, we still hadn't figured out what it was, just mud and rock, we thought, but it was flesh and bone, fucking Japanese flesh and bone, coming showering down, and my buddy McGuiness—he was brushing me off, kinda hard, and he said "Duh-wayne, don't open your eyes, not yet," but I did, I looked down, and I was, everything was moving, maggots were crawling all over me . . . from my helmet down to my boon-dockers. On my hands and up my nose and in my mouth. And in my mouth, and in my . . . Like I was dead. (*Pause*) I want to go home.

ALBERS: We all do, son (*De Lucca re-enters, quietly*) Your buddy's name was McGuiness?

DUANE: Yes sir.

ALBERS: Is he still with you?

DE LUCCA: Right outside.

ALBERS: Then that'll be all, Private Owensby.

DUANE: Sir? Can I ask? What happened to the man who wrote this letter?

ALBERS: He's stateside, now. On leave. With his wife. I imagine—what time is it now in San Francisco?

DE LUCCA: After noon.

ALBERS: I imagine he's still in the rack. With his better half.

DUANE: I hope so, sir.

ALBERS: Are *you* married, Private Owensby?

DUANE: I have a girl. But she sleeps around.

ALBERS: And you don't mind?

DUANE: *I* sleep around. So fair is fair.

ALBERS: You're a very modern man, Private Owensby.

DUANE (*not sure this is a compliment*): Thank you, sir. (*Duane salutes and exits*)

Captain Albers turns to De Lucca)

DE LUCCA: It was kind of you to lie.

ALBERS: You think so? Or do you honest-to-god believe I am soft and old and my brains are turning to sawdust?

(*Pause*)

DE LUCCA: I *don't* think you heard what you thought you did. I don't think there was anyone on the P.A. What you read was just bouncing around in your bean. Having all the men on the ship take a look at this letter . . .

ALBERS: *Everyone* will see the sawdust. Leaking out of my ears . . .

DE LUCCA: No, everyone will react like this poor kid. And the tougher ones will hide it better . . . but all of them will think about dying. Soon. On a Japanese beach. Do you need to remind them?

(*Pause*)

ALBERS: Call in this fellow McGuiness. End it right there. And then I will let my son rest. In a box full of maggots.

(*Pause*)

DE LUCCA: It isn't likely that this is the same McGuiness . . .

ALBERS: I hope not, Lieutenant. I pray to God not.

(*De Lucca exits. Albers stares at the letter. The voice of Albers' son comes over the P.A. again*)

VOICE ON P.A.: ". . . my own men. McGuiness thinks it's funny, whenever he finds a dead Jap, to stand over the wretched creature . . ."

(*Albers suddenly throws his coffee mug at the—offstage—squawk-box. We hear an explosion of static, and then complete silence. As Albers, breathing heavily, looks around him, the lights fade*)

Scene Nine

The galley. Later that day. Billy's peeling potatoes, dumping the ones he's peeled in a big pot of water. Hobie comes in—in his hands a "bra" made of coconut shells, and a fake grass skirt.

HOBIE: What the fuck is this?

BILLY: I'm in the show tonight.

HOBIE: In a pair of coconut hooters?

BILLY: I get a few laughs.

HOBIE: Or snickers?

BILLY: What does it matter to you?

(Hobie throws the costume down on the deck)

HOBIE: You could just wear a sign: *"I'm a pogie."*

BILLY: And what would *your* sign say?

(Pause)

HOBIE: *"I'm a moron."* Great big letters. I *am* a moron, swear to god. You can ask my wife. (*Billy, not rising to the bait, won't enter the conversation*) I don't know why she married me. I reminded her of her father, maybe. *He* was a moron—jesus . . . (*Pause*) You're wasting a hell of a lot of potato.

BILLY: Call the quartermaster.

HOBIE: Let me.

(Hobie takes the paring knife from Billy. As their hands touch, Billy blushes and turns away, bending down to pick up the bra and skirt)

BILLY (*of his costume*): You went through my locker?

HOBIE: Who are you? That's all. I wanted to know.

BILLY: Why? (*Hobie, unable to answer, keeps peeling potatoes. Billy feels an urge to get away*) I'm gonna be late for rehearsal . . . (*Billy starts to put on the coconut "bra" and grass skirt*)

HOBIE (*to keep him from going*): What was your buddy's name?

BILLY: Johnny.

HOBIE: Johnny What?

BILLY: I don't remember. Johnny the Dead Guy.

HOBIE: Do I look like him?

BILLY: I guess. In the dark. (*Billy's got the hula outfit on by now*) Do I look like your wife?

HOBIE (*an uneasy joke*): In that get-up? You could be her twin.

BILLY (*of the costume*): She's a native?

HOBIE: Of Indianapolis.

(*Pause. Despite himself, there's something Billy has to ask*)

BILLY: You told me she was a better lay. Than me. So what does she do?

HOBIE: What does she do? It's been a long time . . . She starts off in the shower. Singing. Sounds like a cat being swung by the tail.

BILLY: I can sing better than that.

HOBIE: So can I. I say, "Drive it in the hangar, doll, and turn the motor off, for crissakes." She can't hear me over her yowling, though. So I have to shut her up.

BILLY: How?

HOBIE: I get into the shower *with* her. I stick a finger inside her. And she's already wet. She told me one time, just the sound of my voice . . .

BILLY: Saying what? What you said to me? "I'll beat you to a bloody pulp."

(*Pause*)

HOBIE: I'm sorry.

BILLY: Sorry? Or horny?

HOBIE: Both? (*Billy starts to exit. Hobie grabs him*) That was a joke.

BILLY: No it wasn't.

(*Hobie stares at Billy, letting him go but still wanting to touch him*)

HOBIE: No. It wasn't.

(*Pulled by the tension between them, the two men move closer, almost embracing. At that moment Chotkowski enters, still angry at the grilling he got. He stops short, seeing the men about to kiss*)

CHOTKOWSKI: At ease, ladies.

(*Billy and Hobie, caught by surprise, jump apart*)

HOBIE: This is not—jesus christ—this is not . . .

CHOTKOWSKI: Oh? The way it looks? It never is.

BILLY: We were rehearsing. (*Both embarrassed and frightened by Chotkowski, Billy quietly starts to slip out of his "bra" and skirt*)

CHOTKOWSKI: You coulda fooled me. (*To Hobie*) I thought you had found you a navy pussy-mouth. Get him down on his knees. Get your rocks off. More power to you.

HOBIE: You don't care?

CHOTKOWSKI: What you do with your dick is your business, Hobart. Long as you cover my ass when we hit the beach. Maybe "cover my ass" is the wrong way of putting it. Given that gleam in your eye.

HOBIE: Fuck you.

CHOTKOWSKI: No I think I will wait for the genuine article, thanks. (*To Billy*) Any room in your show for *another* novelty number?

BILLY (*shaking his head*): We do it up top, at the end of the day . . . and we only have till the light fades out . . .

CHOTKOWSKI (*ignoring*): 'Cause I got me a sorta impression I thought I would try. Of a man pinned down in a foxhole . . . right next to some Nipponese carcasse . . . (*To Billy*) Your Captain don't seem to understand—you stare at a mangled body too long, and you have to go this way or that: either "that could be me, with the hole in my skull, and the rainwater filling it up"—which'll give you the horrors, I know—or "that wasn't *ever* a man like me. That has never been anything else but a chunka the landscape. Target practice." So . . . (*He picks up a load of potatoes*) "A man pinned down in a foxhole, with a dead body, passing the time . . ." And you have to imagine that pot is a dead Jap's skull . . . and these spuds are rocks . . . Goes something like this . . .

(*Chotkowski starts to lob the potatoes into the pot of water. Each hits with an audible splash. Chotkowski takes his time, to make his point: splash . . . splash . . . splash . . . till he's out of ammo*)

I think you two should fuck each other's brains out. While you still got 'em—dicks, brains, arms, legs, faces . . . (*He gets some more potatoes and starts to toss them: splash . . . splash . . . splash . . . splash . . .*)

(*With the kind of desperate urgency Chotkowski's talking about, Billy and Hobie suddenly grab each other, in an embrace that sinks them down to the deck. Chotkowski watches them, continuing to dunk potatoes: splash . . . splash . . . splash. . . . The lights fade*)

Scene Ten

The wardroom. A few moments earlier. McGuiness is in the chair, in the pool of light. Albers and De Lucca stand nearby.

ALBERS: So you *did* know my son.

McGUINESS: Rusty Albers?

ALBERS (*correcting*): David.

McGUINESS: We called him "Rusty." Because of his hair. Sure . . . he saved my ass one night, I was tight as a tick from some jungle-juice the men had been cooking up on the beach. What happens is, I get to the sentry, this two-bit Patton wants to hear the password, and—it's "lullaby"—which is so far gone from my pickled brain that I couldn't have said "lullaby" any better than fucking Hirohito could . . . and this by-the-book little bastard's really going to shoot!—when Rusty—he's walking the line that night, he tells the sentry to hold his fire, he knows me, useta sing me to sleep when I was a lad, and now don't I remember?—He's winking at me and I finally get it, I say to the sentry: "*Lullaby!*—motherfucker!" I tried to thank your son, the next day, he just told me not to drink so much. Or write the password down on me, some place I couldn't miss it. Like my asshole, he said, where I seemed to have wedged my head.

ALBERS: Did David talk like that?

McGUINESS: Sure he did. He was one of the guys. That's why we all liked him.

ALBERS: You know he died.

McGUINESS: Yes sir . . . see, we'd lost so many men by then, I was shipped out of Rusty's company—'cause there *was* no company, anymore—I was posted to the buncha gorillas I'm sharing a cage with now . . . I guess Rusty was on his way to Iwo Jima . . .

ALBERS: That's right.

McGUINESS: I'm sorry for your troubles, sir.

ALBERS: Thank you, McGuiness.

McGUINESS: And I ended up on his old man's ship. Small fucking world.

ALBERS: War seems to make strange bedfellows.

McGUINESS: That it does, sir. The strangest.

(*Albers hands McGuiness the letter*)

ALBERS: Have you see this letter?

McGUINESS (*puzzled*): Sir?

ALBERS: It was sent to me . . . a few weeks after David was killed. It's *from* David—Rusty . . .

McGUINESS: To you? (*Albers nods. McGuiness offers the letter back*) Then it's gotta be private?

ALBERS (*taking the letter*): Didn't you hear it this morning? Booming over the squawk-box?

McGUINESS: You read it out loud?

ALBERS: No, I didn't. *Someone* did. Would you like to hear it?

DE LUCCA (*more and more alarmed*): Captain . . . (*of McGuiness*) *Was* it this man's voice you heard?

ALBERS: I don't believe it was.

DE LUCCA: Then—let him go.

ALBERS: I won't keep you, young man. But listen to this . . . (*reading from the letter*) David writes, "I'm afraid—"

McGUINESS: You would never have guessed that, sir.

(*Albers gives him a look that shuts him up, and hands him the letter again*)

ALBERS: *You* read.

(*McGuiness, sensing big trouble, starts to read*)

McGUINESS: "I'm afraid of the men. My own men. McGuiness thinks it's funny, whenever he finds a dead Jap, to stand over the wretched creature and piss in its mouth."

(*The Captain stares at McGuiness. McGuiness looks at his boots. No one speaks*)

ALBERS: I believe it continues . . .

McGUINESS (*reading*): "I was horrified, at first, and then ashamed. And now I'm not. I'm not anything. Now I just watch. Now it just seems like war. I'm afraid of *myself*."

(*A very uncomfortable silence*)

DE LUCCA: Sir?

ALBERS (*to De Lucca*): I want you to wait for me in your quarters.

DE LUCCA: But sir—

ALBERS: That's an order, Mister.

(*De Lucca reluctantly exits. Albers stares at McGuiness*) Do you know how David died?

McGUINESS: He was shot—

ALBERS: He shot himself. With his service revolver. One round to the head. (*De Lucca silently comes back in, unseen. He's afraid for the captain*) The commanding officer tried to cover it up. To spare my feelings. But David was behind the lines—so how could a Jap have gotten that close? There were powder burns on the skin around the entrance-hole . . . (*Listening to the sound of the words*) Entrance-hole . . . exit-hole . . . (*Pause. The Captain suddenly screams at McGuiness*) You pissed in a dead man's mouth? (*McGuiness twitches, mortified. Suddenly the Captain hauls off and slaps him, hard, in the face. McGuiness doesn't try to get away. De Lucca steps forward, making his presence known. But he Captain ignores him*) My son lay where he fell, on that jungle path, for a day and a night . . . There was serious sniper-fire, I'm told . . . so they couldn't recover his body. Not for a day and a night . . . and I wonder if, during that night, in the jungle—and *nothing* is darker than night in a jungle . . . a Jap stepped out from behind a tree, in the dark, and unbuttoned his fly, and pissed on my son. All over my dead son. *Pissed* on him. (*Again without warning, the Captain slaps McGuiness*)

DE LUCCA: Sir . . .

ALBERS (*to De Lucca*): Would you like to spend a few days in hack? I told you to stay in your cabin. (*De Lucca says nothing. McGuiness starts to grin, though his mouth is bloody*)

McGUINESS: You know what the Japs do. Cut our dicks off. Stuff them in our mouths.

(*The Captain slaps McGuiness again. McGuiness spits some blood and smiles*)

ALBERS: Good for you. Don't break.

McGUINESS: I won't. I don't make any friends. So nobody can hurt me. All I can do is die. (*Pause*) Your son had a buddy. And his buddy blew up. He stepped on a mine. Right next to Rusty. *David*. This bright red haze. We inhaled him. (*Pause*) Rusty cried for a long time. We all knew what that meant. So we let him be. Maybe we shouldn't have. Maybe he shouldn't have been alone so much. (*He puts a finger to his head, like a gun*) Pow . . .

(*Pause*)

ALBERS: Are you saying my son was a faggot? (*McGuiness smiles*) My son has a wife. And a baby on the way.

McGUINESS: Then let's hope the kid is his father's spitting image.

(*The Captain hits McGuiness a final time*)

DE LUCCA: Don't hit this man again. Sir.

ALBERS: No. I won't.

(*Pause*)

McGUINESS: I didn't get that you *minded* homos.

ALBERS: What the hell are you talking about?

McGUINESS: On this ship. There are *clouds* of fairies.

(*Pause*)

ALBERS: Name one.

McGUINESS: Billy. Billy Somebody. He asked me to meet him tonight. By the number-five gun.

ALBERS: I don't believe you.

McGUINESS: Come and watch, if you want. Hang around. Till he puts his hand on my dick. Then arrest him. Or let him go. Let him jerk me off. Nothing wrong with that. Now, pissing on the enemy . . . *that's* a court-martial. Am I right? Or am I right? (*McGuiness smiles again—a bloody smile—at the Captain*)

(*The lights fade*)

Scene Eleven

Beside a gun turret. Night. Billy waits for McGuiness. He's gripping a heavy metal stanchion, beating a rhythm out on the palm of his other hand. McGuiness, in fatigues and T-shirt, sneaks up and speaks to him from the shadows.

McGUINESS: You signalling? To the enemy?

BILLY (*turning, oddly calm*): Which enemy?

(*McGuiness looks out*)

McGUINESS (*with total certainty*): There is somebody out there.

BILLY (*looking out*): Nothing. Dark as an asshole.

McGUINESS: You should know. (*All this time, Billy's kept the percussion up, on his palm, with the metal bar*) So what's the ditty, Mr. Krupa?

BILLY: You don't recognize it? No. Why should you? (*Billy sings, in* *rhythm to this thumping*) "Eternal Father, strong to save, Whose arm hath bound the restless wave . . ."

(*Something about Billy's manner is making McGuiness uneasy*)

McGUINESS: Hot below.

BILLY: Like sleeping in an oven. They say. Not that I've ever slept in an oven. Have you? Sometimes it felt like an oven—my own body, when I was fucking. I'd wake up, and the man would be gone . . . like I'd burned him up and he'd blown away . . .

McGUINESS: Take your clothes off. (*Billy stares but doesn't move*) Come on. Hot night, two lonely guys . . . (*He moves closer, stepping out of the darker shadows*)

BILLY: What happened to your face?

McGUINESS: You should see the other guy.

BILLY: I just want to see you.

McGUINESS: Propeller-wash. You are fucking your way through the whole duty-roster.

BILLY: Trying to find somebody.

McGUINESS: Who? (*McGuiness is getting too close to something. The mood begins to evaporate. McGuiness tries to pull Billy back, by singing to him*) "Oh hear us when we cry to Thee—"

BILLY (*surprised that he knows the hymn*): I thought—

McGUINESS: You were a Cub Scout. I was a choir-boy. We *all* had lives. (*Singing again*) "—for those in peril on the sea." (*Pause. He's got Billy back, for a moment*)

BILLY: Who hit you?

McGUINESS: The Captain.

BILLY: Why?

McGUINESS: Because he can.

(*Pause*)

BILLY: They don't lay a finger on us, faggots they catch in the act. They don't have to. But they make you strip, in front of them—then you stand there, with this hot light shining down and your arms at your side, you can't cover yourself, and they ask you, over and over, "Why the hell did you ever enlist?"

McGUINESS: Bullshit. That's a campfire story. That's you nellies trying to scare yourselves.

BILLY: One guy I heard about, he was so afraid, he pissed himself. And he had to keep standing there. Arms at his side. Naked. In the puddle.

(*Pause*)

McGUINESS: And then what happened? Nothing—right? They kicked him out. He was free.

BILLY: Except—it said, "Sexual psychopath," right there on his discharge papers. He could never get a decent job. He could never go home. He's still standing there—in that light. In that puddle. Hearing voices: "Why did you ever enlist?" (*Pause*) "Are you tight? Is an asshole tighter than a pussy? Why don't you gag, when it's down your throat? Are you always the woman? Or do you switch?" Over and over and over: "Why the hell do you like to suck dick?"

McGUINESS: We could give 'em the dog joke: "Why does a dog lick its balls?"

BILLY (*surprised by the "we"*): "Because it can."

McGUINESS: And how can they argue with that? So they stick us with lousy discharge papers—so what? We'll be off of this ship. We'll be alive. I don't think there's a problem.

(*Billy thinks he's finally figured McGuiness out*)

BILLY: You want to get busted.

McGUINESS (*agreeing*): Come here.

BILLY: And your buddies?

McGUINESS: Fuck them if they can't take a joke.

BILLY: Just leave 'em behind.

McGUINESS: *Fuck* 'em. (*McGuiness' coldness almost convinces Billy he's sincere*) Take your clothes off.

BILLY: They say, "Strip." Just so you know: when they have *you* standing there, in the light.

McGUINESS (*nodding*): "Strip." (*Getting into it*) Faggot. (*At that moment, Hobie wanders in—unseen at first by the others. He watches from the shadows, as Billy starts to unbutton his shirt. McGuiness continues to play "Investigator"*) *Is* an asshole tighter?

BILLY: I don't know.

McGUINESS: Is it hotter? We *know* it's darker. (*Billy, intent on undressing, doesn't answer*) Why do you like to suck dick?

BILLY: Because I can.

McGUINESS: Are you thinking about it, now? Or is that a banana in your pants?

(*Out of a pocket, Billy pulls the banana peel he'd tucked away in Scene One. He tosses the peel aside*)

BILLY: No sir. I'm just glad to see you. (*By now, Billy has stripped to the waist*)

McGUINESS: Why?

BILLY: Because I don't have to hide anymore.

(*McGuiness is startled. He's closer than ever to what makes Billy tick*)

McGUINESS: Why did you enlist?

BILLY: To be a man.

McGUINESS: But you aren't a man.

(*As if accepting this judgment of himself at last, Billy pulls off his T-shirt. Now Hobie can't take it anymore—he steps forward*)

HOBIE (*to Billy*): What are you doing?

McGUINESS (*intense*): Beat it, Hobie.

(*Hobie grabs Billy roughly*)

HOBIE: What the fuck are you doing?

(*Billy speaks, as if Hobie were now the Interrogator*)

BILLY: Nobody could sleep below. That's all. Hot night—two lonely guys—

HOBIE: You're lonely? I was down there, too. Wide awake. You could've—

BILLY: What?

HOBIE (*not sure himself*): I don't know. I can smell you on my hands . . .

(*Billy pulls away. McGuiness shoves Hobie off to the side, to whisper*)

McGUINESS: Back off. I got orders, Hobie—from the Captain. He said, "Hey, I got an idea—why don't you guys put on a show?"

(*Before Hobie can figure out what to do, Duane enters, looking haunted. Chotkowski follows him in, concerned. Duane heads for the rail, away from McGuiness, who's moving back to Billy. Hobie, adrift in the middle, moves to his buddies—but keeps a worried, possessive eye on Billy*)

CHOTKOWSKI: Duane? You okay? You were yelling.

DUANE: I had a bad dream.

CHOTKOWSKI: Wanta tell me about it?

(*Duane stares out at the dark*)

DUANE (*speaking of Japan*): What'll we see? When we see it?

HOBIE (*trying to reunite with his friends*): We aren't even close.

CHOTKOWSKI: Lotta miles and miles . . .

DUANE (*answering his own question*): Pagodas, right? Little bridges, cherry trees . . . In the dream, they were right out there . . . (*He points out at the dark*)

HOBIE: Bullshit. We're a thousand miles away.

(*Behind them—noticed only by Hobie—Billy's moved up to McGuiness, putting his hand on the other's chest. He tries to unbutton McGuiness' shirt—but Mac firmly moves Billy's hand away. Hobie, unable to help himself, turns his back to the sea, and watches, as Billy sinks to his knees in front of McGuiness. Oblivious, Chotkowski tries to steady Duane*)

CHOTKOWSKI: Duane?

DUANE: What?

CHOTKOWSKI: Don't run.

DUANE (*a whisper*): I want to go home.

CHOTKOWSKI: No shit. So do I. That's why *I* ran. In the valley. Remember? (*As Chotkowski talks, Billy nuzzles McGuiness' crotch with his head. McGuiness makes a point of not responding—holding his arms at his side, not touching the sailor kneeling in front of him. Dazed, Hobie looks up and sees that Albers is coming onto the bridge. The Captain stares down into the dark, trying to spot McGuiness*) Now I can't sleep anymore. I'm afraid of the things I can do. All the terrible things. Hold on. A little longer.

(*De Lucca—worried about the Captain—joins him on the bridge. The moon comes out for a moment, disappearing again behind a cloud*)

Anyway, the Captain's off his nut. Don't worry about the Mainland. We are all gonna die a lot sooner than that. *Zig-zag, you son-of-a-bitch!*

HOBIE: He can hear you.

CHOTKOWSKI: Who?

(*As the moon comes out again, brighter than ever, Hobie points at Albers, on the bridge above them*)

HOBIE: The Captain. Up on the bridge.

CHOTKOWSKI: Fuck him. (*He shouts*) The moon's come out! We're sitting ducks!

(*The moonlight also clearly reveals McGuiness and Billy, about to have sex. Astonished, De Lucca looks to Albers to act—but the Captain, grim, does nothing*)

DE LUCCA: *Sir?*

(*Duane sees McGuiness and Billy and stares, not understanding*)

DUANE: What is McGuiness . . . ? Hobie—look.

HOBIE: No thanks.

DUANE (*more urgent*): Chotkowski. What are they doing?

CHOTKOWSKI: Deserting.

DUANE: No, somebody *tell* me!

HOBIE: Escaping.

(*At this moment, as Billy starts to unbutton McGuiness' fly, Captain Albers calls down from the bridge*)

ALBERS: You there—on the deck! Would you move whatever it is you are up to—

McGUINESS (*stepping back from Billy*)**:** A blow-job, sir.

ALBERS: —to the shadows under the gun? Where I think you would have more privacy?

(*McGuiness isn't sure the Captain understands what's happening. Hobie, Duane, and Chotkowski uneasily watch*)

McGUINESS: *This man is a pervert, Sir! Undermining morale! Creating dissension—*

ALBERS: *Then give him a very wide berth.*

(*McGuiness is stunned. Billy gets to his feet,* knowing *what he was afraid of, all along—that McGuiness was trying to set him up*)

McGUINESS: *I don't think you understand: he was trying to give me a blow-job! Sir!*

ALBERS: *You remind me of the man who complains of a fly in his soup. And the waiter replies, "Would you keep it down? Or everyone will want one."*

(*While the other men are distracted by this shouting match, Billy picks the stanchion up again. He approaches McGuiness, hiding the metal bar behind his back, intending to kill his tormentor*)

McGUINESS: *They all* **have** *one! He is fucking every man on this ship! From the fo'c'sle clear to the taff-rail! Trying to* **find** *somebody! But where is he looking? Down our throats? There is no one down my throat! Or up my heinder! Why is he searching us there?*

(*Now Duane sees Billy closing in on McGuiness, metal bar in hand*)

DUANE (*poking Chotkowski*)**:** Jesus Christ—

CHOTKOWSKI: McGuiness! Watch your back! (*McGuiness turns and sees Billy raising his arm to conk him. Startled, McGuiness takes a step* *backward and slips on Billy's discarded banana peel. He takes a pratfall, landing with a bang on his ass. Billy, startled, lowers his club. For a moment, no one speaks or moves. Then the craziness of the situation finally sinks in)* Saved by a fucking banana peel.

(Chotkowski starts to laugh—and Hobie, and finally Duane, join in, the laughter close to hysteria)

McGUINESS: He was trying to kill me! *That's funny????* *(This shuts the men up, for a second—then they burst out laughing again, even harder. The laughter starts to die down. McGuiness stares, hurt, at Duane)* Fuckit, Duane—even you?

(Abashed, Duane turns away—and sees something out in the water)

DUANE: What the hell is that? *(Chotkowski turns to see what Duane is pointing at. Duane is paralyzed with fear)* It's fish . . . two fish . . .

CHOTKOWSKI: You've seen 'em before. And they always amaze you—

DUANE: No, *fish! Torpedoes!*

ALBERS *(on the bridge)*: *WHERE?*

DUANE: Off the starboard—

(The ship is suddenly rocked by a huge explosion. All the men still standing fall to the deck. Another explosion. The lights change)

Scene Twelve

A small life-raft—just a wooden ring with a bottom of wooden strips. Mid-ocean. Lying in the raft, badly wounded, are Hobie and De Lucca. De Lucca's right leg is broken; Hobie's eyes are protected by a strip of cloth someone has tied around his head. Clinging to the sides of the raft—to avoid the punishing sun—are Albers, Billy, Chotkowski, and McGuiness, who's looking around for Duane. Duane seems to be missing. De Lucca and Albers are wearing life jackets. The rest are not. Since the night the ship sank, the men have been in the water for the following day and night. Now they've come to the end of the second day—almost forty hours. The men are weak, dehydrated, close to delirium. Late afternoon. Still bright, but soon the light will begin to fade, very rapidly.

McGUINESS: I shouldn't have let him—*Duane!* Why the hell did I . . .

CHOTKOWSKI: Down the red lane. Down the shark's red lane—

McGUINESS: *Fuck You! Duh-WAYNE!*

HOBIE (*for the umpteenth time*): I can't see.

ALBERS: It's the glare—off the water.

HOBIE: What glare? I don't see any glare—

McGUINESS: *Fucking DUANE! You son-of-a-bitch . . .*

ALBERS (*to Hobie*): It was driving you crazy, son. So we had to cover your eyes.

(*Hobie touches his face and feels the blindfold; again, he's done this many times. He's confused*)

HOBIE: Why? What did I do? I'm blindfolded. *What did I do?*

(*Suddenly Duane pops up from underwater, near McGuiness*)

DUANE: It's there!

ALBERS: I don't think so.

(*Furious with relief, McGuiness reaches out and grabs onto Duane, who isn't wearing a life jacket either*)

McGUINESS: You goddamn goober. (*He pulls Duane back to the raft*) Stay fucking put.

CHOTKOWSKI: What's down there?

DE LUCCA (*emphatic*): Nothing.

DUANE: The ship!

CHOTKOWSKI: What ship?

DUANE: It's right below us! (*Pointing down*) See? That's the top of the Number Two stack. Right under our feet.

(*Hearing Duane ranting, De Lucca tries to sit up in the raft. The effort makes him gasp*)

ALBERS (*to De Lucca*): Where the hell are *you* going, mister?

DE LUCCA: Trading places. (*Referring to Duane*) You'd better get that man in the raft.

ALBERS: But your leg—

DE LUCCA: He keeps drinking sea water.

DUANE (*proudly*): Not now!

ALBERS (*to De Lucca*): I can see all the way to the bone. You can't put that leg—

DUANE: I don't have to drink sea water now. It's fresh. Right out of the scuttle-butt. Cold as ice. I drank till I just about bust a gut.

HOBIE (*looking blindly around*): Where?

CHOTKOWSKI (*confused*): The ship didn't sink?

DUANE: Not all the way down. Just a couple of feet. Like it's waiting for us. You just have to swim in and you open a door . . .

CHOTKOWSKI (*trying to reason this out*): That'd flood it . . .

DE LUCCA: That's right. The man's gone. Flying one wing low. Get him into the raft.

DUANE: I'm *thirsty!*

McGUINESS (*holding onto Duane*): You think I'm not, you bobbing turd?

HOBIE: I'm burning up.

ALBERS: The sun's well under the yard-arm. Wait it out.

HOBIE: But I have to get into the water. Just to cool off.

ALBERS: You can't see.

BILLY: I can hold him.

McGUINESS: I bet.

(*Hobie blindly tries to clamber out of the raft*)

CHOTKOWSKI (*out of the blue*): I can see an island.

(*Pause*)

HOBIE: Help me into the water. Somebody. Please. I'm burning up.

(*Chotkowski and Billy awkwardly help Hobie over the side of the raft, and into the water. As they do so, Albers wriggles out of his own life jacket*)

DE LUCCA (*almost crazy with pain, gritting his teeth*): There has to be order. Somewhere. Why were we fighting? Why did we go to war? That man should be in the raft.

BILLY (*to Hobie, as he holds him in the water*): Better?

HOBIE: Than what?

(*This cracks up Chotkowski and Billy. They laugh, a little crazily. The Captain passes his life jacket over to Billy*)

ALBERS: Get a jacket on this man. On the double.

(*Billy helps Hobie get the life jacket on*)

DE LUCCA: Captain. I think—if you won't wear a life preserver yourself, then get back in the raft.

ALBERS: When the sun has set. My burns are already bad enough . . .

DE LUCCA: And when it gets dark? Will you, quiet as a rat, let go of the side? Splash . . .

(*Pause*)

ALBERS: I don't like you, Mr. De Lucca. I never have.

(*Pause*)

CHOTKOWSKI: I can see a goddamn island. There's a long white beach, what looks like a valley above it . . .

McGUINESS: I thought you'd seen enough valleys. You and me both, chicken shit.

CHOTKOWSKI: And this line of silver, must be a river, falling down into the valley. Can you see it? Can anyone see it?

BILLY: No.

CHOTKOWSKI: If I could haul my raggedy ass that far . . .

ALBERS (*wanting De Lucca's life jacket*)**:** Mr. De Lucca—

DE LUCCA (*knowing what Albers wants*)**:** No. Sir. There is nothing out there.

DUANE: Lotta miles and miles . . .

DE LUCCA: Listen: if there was a shore, we could hear the surf. This steady roar . . .

ALBERS: But he needs to go.

DUANE (*to Chotkowski*)**:** You said don't run.

CHOTKOWSKI: I ain't running. If I could get help . . . Save one of you pitiful bastards . . . I *swear* I can see a beach.

DUANE: All the terrible things you can do . . .

CHOTKOWSKI: And palm trees. Tall ones . . . Shifting in the breeze.

DUANE: All the terrible things . . . (*Pause*) Remember how that valley felt? Like the mouth of an animal. I looked around, and—everyone was gone.

(*Pause*)

McGUINESS: *I went back for you!* (*Pause*) *Chotkowski* said, "Fuck him. He's a piece of dead meat. Lying there with his cock in his throat. Let him lie."

(*Pause*)

DUANE: It's all right. The reason *I* didn't run—I was so scared shitless— down my leg, I mean, shit— how *could* I run?

CHOTKOWSKI: Don't *forgive* me, you son of an apple-knocker.

DUANE: I'm not—

CHOTKOWSKI: I said *don't forgive me!*

ALBERS (*offering Chotkowski permission*): *Is* that surf?

DE LUCCA: I'm not giving this man my jacket.

ALBERS: You are if I—

DE LUCCA: No. I'm relieving you of your command. Sir.

(*Pause*)

ALBERS: I will see you in hell.

DE LUCCA: If you let us die, I believe you will. You knew the moon had made us a target. What did you say? You said, "Good." I *heard you.* "Good." (*With the other men distracted by this fight, Chotkowski starts to swim away. De Lucca to Albers*) Let go of the side. If that's what you want. Rat-bastard. Splash. You don't give one rusty fuck for the men in your charge. You don't give a fuck about anything. Only your son. And your son is dead.

(*Pause*)

DUANE (*to the Captain*): Does he look like you?

ALBERS: No. Handsome. At least a head taller.

DUANE: I saw him.

ALBERS: *What?*

DUANE: He's on the ship. Right below us. Chug-a-lugging champagne. With a beautiful woman—

DE LUCCA: Shut up.

DUANE: A blonde. With legs up to here. Is that his wife?

DE LUCCA: Gyrene, that's an order—*Shut Up!*

(*In his agitation, De Lucca jars his broken leg and screams in pain. No one moves to help him*)

DUANE: Like Veronica Lake, a little? Except in a family way?

(*Chotkowski is far away from the life raft now. At last he disappears*)

ALBERS: My son is dead. And my ship is on the bottom. Miles below us. Please be still. The sun is almost down. You can climb back into the raft, for the night—

DUANE: But I'm *thirsty now!*

ALBERS: All of us are.

McGUINESS (*shaking Duane*): Did I tell you not to drink salt water? Did I? "Bonk . . . bonk . . . bonk . . . bonk . . ."

DUANE (*looking down*): I think they're dancing. (*Looking closer*) Making love? No, dancing. Can you hear—I can't hear the music . . .

(*Pause. Billy starts to sing*)

BILLY: "Down in the jungle lived a maid, of royal blood though dusky shade . . ."

DE LUCCA: Tell the invert to button it, would you? Also tell the invert he's on report. I saw the advances he made. When they pick us up—

HOBIE: *Nobody is picking us up! We lost our power before the ship could send out an S.O.S.!*

ALBERS: You don't know that.

HOBIE: Ask my wife. We are all gonna die. (*Pause*) Where is Chotkowski?

(*Pause. The others finally realize Chotkowski is gone*)

BILLY: He went to get help.

HOBIE: There is no help. *Chotkowski!* (*Pause*) Can you see him?

McGUINESS: Hard to look that way. He must be swimming right into the sun.

HOBIE: Is the sun that low? (*Hobie takes the blindfold off, but still can't see*)

DUANE: They've started turning on the lights. Down there. See that watery glow? This handsome man and this beautiful woman . . . dancing on the bridge—

ALBERS: *My son is dead!* (*Captain Albers starts to cry*)

HOBIE: Somebody is crying . . .

BILLY: The Captain.

DE LUCCA: He isn't the Captain. (*Pause*) There has to be order. Or why did we fight?

(*The light begins to fade more rapidly, now*)

DUANE (*looking down*): Wait a minute—that's *my* girl! On the dance floor . . . wrapping all of her legs around his . . . I *told* you she was a whore.

DE LUCCA: You said you were, too.

(*Pause*)

DUANE: I'm thirsty.

(*Pause. Duane suddenly pulls away from McGuiness. He dives beneath the surface, disappearing*)

McGUINESS: *Duane!*

DE LUCCA: Let him go.

McGUINESS: Fuck *you*, buddy. *Duane!* Oh Jesus, Duane . . . I was holding on, this time, I was holding *on!*

DE LUCCA: He was out of his mind. And he wanted to die. Do you want him to kill *two* men? Let him go.

McGUINESS: I *won't!*

(*McGuiness swims away from the raft. Frantically he searches for Duane. But Duane is gone, and McGuiness himself is exhausted. He starts to go under. Billy—who's been holding Hobie up in the water—moves Hobie up to the raft*)

BILLY (*to Hobie*): Hold on to the raft. Can you do that?

HOBIE: Where are you—no. Don't leave me.

BILLY: Your buddy's in trouble.

HOBIE: Don't leave me!

(*Billy kicks away from the raft, to rescue McGuiness. De Lucca reaches out a hand and grabs Hobie*)

DE LUCCA: I've got you, okay?

HOBIE: Tell my wife she was right to stop sending me letters. She knew. Tell her—

DE LUCCA: Tell her yourself. You aren't dying.

HOBIE: Tell her women know everything.

ALBERS (*more to himself than the others, starting to lose it*)**:** My wife said good-bye to us both. At the station. My son and I. She held onto me long enough to whisper: "Bring him back." That was all she would say to me. "That's an order, Mister. Bring him back."

(*At this moment, Billy reaches McGuiness. He grabs the Marine by the neck of his T-shirt, starting to drag him back to the raft. McGuiness struggles feebly*)

McGUINESS: Let go of me, you faggot—*Duane!* Let me *go!* I *had* him!

ALBERS: Every mother's son . . .

McGUINESS: —by the hair . . . *DUANE!* But he started to slip away . . .

ALBERS: "Bring him back."

McGUINESS: . . . through my hand . . .

(*Billy has pulled McGuiness back to the raft*)

BILLY (*to De Lucca*)**:** Can you help me?

HOBIE (*calling out to Billy*)**:** Where are you?

BILLY (*to Hobie, as De Lucca lets go*)**:** Hold on till we get this man in the raft.

(*De Lucca, grunting with pain, grabs hold of McGuiness, weakly pulling him in as Billy—in the water—pushes. Finally McGuiness flops onto the bottom of the raft, gasping and coughing up water. Billy now grabs hold of Hobie again, holding him up*)

HOBIE: Hey sailor . . .

(*Hobie clings to Billy. For a moment, everyone is still—from shock or exhaustion. Billy holds onto the raft and buoys up Hobie. Hobie floats, held up by Billy's arm. McGuiness, coughing less, is trying to catch his breath. De Lucca grits his teeth, riding out a wave of pain in his broken leg. Captain Albers bobs in the water, holding onto the raft and watching the other men. Then—quietly and deliberately—Captain Albers lets go of the side of the raft. He sinks into the water, disappears. No one sees him go. With great tenderness, Billy kisses Hobie—his face, his hair, his neck—as Hobie dangles in his grasp. McGuiness, hearing something, stirs*)

McGUINESS: Hobie . . .

BILLY: He's dead. (*Billy continues to kiss the lifeless body*)

DE LUCCA: Then let him go. Save your strength. *Let him go!*

(*Billy ignores him. Offstage, the men who drowned begin to make the sound of breakers on a shore: "Poosh . . . poosh . . ."*)

McGUINESS: Listen . . .

DE LUCCA: What is it? (*De Lucca scans the horizon, terrified*) What *is* it?

BILLY: Why are you so afraid?

McGUINESS: I think it's surf . . .

(*Billy, still in the water, holds onto Hobie, tighter. McGuiness and De Lucca strain to sit up in the raft. They look out at the swelling dark*)

DE LUCCA: Waves on a fucking beach. We are not gonna make it. All of us are insane.

(*The sound of surf. The light, very rapidly fading, suddenly swoops to almost black*)

McGUINESS: No: I can hear it too. I *think* I can . . . I can hear the shore . . .

(*As McGuiness and De Lucca wonder if rescue is possible, Billy starts to kiss Hobie's body again, in a fury. The dim light fades—in a second—to black*)

NEGOTIATIONS

CLOCKS AND WHISTLES

by Samuel Adamson

Clocks and Whistles was first presented at the Bush Theatre, London, on April 2, 1966, directed by Dominic Dromgoole, with the following cast:

Henry	John Light
Anne	Kate Beckinsale
Trevor	Neil Stuke
Alec	Michael Cashman
Caroline	Melanie Thaw

Dedication

For Dominic Dromgoole, and for the late Paul Andrews.

Characters

Henry—25
Anne—26
Trevor—25
Alec—late 40s, early 50s
Caroline—Late 30s

Setting

London, The Present

AUTHOR'S INTRODUCTION

I'm delighted that *Clocks and Whistles* is part of this "gay play" anthology (and ecstatic that it's being published in America for the first time) but I would have been as delighted if it had been part of a "first plays" anthology, or a "friendship plays" anthology, or a "London plays" anthology, any kind of anthology at all. The main character, Henry, sleeps with men and is, I think, content with that, and would probably describe himself as "gay." Of course this is reductive. For a start, he rejects many of the clichéd signifiers of "gayness" that the other characters dangle in front of him. And I think when he says he loves *Singin' in the Rain* it's because it happens to be a good film. If he understands the absurdity of a production of *La Vie Parisienne* set in the roaring nineteen-forties, perhaps its because he happens to appreciate the melodies of Offenbach, and happens not to appreciate the cult of the revisionist director. If he doesn't have a clue what the men on London's Old Compton Street (a center of gay night life) are wearing this season, perhaps it's because he happens to forget to take notice. To call him "camp," or an "opera queen," or "un-trendy" might be fun, but is probably too convenient. What Henry deals with in *Clocks and Whistles* is the fickle nature of love. And so do Anne, Alec, Caroline, and Trevor, none of whom would call themselves gay, but all of whom still *might* love *La Vie Parisienne* or *Singin' in the Rain* because of Offenbach's catchy tunes or Donald O'Connor's nifty feet.

SAMUEL ADAMSON
London, June 2000

Scene One

A wine bar, SW3; Henry and Anne, sitting at a table. Soft music. Henry is writing in his diary. Anne has been drinking, but is in control. She raps her fingers on the table. She sighs.

ANNE: Alec is due at my place this afternoon. (*Beat*) He might take me to a film. (*Beat*) Well, I know what you think of Alec. (*Beat*) Frappy?

HENRY: I don't think anything about Alec.

ANNE: I don't like him much, either.

HENRY (*head down, writing*): I know too little about him to have an opinion either way. As you know.

ANNE: Do you know what I hate? I hate super models, minor royalty, and finely featured English actresses with dead—or alive—French husbands . . .

HENRY (*not looking up*): Do you want another one?

ANNE (*fed up*): Do I? No, no more.

HENRY: Okay.

ANNE: This is very rude.

HENRY: What?

ANNE: Writing in your diary, while you're with me. I'm bored.

HENRY: Have another drink. I won't be long—you've never minded before.

ANNE: What does it say?

HENRY: Stuff.

ANNE: That's not an answer. Stuff. Have you written things in there about Alec? I bet you have. You hate Alec.

HENRY: Tell me about him. (*Anne doesn't answer. Patiently*) No, I don't. Hate him.

ANNE: What does it say, there? I shouldn't let you do this. I should be the one writing in my diary, being all creative, showing off in public, while *you* sit staring into thin air—

HENRY (*busy*): I'm not . . . showing off . . .

ANNE: Heigh, ho. (*Beat*) Go back a few pages.

HENRY: No.

ANNE: Go on, go back, tell me what's written on . . . March the fourth . . .

HENRY: No.

ANNE: Pleeeaassee.

HENRY (*flicks back a few pages*): "Meet Anne . . . lunch. Palaminos." Happy? That's you. You're in it.

ANNE: I know it's not an appointments diary.

HENRY: It's that too.

ANNE: I'm not going there any more, it's revolting. I said to you, cannelloni has meat in it, you said, "Um, I don't know . . . I think cannelloni has whatever you want to put in it, it doesn't have to be meat. What's it say on the menu?" We look at the menu and it just says "Cannelloni." Cannelloni *has* meat in it, Frappy. I've never, *ever* known cannelloni not to have meat in it. And I tasted the gelatine in my pudding. I'm not going there any more.

HENRY: All right. That's fine with me.

ANNE: The waiters aren't what they were, anyway.

HENRY: No, they're not . . .

ANNE: Very nice once, I remember.

HENRY: Me too.

(*Beat*)

ANNE: There was a film on last night with a friend of mine in it, did you see it? She was *ghastly*.

HENRY: Are you sure you don't want another one?

ANNE: I'll finish yours. (*Takes it; it's a coffee*) Don't you like me any more, Henry?

HENRY: Of course . . . what's the matter?

ANNE: Nothing, except you're not taking any notice of me. (*Beat*) Here's to two-bit little south London theatres. (*Drinks*) Uuurgh, it's cold.

HENRY: It isn't two-bit.

ANNE: It *is*. The only thing I liked about that place was the smell.

HENRY: Smell?

ANNE: That incredible backstage smell. The floor boards . . . old adrenalin. What does it say in your diary about it, bumping into me?

HENRY: I think I thought of Sibyl Vane.

ANNE: Who's that?

HENRY: *Dorian Gray*.

ANNE: Yes, right. You in a box watching me . . .

HENRY: . . . playing who?—Rosalind . . . your white, soft skin, with flushes of pink on the cheekbones, glowing radiantly . . . (*He continues*)

ANNE (*over this*): You're sweet, Frappy, but—

HENRY: . . . your pouting lips, your piercing eyes, your powerful, bony figure that spoke "Actress," not like Sibyl Vane at all, more like a forties movie star. Hepburn in *Holiday*.

ANNE (*depressed*): Oh, Hepburn . . . why can't I be like her? Don't laugh.

(*Beat*)

HENRY: You'll get work.

ANNE: Guess what. I had an audition.

HENRY: Oh, Anne! You didn't tell me? Is it a film, what?

ANNE: A play. You won't believe it. *Who's Afraid of Virginia Woolf?*

HENRY (*incredulous*): Really?

ANNE: Yes.

HENRY: Elizabeth Taylor?

ANNE: No, of course not Elizabeth Taylor, I'm not a hundred and five, I went for Honey, you know, the other one, the wimp. (*Henry smiles*) That was made in the thirties.

HENRY: What?

ANNE: *Holiday*.

HENRY: Wasn't.

ANNE: Was.

HENRY: Wasn't.

ANNE: Fuck it. Should I have another drink?

HENRY: I really don't care now.

ANNE: I can't afford it today.

HENRY: Please. I offered anyway.

(*Beat*)

ANNE: I'm not besieging you, am I?

HENRY: No.

ANNE: It's just . . . (*Suspicious*) Who's new?

HENRY: No one.

ANNE: There is somebody, I can tell. That's why you're being so distant—I know you—sitting there with your diary, not even getting a drink, having a bloody cappuccino on a Saturday afternoon . . .

HENRY: What's wrong with that . . . ?

ANNE: There is somebody.

HENRY: There's not.

ANNE: There is.

HENRY: No, there's not.

ANNE: Well, that's a shame.

HENRY: Oh, Anne.

(*Beat*)

ANNE: What about that primitive guy you were talking about? A few weeks ago you were talking about someone you met in a club. You said he was primitive. (*Beat*) Do you want to know the painting I like most in the National Gallery?

HENRY: Umm . . . no.

ANNE: It's very pedestrian to people in the know, I bet.

HENRY: Probably. Come on . . . have another drink . . .

ANNE: The people who really know about *art*. But it's my favourite, favourite, favourite. "Ophelia Among the Flowers".

HENRY: I know that one . . .

ANNE: It was ruined for me the other day when an American couple started looking at it though.

HENRY: Why?

ANNE: We shouldn't share our art with the Americans. Maybe there should be prescribed American days.

HENRY: Alec's American.

ANNE: He's not American really.

(*Beat*)

HENRY: What?

ANNE: What?

HENRY: Alec's not American?

ANNE: He has the accent because he lived there. I'm hungry.

HENRY: They have nuts.

ANNE: Do they have ice cream?

HENRY: No . . . I don't think so.

ANNE: I'll have zabaglione!

HENRY: Zabaglione?

ANNE: Gelati, Frappy. Zabaglione gelati.

HENRY: There's none, Anne. They don't have it.

ANNE: Well they should.

(*Beat*)

HENRY: I'm really surprised to hear that Alec isn't American.

(*Beat*)

ANNE: My audition was a calamity. I was very bad. W.I. stuff, church hall.

HENRY: I bet it was fine.

ANNE: I was bad. Fine isn't good enough, anyway. Critics say that. (*Pause. Henry starts writing again*) Oh, bloody hell, don't start writing again. (*Henry looks up briefly, then continues writing*) Oh sod bucket pooh shit. I know you're seeing someone. I'll have another drink. Gin. Another gin.

(*Music. Crossfade*)

Scene Two

Hyde Park. Henry and Trevor, sitting on the ground. Trevor drinks from a large bottle of Coke.

TREVOR: There's a piece of fluff, still stands down there . . .

HENRY: I've seen her!

TREVOR: She's probably been there for five 'undred years—she's got worn-down stilettos and a tatty leather jacket . . .

HENRY: That's it. I saw her the other day, she stands near a phone box . . .

TREVOR: She needs 'er roots done.

HENRY: It's so blatant. She's not really, is she . . . ?

TREVOR: She is! She doesn't get anyone though, never.

HENRY: It's not surprising.

TREVOR: Nah, not lookin' like that. She doesn't pull a thing these days . . .

HENRY: What have you tried, or something?

TREVOR: Yeah, right.

HENRY: No, of course not . . . I didn't mean . . .

TREVOR: You 'ave to go to other places for that sort of thing.

HENRY: I'm not . . . Oh, do you?

TREVOR: She's cheap, what d'you reckon?

HENRY: I suppose she would be.

(*Beat*)

TREVOR: Why were you around this area, then? (*Beat*) You said you were 'ere the other day.

HENRY: I . . . I had your address, and I . . .

TREVOR: You chickened out. (*Henry is silent*) Did you see me flat?

HENRY: No, I gave up.

TREVOR: Well, there's not much around here but me, all the trade's pretty straight . . . you should have come over.

HENRY: I . . . just wanted to see you.

(*Trevor smiles*)

TREVOR: It's over there, five minute walk. All in good time. Where do you live, then?

HENRY: Clapham.

TREVOR: Hardly ever get down that way any more. Occasionally I do, quite recently in fact—there are a few places I go to sometimes. Two Brewers, know it?

HENRY: Yeah.

TREVOR: I suppose you've got a great place.

HENRY: Why do you suppose that?

TREVOR: I dunno, somethin' about you, your manner. I thought you probably lived in this really expensive 'ouse in Pimlico or somethin'.

HENRY: It's cheap, where I live.

TREVOR: No kiddin'?

HENRY: Really cheap.

TREVOR: Just like that prozzie.

HENRY: Cheaper, I'd say. We shouldn't talk about her like that.

TREVOR: Why not? She's a lost cause. (*Eyes Henry up and down*) Love that shirt you're wearing.

HENRY: Do you?

TREVOR: I couldn't see myself inside it though.

HENRY: I could.

TREVOR (*mischievous*)**:** Aaaahh, nice one. (*Beat*) D'you live with anyone?

HENRY: Yeah. Another guy. Martin.

TREVOR: Oh . . . 'e's your significant partner, then.

HENRY: Significant other.

TREVOR: What?

HENRY: I think they say significant other.

TREVOR: Yeah, well it's crap i'n't it. Words, words, words, words.

(*Beat*)

HENRY: He's not anyway. His girlfriend spends most of her time there.

TREVOR: I hate that. That's why I live on me own.

HENRY: It's pretty dingy to be honest.

TREVOR: I wouldn't worry. You can find somewhere else.

(*Beat*)

HENRY: Am I a disaster?

TREVOR: What?

HENRY: Nothing . . . I just . . .

TREVOR: You're the fucking *Titanic*, you are (*laughs*): look at you.

(*Beat. Trevor drinks*)

HENRY: Trevor?

TREVOR: Yeah?

HENRY: I was being a bit . . . well, dishonest before, about that . . . woman
. . . you know, because I didn't want to sound so surprised, or anything,
because the other day I . . .

TREVOR: What?

HENRY: I rang, um . . . an escort agency . . . isn't that sad?

TREVOR: No . . . no, no.

HENRY: It is . . .

TREVOR: No, but mate, there's no need to spend all that money, you know. I can't imagine you needing to call out, I 'ave to say, you *don't* need the practise . . .

HENRY: Trevor.

TREVOR: Well . . . (*Brings fingers up to his lips and blows a kiss into the air*)

(*Beat*)

HENRY: This woman arrives.

TREVOR: Woman?

HENRY: And we have a bit of a chat. She says hello, I say hello back. "This is nice, here," she says. "Hello," I say, gulping. "No, it's not," I say, "it's a dump." "Hi!," she says, "Hi," I say. "That's nice," she says, looking at my poster of Julia McKenzie and Millicent Martin in *Side by Side by Sondheim*. It was awkward.

TREVOR: Sounds it.

HENRY: And I try to have sex with her, right, and she tries to have sex with me, but it doesn't work . . .

TREVOR: Oh . . .

HENRY: And she says "Bye" and I say "Bye" . . . and that was a really, really, really, *really* stupid thing to do—

TREVOR: No it wasn't mate, I'd—

HENRY: "Bye" I said, and she walked down the stairs and her skirt rode up her arse, you know, really, really corny, it was, it made me feel as if I was—

TREVOR (*over this*)**:** Yeah, seen it.

HENRY: —in a movie or something . . . and that was, I'm not sure, eighty pounds down the drain, all on Barclaycard—(*ashamed*) imagine Penelope's face . . .

TREVOR: Who's Penelope?

HENRY: My mother.

TREVOR: You call her Penelope?

HENRY: That's her name. (*Beat*) Stuff Penelope.

(*Beat*)

TREVOR: Does she know about you?

HENRY: Who, Mum?

TREVOR: Yeah.

HENRY: She doesn't know anything. (*Beat. He sighs*) Everything's so static, lumpish.

(*Trevor smiles*)

TREVOR (*flirtatious*): I feel like dancing.

HENRY: It's a bit early, isn't it?

TREVOR: Never too early. I know a place. I'll show you the flat next time. (*Beat*) Yeah, I wanna dance.

(*Music. Crossfade*)

Scene Three

Anne's flat, Chelsea. Alec and Henry. Uncomfortable pause.

HENRY: So you're not American?

ALEC: Pardon me?

HENRY: Anne told me that you aren't—actually—American.

ALEC: She did?

(*Beat*)

HENRY: She was quite drunk, I don't know whether maybe, she was . . . So are you, or not?

ALEC: Actually, no I'm not.

HENRY: I never thought to ask, I always assumed you were. You just spent time there?

ALEC: You make it sound like a prison sentence: the U.S. is my home, spiritually, constitutionally, intellectually—my God, intellectually. Sure, I spent time there, late seventies, all of the eighties, ten years, more. And I go back all the time. You're in business right, talking all day—it's a very verbal culture, more verbal than here, right, *much* more—so, you pick up the accent, you can't help it.

HENRY: Oh.

ALEC: And, to be perfectly honest, I decided to retain it: anything to keep others from the God-awful truth.

HENRY: Which is what?

ALEC: It's a great liability, Henry, if people know you were actually *born* on this dreary little island.

HENRY: Really?

ALEC: The only English who foreigners have any requirement for are either dead, or actors.

HENRY: Why did you come back, then?

ALEC: No choice. Anne. She needs me. (*Beat*) Do you want a drink of some sort?

HENRY (*uncomfortable*): Um, no thanks—I just called in, that's all.

ALEC: On your way somewhere?

HENRY: No.

ALEC: You're in Chelsea a lot?

HENRY: No.

ALEC: Go on. She might be a while—I suppose you know what she's like once she gets on that blower.

HENRY: All right . . . a small one, shall I . . . tell her?

ALEC: I think I should know where they are, by now. What do you want?

HENRY: Umm, a beer will be fine.

ALEC: Well, we only got cool designer beers here, is that a sure thing with you?

HENRY: Sure. I mean . . . Okay.

(*Alec hands Henry a beer and mixes himself a drink*)

ALEC: I'm just here for the morning, Henry; I've got to go over some figures with Anne. She has an audition, did you know?

HENRY: Yes she told me.

ALEC: It's damn good news: she's had no work for some time . . .

HENRY: No.

ALEC: Not only that though, no prospects of work, either—she wasn't auditioning for anything.

HENRY: It's tough work.

ALEC: All work's tough. Tough is good. There was something wrong, right, it was laziness: pure, simple. She should be at two, four, six, seven auditions a week. She gets lazy. She never rings her agent. I got her that agent. Which is why I have to keep coming back to London, to get her moving.

(*Beat*)

HENRY: We all have our off periods, I suppose.

ALEC: No, Henry, not all of us. She was . . . out of the right circles. (*Smiles*)

HENRY: I see her a bit, I thought she was—

ALEC: You know it then, you know how lazy she was getting.

HENRY: She always seems on the go to me.

ALEC: Doing the wrong things: she wasn't looking for any work. Just relied on the hand-outs.

HENRY: Hand-outs?

(*Beat*)

ALEC: That's what they are. I don't suppose she's told you that, though.

HENRY: Well, um— (*Drinks his beer*)

ALEC: Just how close are you? (*Doesn't wait for answer*) I look after her financial interests, Henry, did you know that?

HENRY: Well, sort of, but . . . I just assumed . . .

ALEC: I've done it since her parents went AWOL.

HENRY: AWOL?

ALEC: Yes, Henry. I've always thought drinking too much then disappearing off the face of the earth is AWOL. That is not responsible. Behaviour. (*Smiles*) If I was family, I'd be perturbed about that kind of unfaithfulness. But: I'm not family, so it makes no odds to me.

HENRY: But . . . it was a car accident.

ALEC: I'd be careful about your use of the word "accident." But that's past history. (*Charming, smiling*) She's known me all her life. It feels like I've known her all mine, too. She's stayed with me in New York many, many times. When she was younger. "Shazam, Anne!", I used to say when she walked in. The father was useless in business, useless; I was grateful to take over some very frayed reins, 'cause I got what he didn't: (*taps head*) nous . . . (*Smiles*) So, you see her a lot?

HENRY: She's a good friend.

ALEC: Yes. (*Beat*) Thank God things are looking up. She'll get this play. She's perfect. *Who's Afraid of Virginia Woolf?*, it's one of my favourites.

HENRY: Is it?

ALEC: Certainly . . . I saw it in the States once, with, oh, Jesus, what's that girl's name? God . . . Elaine Stritch. That's the role Anne should be playing, given her temperament . . . she should be playing that role.

(*Anne enters*)

ANNE: What role?

ALEC: Shazam!

ANNE: I'm sorry for leaving you two together.

ALEC: There's no need to apologize for anything, Anne.

ANNE: On your own, I meant.

ALEC: How is your friend?

ANNE (*ignoring this*): Henry, I'm sorry.

HENRY: I should have rung first?

ANNE: Maybe.

ALEC (*smarmy*): He said he was just passing through this neighbourhood.

HENRY (*getting up*): I am . . . I'm sorry . . .

ALEC: We've been confabulating agreeably.

ANNE: Never mind.

ALEC: Isn't she a card? (*He touches her fondly, intimately. She reacts a bit. Henry stares. Alex starts to exit*) I'm going to the restroom.

ANNE: All right.

ALEC: Then we'll get down to business. Nice to see you, Henry. We'll have to trade stories, some time.

(*He exits*)

ANNE (*brusque*): I apologize for this. I forgot you were coming. This is a double booking.

HENRY: I don't really understand why it's so embarrassing. He could leave. (*Anne doesn't look at him*) Can I stay, perhaps? I'll wait in the garden until you've finished.

ANNE (*firm*): No. (*Beat*) It's freezing outside.

HENRY: I don't like him, Anne. He's . . . he's such a phoney.

(*Anne doesn't answer. Henry sighs. He is about to leave*)

ANNE: How's your man?

HENRY: What?

ANNE: Your new man.

HENRY: He's . . . (*Smiles*) Good.

(*Beat*)

ANNE: Jesus, why can't he call it the loo like everyone else?

(*Music. Crossfade*)

Scene Four

Outside Trevor's block of flats, Paddington. Late morning. Trevor is seen sitting on the steps to the main entrance as Henry enters.

HENRY: Hi. Trevor?

TREVOR: Hey!

HENRY: Hello.

TREVOR: You came this time!

HENRY: Yeah.

(*Trevor smiles*)

TREVOR: I didn't know if you would.

HENRY: Here I am . . .

TREVOR: Didja get out at Paddington?

HENRY: Yeah.

TREVOR: Well this is it. Shocking isn't she. You do get a view of Hyde Park if you climb on the roof though. Ugliest building in W2.

HENRY: I like it . . .

TREVOR: Nah, it's mediocre. Who'd live in Paddington, eh?

HENRY: You.

TREVOR: Yeah, me. (*Pause*) It's good to see you, Henry. I'm glad you came.

HENRY: So am I.

TREVOR: Yeah.

(*Beat*)

HENRY (*awkward*): Are you . . . going to take me in?

TREVOR: Nah. Not yet. Take a seat 'ere. (*Pause. Henry sits*) I can keep check on life from here, yeah? (*Gets out cigarettes*) Dodgy area, this. Too many cheap hotels, one after the other. Full of people who have just got off the boat, you know, or swum the channel. (*Lights up*) Fag?

HENRY: No thanks.

(*Trevor looks about, smokes*)

TREVOR: I used to live in that one.

HENRY: On the ground floor?

TREVOR: Yeah, but I 'ad to get out. I mean it's not much better upstairs but you don't get people pissing on your window sills.

(*Beat*)

HENRY: Cats.

TREVOR: Look at 'em all . . . strays, all of 'em. Like a bloody ménage . . . Psstt! Is that what I mean? No, a menagerie. Yeah, that's what I mean. Disgusting . . . They're always half-moulted like that . . . mangy, dirty bastard.

HENRY: They look hungry.

TREVOR: Well I'm not gonna feed 'em, they'll follow me up. There's no way I'm lettin' 'em in . . . Suffer.

HENRY: Poor things.

TREVOR: Don't you start. All day they look up . . . I get sick of 'em lookin' up at me. (*Beat*) This feels weird. I don't do it like this, you know, usually. I mean usually I bring people straight back. But you, you're different. (*Beat*) How long's it been now?

HENRY: Four weeks.

TREVOR: Four weeks! I've known you for four weeks! Can't believe we 'aven't made it back 'ere in all that time.

HENRY: I was thinking of coming last night.

TREVOR: Yeah? It's for the best this way. I looked at you when I first saw you, I thought . . . I would normally, straight away, bring you back . . . but something told me to wait, I'll wait for you to see my gaff of your own accord. Four weeks! I'm kickin' myself!

HENRY: Well, I'm here now.

TREVOR: Good.

HENRY: It's nice.

TREVOR: Been here three years, maybe four, pretty lucky to get it really. Contacts, y'see? Someone once told me I'm the friendliest person in the block, you know. 'Er upstairs laughed 'er 'ead off.

HENRY: What—you do live with someone?

TREVOR: No. Her up there. (*Points*) She lives in that one. Closest to the sky. She'll be on 'er backside now, painting or something.

HENRY: Oh.

TREVOR: Not 'er flat, she's an artist. Her name's Caroline. She takes no notice of me. Bitch. (*Beat*) You eaten yet?

HENRY: No.

TREVOR: Good. (*Pause. They look at each other*) Caroline's middle-aged.

HENRY: Is she?

TREVOR: Yeah. It's amazing how many middle-agers I know, they're the only proper sort of people I seem to meet, actually.

HENRY: Well, age doesn't matter.

TREVOR: Nah. Every night you 'ear 'er mixing plaster of Paris, for casts and that. She is the *queen* of plaster.

HENRY: Really?

TREVOR: Oh yeah. She's got no taste. Listens to Jackson Browne.

HENRY: Has she lived here long?

TREVOR: Years. It's amazing, but I've never seen a thing, not prop'ly . . . not a paintin', not a sculpture, nothin'. She won't let me. (*Beat*) She's got abnormal friends, Henry. From Notting Hill. She's got stuff in a gallery there.

HENRY: Well . . . why don't you go in? Then you'd see some of her work.

TREVOR: No. No, I don't wanna go in there. No way. (*Beat*) Do you think she's got any talent?

HENRY (*surprised*): What?

TREVOR: Do you think she's got any talent?

HENRY: But I've never met her.

TREVOR: Yeah, well you will. (*Long pause*) Well . . .

HENRY (*awkward*): Well . . .

TREVOR: Henry. Great name. Royal, like.

HENRY: I suppose.

(*Beat*)

TREVOR: I got somethin' in the oven.

HENRY: Oh.

TREVOR: Yeah. We'll go inside.

HENRY: All right then.

(*Beat*)

TREVOR: Do they call you 'arry?

HENRY: Never, no one.

TREVOR: Hen, then.

HENRY: Maybe.

TREVOR (*smiles*): Good. (*Stretches himself out on the steps*) Let's go up.

(*Pause. They are still sitting. Crossfade*)

Scene Five

A square, near Anne's flat. Henry and Anne are sitting.

HENRY: He's got more 501s than you could ever think possible, pairs and pairs of the bloody things . . .

ANNE: I thought you were passé for gay men.

HENRY: I don't know, you're asking me? Anyway, it's against the rules of the building to hang washing out on the balconies but he says he doesn't give a shit about anything like that, "You've got to make the most of this good weather," he says . . . so they hang there, it's like a Chinese laundry.

ANNE: It sounds a bit sordid.

HENRY: Yes, sordid. They've probably spent more time around his ankles than . . . (*Trails off*)

ANNE: Oh, he gets about?

HENRY: He gets about. His name is Trevor. He's completely strange.

ANNE: Trevor?

HENRY: Yes.

ANNE: I don't know any Trevors. (*Beat*) I got the play.

HENRY: What?

ANNE: I got it. Remember that audition? I had two call-backs. They were cunts, Frappy, absolute cunts. They offered it me yesterday.

HENRY: Anne! Congratulations! Why didn't you tell me? Before?

(*They hug*)

ANNE: I'm relieved.

HENRY: I bet. This is . . . amazing. Well done.

ANNE: It's about time, Frappy.

HENRY: Oh, I know, but . . . you've got it now. Where is it?

ANNE: Islington.

HENRY: Brilliant, it's what you've wanted.

ANNE: Yes, I know all that carp. (*Beat*) It is about time, you see: say it. I've been out of work for ages. Say it's about time.

(*Beat*)

HENRY: Okay. It's about time.

ANNE: But money's not a problem for me, is it? Say that.

HENRY: Anne, this is great news, you deserve it. I'm so excited . . .

ANNE: Oh . . . bloody platitudes. Money's not a problem. Say that.

HENRY: No.

ANNE: Damn, Henry . . .

HENRY: I don't know anyway, Anne. How should I know what your situation is? You've got work, this is . . . let's celebrate . . .

ANNE: I didn't go to drama school, Henry.

HENRY: So?

ANNE: I didn't go to Oxbridge or some middle-class, recently accredited university, I didn't do all the things you're meant to do, to get work, and I ask myself, should I really feel right about this? . . . When I see . . . people like—

HENRY (*interrupting*)**:** Anne. I'm so happy for you, don't spoil it. Congratulations.

(*Beat*)

ANNE: Thank you, Frappy.

HENRY: I'll help you with your lines.

ANNE (*guffaws*)**:** It's not the school play. (*Beat*) Yes. Henry. (*Beat*) What's this guy look like? He's the primitive one, isn't he? It is him.

HENRY: Yes. There's nothing in it . . . he's simply . . . he's not . . . very attractive, if you must know.

ANNE: Yes, but has he got a nice (*gestures*) . . . ?

HENRY: He's got a pimply forehead. His nose and mouth are always pouting, sort of, contorted into a snigger. He walks about . . . appropriating everything.

(*Beat*)

ANNE: I had grapefruit today.

HENRY: Did you?

ANNE: It went everywhere, dripped, all over my chest and all over the duvet cover.

HENRY: Bad luck.

ANNE: It was careless . . . all over my brand-new duvet cover. Then I spilled coffee on it as well. Still, a lovely big fat cheque bounced over the other day. (*Uncomfortable pause, then they laugh*) Lucky me.

(*Anne looks away. Music. Crossfade*)

Scene Six

Trevor's flat. Caroline and Trevor are seen at the balcony, drinking red wine and smoking, as Henry enters.

HENRY: Hello?

TREVOR: Hen! Come and join us. Over here.

(*Henry walks to them*)

HENRY: Hi.

TREVOR: Hi! Caroline's come down for a drink. For one of our balcony sessions. This is Henry. Henry: Caroline.

CAROLINE: I've seen you. You've been here quite a few times, haven't you?

HENRY: I suppose I have.

CAROLINE: Hello anyway.

HENRY: Hello.

CAROLINE: Better late than never.

TREVOR: Good.

(*Beat*)

CAROLINE: I come out to my balcony and I look down from above. I see everything.

HENRY: Right.

TREVOR: Nice evening for it, though, i'n't it . . . Dusk . . . My favourite. We come out 'ere at dusk like the crickets do.

HENRY: It gets quite noisy around here, doesn't it?

TREVOR: Tourists comin' in and out of Paddington—everywhere. Continental delights. You stayin'?

HENRY: Thought I might.

TREVOR: Have a drink then.

CAROLINE: It's Bulgarian. Do you want some?

HENRY: Oh, that's kind.

CAROLINE (*as she pours*): From Trevor's cellar.

HENRY: I should have brought something . . .

TREVOR: Henry, sit down . . .

HENRY: Thank you.

TREVOR: We were just discussing, Henry, about film stars. Caroline and me, we talk about film stars a lot—

CAROLINE (*overlapping*): Trevor . . .

TREVOR: Caroline goes for the older man, of course—

CAROLINE: Oh for goodness' sake . . .

TREVOR: I was saying, Winona Ryder is brighter and sexier than Sandra Bullock—

CAROLINE (*interrupts*): Trevor. (*Beat*) So, are you two (*indicates with her hands "a couple"*) . . . ?

TREVOR: No . . .

HENRY: No . . . not . . . really.

(*Trevor smiles*)

CAROLINE (*casually*)**:** Well, you're sensible.

HENRY: Why is that?

CAROLINE: He isn't faithful to anyone.

(*Beat*)

HENRY: Trevor . . . ?

(*Trevor doesn't answer*)

CAROLINE: We all see him go out . . . he returns late at night with a stranger in tow, sometimes a woman, sometimes a man. He thinks he's Joe Orton. The pick-up often stays all night. But in the morning, the daytime light ekes its way into Trevor's flat and it's insulting enough to reveal just how plain he really is, and I see the pick-up walk regretfully down the street. Every time . . .

(*Pause*)

TREVOR: Caroline is very very very very—parochial. She goes down to Westminster underground just to see the looks on tourists' faces as they come out and see Big Ben for the first time. She's been at work on a guidebook for years.

HENRY: Have you?

TREVOR: But she can't finish it.

CAROLINE: I'm too busy with my art.

HENRY: What sort of guidebook?

TREVOR: It's called *The Tribes of London* . . .

CAROLINE (*ignoring Trevor*): I'm trying to characterize the city in—yes, Trevor—a tribal sense.

TREVOR: Very anthropological it is.

CAROLINE: How types of people . . . have congregated . . . creating, sort of, villages, with particular characteristics.

TREVOR: It's all about *ghettos*! She even includes Clapham, Hen!

CAROLINE: Anyway, the point is, it stays unpublished.

TREVOR: I've got friends in publishing, from the factory. Perhaps they could help.

CAROLINE: If you really did, you wouldn't be saying that.

TREVOR: She told me to go to Tesco's to buy myself an existence last week.

CAROLINE: They were on special.

HENRY: I'm in publishing.

CAROLINE: Are you?

TREVOR: I've never asked, you know, never even asked what you did.

HENRY: Just starting out, really.

CAROLINE: An editor once told me my writing was too "ebullient," can you believe it, that was her very word.

TREVOR: I've seen it . . . I saw some of the manuscript . . .

CAROLINE: A very small section, Trevor . . .

TREVOR: There's a chapter about Paddington.

CAROLINE: Paddington! Hah, there's nothing in Paddington.

TREVOR: What about you Hen, were you born here?

HENRY: No . . . not a real Londoner.

TREVOR: None of us are, none of us.

HENRY: I thought you were from London.

TREVOR: My parents are on a dairy farm. In Dorset.

HENRY: Oh.

TREVOR: Why the surprise?

HENRY: Nothing. I just thought you were from London.

TREVOR: Well I am really. Been here long enough.

CAROLINE: Surely it's time to return, then? To the womb.

(*Trevor looks at Henry. Beat*)

HENRY: Where are you from, Caroline?

CAROLINE: Oh, I can't remember now. There's too much here for the tourists.

TREVOR (*confidentially, mocking*): You've got to live amongst the tribes.

CAROLINE (*to Henry*): He's too busy with other things, like personal gratification, to even begin contemplating the beauty, or non-beauty, of his surroundings . . . he's an innocent. Here, back on the farm, every-where. Don't take any notice of *anything* Trevor says.

TREVOR: She loves me . . .

CAROLINE: Yes. Absolutely. I have work to do. (*Finishes her wine*) Nice to meet you, Henry. Bye-bye.

HENRY: Bye. (*Caroline exits*) She's very attractive.

TREVOR: I know.

HENRY: Why does she live here?

TREVOR: What do you mean?

HENRY: She's not suited to these flats, not like you . . . or, or, or me even.

TREVOR: Because she walks about the place as if she was this mega-successful artist?

HENRY: Well, yeah.

TREVOR: What a put-on.

HENRY: Maybe it's not.

TREVOR: It is.

HENRY: I can picture her at the opening of an exhibition in a small gallery—sipping champagne under the bright spotlights.

TREVOR: Yeah. (*Beat*) She's gone upstairs to work. She does it every evenin'. Cue Jackson Browne. (*Beat*) And then she goes out. I'm not the only one. She goes out too.

HENRY: Do you mind?

TREVOR: No. (*Beat*) I see 'er. I see 'er trundle down the road with 'er purple batik sling-bag over 'er shoulder and 'er daffodils and 'er bottle of wine . . . (*Beat*) She's 'avin' an affair with a priest.

HENRY: Really.

TREVOR: Oh, yeah. She won't talk about it, but I know.

HENRY: How?

TREVOR: I spied on 'er once.

HENRY: What?

TREVOR: I spied on 'er. Dark glasses, other side of the road, that sort of thing. Done it a few times.

HENRY: Why did you do that?

TREVOR: Because I did. (*Beat*) We'll go out. (*Beat*) I've just got to get ready, like. (*Beat*) We'll go out.

(*Long pause. They sit and drink. Crossfade*)

Scene Seven

A West End nightclub, just before closing. Flashing lights, thumping music. Henry and Trevor are on the periphery. Henry has a Budweiser. Trevor has a bottle of Evian. He is very drunk.

TREVOR: I kept my promise.

HENRY: Yes, you kept your promise.

TREVOR: To see you through till the evenin' is out.

HENRY: I think that's about now. Look, Trevor, I've really had enough. Can we go?

TREVOR (*looking out over the dance floor*)**:** Comin'?

HENRY: No, I think it's time . . . It closes soon. (*Looks at his watch, taps it*) Four-thirty.

TREVOR: I'm out there . . .

(*Trevor dances, centre. Henry looks on hopelessly. Trevor comes back to Henry, still dancing*)

HENRY: Look at you!

TREVOR: Can't stop, 'ave to keep moving. It's called "Bill and Coo" on Sunday nights. Goes all queeny.

HENRY: Does it?

TREVOR: It's fantastic. I love all that shit. My friend Moana, you'll 'ave to meet 'er.

HENRY: Yeah.

TREVOR: I thought you probably wouldn't 'ave been here. I sized you up, and I thought, where can I take 'im where 'e 'asn't been.

HENRY: Well, we've done it now.

TREVOR: It's a bit different from where we met, eh? Yeah. I come here on and off, actually. It's my safe haven if you know what I mean? Always lots of pretty boys, a few pretty girls. (*Dances, offers popper*) Popper?

HENRY: Err, no thanks.

TREVOR (*offers drink*): Evian?

HENRY (*accepts*): Thanks.

TREVOR: You needed that, hey? Gets hot in 'ere.

HENRY: Damn hot.

(*Trevor dances, Henry half-dances; they look out at the dance floor*)

TREVOR: I've been told that I excel on the floor . . .

HENRY (*shouts above the music*): What . . . ?

TREVOR: That's what somebody said, that I excelled! (*Dances*) See anything you like?

HENRY: What?

TREVOR: Now that's a nice face . . . see that guy, pull him your way! He was ugly at the bar, I saw 'im but out there!

HENRY: Out there . . .

TREVOR: Delicious!

(*They watch*)

HENRY: . . . four-thirty . . .

TREVOR: Yeah.

HENRY: Come on, then.

TREVOR: All right, Henry. All right, mate.

(*They move off, out of the club*)

HENRY: Should we get a taxi? It'd be easier. Trevor?

TREVOR (*takes a sniff of the popper*): Come 'ere. (*He pulls Henry roughly and kisses him, passionately. It lasts a while*) You're great. (*Beat*) Yeah.

(*Beat*)

HENRY: Trevor?

TREVOR: Yeah. What? No taxis, no. I may be smashed, but I'm not gullible. (*Drunkenly*) I'm not danced-out! I'm walking home!

HENRY: Trevor, I'll walk you to the bus.

TREVOR: No! come on. (*They walk away from the club; the music fades*) Here begins the new life!

HENRY: What?

TREVOR: Here begins the new life! (*Runs his fingers through his hair, loses his balance and falls to the ground*)

HENRY: Trevor . . .

TREVOR: Here *beginneth* the new life!

HENRY: What are you talking about, Trevor . . . ? How are you getting home?

TREVOR: Bus.

HENRY: Come on then.

TREVOR: Where to?

HENRY: Trafalgar Square.

TREVOR: Follow me.

HENRY: What?

TREVOR: Let's go this way.

HENRY: Are you sure?

TREVOR: This way!

HENRY: Okay, Okay. (*They begin to walk*) Trevor . . . ?

TREVOR (*mumbling and declaiming, apropos nothing*)**:** Caroline . . . and all those goddamn geraniums . . . new life . . . in a desert by the Nile . . . crocodile . . . saw a smile . . . for a while . . . over a stile . . . got a pile . . . eat some bile . . . "Edgware Poetry Society!" Henry!

HENRY: What?

TREVOR (*making a sign in the air*)**:** "Edgware Poetry Society." That's me!

HENRY: Trevor . . .

TREVOR: "Edgware Poetry Society . . . present an evening of new poetry by young writers." Me!

HENRY: What . . . ? Where does it say that, Trevor?

TREVOR: All over London! Billboards plastered everywhere. Last year. Me! I did a reading of some of my poetry there. At the Poets' Warehouse in Lisson Grove.

HENRY: Poetry?

TREVOR: Poetry!

HENRY: You write poetry?

TREVOR: Of course I do! I'm the Bard of Sussex Gardens, if not the whole of Paddington! (*Shouts, over and over, "Me" and then, out of breath, falls to the ground. Mumbling*) And there I left you, sitting on the hedge . . . Abandoning our marriage pledge . . . (*Smiles*) Here begins the new life . . . (*Shuts his eyes*)

HENRY: Trevor?

TREVOR: Here begins the new life . . .

HENRY: Oh. Fuck.

TREVOR: Good-night.

(*Trevor sleeps. Music. Crossfade*)

Scene Eight

A party. Music, lots of people. Henry and Anne stand, drinking. Henry a little drunk; he holds a glass and a bottle of wine.

HENRY (*looking off*): Look who's here.

ANNE: I know. We came together, actually.

HENRY: Oh.

ANNE: Don't be surprised. I owe him.

HENRY: Why?

ANNE: It doesn't matter. I let him mix with me socially once in a while. Makes things easier. Although I didn't know you were going to be here.

HENRY: Yes you did.

ANNE: I forgot. Anyway, how's your friend?

HENRY: What?

ANNE: The boy called Trevor.

HENRY: Fine.

ANNE: Fine. Just fine?

HENRY: Yes.

ANNE: I should meet him.

HENRY: No, no. Not . . . yet.

ANNE: It's been ages.

HENRY: Later.

ANNE: Why? Why? I'm intrigued.

(*Beat*)

HENRY: I met the artist who lives above him, Caroline.

ANNE: So . . . ?

HENRY: Well . . . he has a thing for her. This isn't bad this party . . .

ANNE: Henry . . .

(*Beat*)

HENRY: The other day we went to Notting Hill and we ended up spying on this Caroline.

ANNE: You're kidding?

HENRY: No. She drinks coffee with her friends opposite this gallery that sells some of her sculptures. We walked up and down the street all morning, *spying*.

ANNE: Why?

HENRY: To keep check on her, see what she's doing. He hates the way she holds her cappuccino, he hates her twittering friends.

ANNE: Doesn't she see him?

HENRY: She spotted us once, I'm sure.

ANNE: What did she do?

HENRY: Ignored us . . . Trevor's not what you'd call Notting Hill chic.

ANNE: It's almost sad, Frappy . . . the poor man.

HENRY: Yeah, well. Anyway, he calls them "Geraniums."

ANNE: Who?

HENRY: Caroline's friends. It's his code word. He can't bear them because they're so cold, unapproachable. Here. I've brought this. (*Gets out a scrap of paper*) This is his revenge.

ANNE: What?

HENRY: Bad poetry.

ANNE (*reads*): "Note their hard profiles, their inflated craniums / As they sit and sip their *café-late* / Suits by Gaultier, watches by Cartier / These over-watered, stiff Geraniums." He writes this stuff?

HENRY: Yeah, he says he's a poet . . . he's done readings. What do you think . . . ?

ANNE: He's a nutcase.

HENRY: I like him. I really like him.

(*Beat*)

ANNE (*teasing*): Poetry.

HENRY: Yes.

ANNE: Poetry . . . ! Has he written an epic in honour of you?

HENRY: Anne.

ANNE: Well . . . (*Beat*) I must meet him. It's as simple as that.

HENRY: We'll see.

ANNE: What about this woman though? What's his real—persuasion?

(*Beat*)

HENRY: It's part of his . . . charm. He, collects people.

ANNE: And where does that leave you?

(*Beat*)

HENRY: Do you want another drink?

(*But there's none left*)

ANNE: I shouldn't be too late.

(*They stand for a while, drinking*)

HENRY (*looking off*): Alec's loving it.

ANNE (*likewise*): Poor girl.

HENRY: Who is she?

ANNE: Some inbred heifer.

HENRY: I haven't seen him since your place, that day.

ANNE: Don't harp on that again. It was intended.

HENRY: Imagine, me sitting in your living room. *On my own.* Talking to the dreaded Alec for more than three minutes.

ANNE (*sarcastic*): Sorry about that. (*Blasé*) Must've been hell.

HENRY: It was very enlightening.

ANNE: Henry. I don't care what you think, or even what you know.

(*She looks off*)

HENRY: You've got lines to learn now, I suppose.

ANNE: What?

HENRY: Your lines . . . for the play.

ANNE: Oh . . . something like that.

HENRY: Can I do anything?

ANNE: No. (*Smiles*) You're too busy anyway . . . with your poet from Paddington.

(*Beat*)

HENRY: Look at him—he's doing the rounds. (*Beat*) It's funny how you don't want us to be together.

ANNE: Codswallop. Subject change.

HENRY: I think he's like an anteater, something prickly: he'd bristle if you touched him. Of course, we've got to think of the American equivalent of an anteater, or are anteaters American?

ANNE: Frappy . . .

HENRY: An armadillo?

ANNE: I don't care at the moment.

HENRY: Where do porcupines live?

ANNE: Henry please be quiet . . .

HENRY: Anne . . . ?

ANNE: I'm going to get a drink now.

HENRY: Get one for me, would you?

ANNE: You don't need one.

HENRY: But I do.

(*Anne exits. Henry stands, looking around. Pause. Alec enters behind Henry and taps him on the shoulder. He has a bottle of wine*)

ALEC: Hello!

HENRY: Oh. (*Looks off in Anne's direction*) Hello, Alec.

ALEC: What an enjoyable party!

HENRY: I suppose.

ALEC: Anne's left you here, on your own?

HENRY: No.

ALEC: No? Charming. So.

HENRY: So.

(*Beat*)

ALEC: All right for a drink?

HENRY: Yes. Thanks. I've had a bit too much, if you want the truth.

ALEC: So what have you two been up to?

HENRY: Excuse me?

ALEC: You and Anne. Been up to much lately?

HENRY: No, not really.

ALEC: You're very tight, you two, aren't you?

HENRY (*laughs*): Are you grilling me?

ALEC: No, I'm making conversation, Henry.

(*Beat*)

HENRY: We're, we're close . . . I rely on her, she on me . . .

ALEC: That's so sweet . . .

(*Beat*)

HENRY: I like to think it's because—we're not the same.

ALEC: Uhuh.

HENRY: I think most of her friends are . . . (*looking around*) Sloanes— well you're not one obviously . . . Anyway, I'm a little different.

ALEC: You each fill a void in the other's life.

HENRY: No . . . I suppose you might say that.

ALEC: A Sloane neutralizer. Imagine that. You must bottle that and sell it. Are you in love with her?

(*Beat*)

HENRY: I can't answer that.

ALEC: Aren't you . . . ? How can I put this delicately? . . . Don't you shop at a different department store?

(*Beat. Henry looks at him warily, then laughs*)

HENRY: I could ask the same thing of you.

ALEC: Go ahead.

(*Beat*)

HENRY (*laughs, shyly*): Do you . . . shop at a different department store?

ALEC: From you. I think I do. Or, maybe not. (*Henry laughs, unsure. Alec fills up their glasses from the bottle*) Don't you have someone new, now? Aren't you seeing someone? A new man friend?

HENRY: No, I'm not. (*Drinks most of the glass*)

ALEC: Do you love her?

HENRY: Of course.

ALEC: Sexually? (*Refills Henry's glass*)

(*Pause. Henry drinks*)

HENRY: I . . . I . . . (*Gathers memory; breathes heavily*) The other day we were out . . . at night . . . we were walking around Clapham at night. And Anne collected some pebbles, and as if she were bowling, she rolled them down the road. She made clicking noises with her mouth. They rolled away and her laughter echoed up into the night—and all I wanted to do Alec: was fuck her. (*Alec smiles*) Why are you smiling? (*Alec says nothing; he drinks*) You shouldn't be smiling. No . . .

ALEC (*teasingly, almost flirtatious*): Shouldn't I, why not? You felt like— (*laughs*) fucking her . . . (*Laughs*)

HENRY: Yes.

ALEC: That might be funny . . . some people would consider it a laughing matter.

(*Henry laughs with him*)

HENRY: Would they? I don't know . . . That's what I wanted to do—this urge came over me, but, but I didn't want to seduce her, Alec, I wanted to do it there in the street.

ALEC (*laughing*): There, in the street?

HENRY: Yeah.

ALEC: In the middle of Clapham?

HENRY: Yeah.

ALEC: Goodness, you kill me.

(*Henry bursts into laughter*)

HENRY: I can hardly explain it, you know. This hedonistic sexual feeling for her came over me . . .

ALEC: Well, I know, I've been there . . .

HENRY (*not taking this in, continuing*): Yeah . . . as powerful as any urge I've ever had. It's a heinous thought, I thought . . .

ALEC: Heinous . . . (*Laughs*)

HENRY: . . . wanting to make love to her here right now, in the street . . .

ALEC: . . . in Clapham . . .

HENRY: . . . in Clapham, but I can't—couldn't—help it. "Anne," I wanted to say . . . "Can't we just forget all this . . ." I don't know, "Propriety," "Our lives," whatever it is . . . "Can't we just cut all of this and have each other *right here*!"

ALEC: Right here!

(*They laugh, and drink, and look at each other. The laughing subsides*)

HENRY: Why is this funny?

ALEC: Because look at you.

HENRY: What?

ALEC: Well, you *do* shop at the other department store, *n'est-ce-pas*? (*Threatening*) You worship in the other chapel, yes? Inhabit an alternative chat-room, bat for the other team, bark up a different tree, row a different boat, dance to a different tune? (*Beat*) You play Twister without the ladies? (*Beat*) Never mind, you were saying.

HENRY: Um . . .

ALEC: So, what happened?

HENRY: Nothing. Of course, nothing happened. She left me there. 1:30
A.M. A black cab was going north. That never happens. "Bye, Frappy," she
called, "see you tomorrow!"

ALEC: And you went home?

(*Beat*)

HENRY: No.

ALEC: You were just near Clapham Common?

HENRY: Yes.

ALEC: Well that's convenient for a fuck.

HENRY: Yes. (*Beat*) Hey, fuck you.

(*Alec laughs. Henry stares at him, alarmed. Music. Crossfade*)

Scene Nine

*Outside Trevor's flat. Henry and Trevor are sitting on the steps to the main
entrance. Trevor is stretched out, soaking up the sun, smoking. Henry reads.*

TREVOR (*languid*): In a desert by the Nile . . . I saw an angel smile a
smile . . . (*Beat*) What you think of that? Yeah. Smile a smile. Hen?

HENRY: Great.

(*Beat*)

TREVOR: It made me think of hugging trees. And brought me crashing to
my knees . . . (*Beat*) Yeah.

(*Sound of a car. Trevor looks up as it drives past. Henry keeps reading*)

Who's this? Not seen this one before. Green Renault. M759ADP.

HENRY: What?

TREVOR: Nothing. (*Beat*) Hugging trees. No. (*Looks off*) Holy McFoley, watch it!—Jesus!

(*Crash! Henry looks up*)

HENRY: What's going on?

TREVOR (*over this; getting up*): Straight into it!

HENRY (*overlapping*): What's happened—?

TREVOR (*overlapping*): She drove straight into it! Bloody hell, look at that! Didn't even see it!

HENRY: I don't believe it . . .

TREVOR: Look, look, some nutter's driven into Caroline's scarecrow!

(*Anne enters, holding a piece of tin. She carries a Harrods bag*)

HENRY: Anne?!

TREVOR: Did you see what you did! Straight into it!

ANNE: Excuse me, Frappy, what's that ridiculous thing back there?

HENRY: What are you doing here?

ANNE: I followed you. What's this?

HENRY (*distracted*): It's a sculpture.

TREVOR: Caroline's scarecrow! (*Bursts into laughter*) You've hit the scarecrow!

ANNE: A scarecrow?

HENRY (*sotto voce*): Thank God she's not here.

TREVOR (*still laughing*): Look what you've done! Pranged right into it! (*He runs off to have a look*)

ANNE: Is he serious?

HENRY: Yes . . . right into Ray Bolger.

(*Trevor runs back on with another piece*)

TREVOR: Yeah . . . yeah . . . "We're off to see the wizard . . ." (*Bursts into laughter*)

HENRY: It's a scarecrow, of sorts . . . it's art . . . you know . . . Caroline's, the artist, she lives upstairs. What are you doing here?

ANNE: A scarecrow . . . ?

HENRY: Yes.

ANNE: Made from . . . this?

HENRY (*cross*): Yes. Tin, pipes, and push-bike. Caroline usually welds on a new part at the weekends if the weather is nice. Very Turner Prize.

TREVOR: It'll probably win now!

HENRY: There have been complaints but I don't think it can be moved.

ANNE: Oh dear. (*Holding up the tin*) This came off, Frappy.

TREVOR: It's the flag, you know, the pennant! The flag the scarecrow was holding!

HENRY: How's your car?

ANNE: Not a scratch.

TREVOR: Ha!

ANNE: Oh well.

HENRY: Yes, don't worry about it, now.

ANNE: Okay, I won't. (*Moves towards Henry and gives him a kiss; she looks at Trevor*) Hallo, Frappy darling. I've brought poppy seed rolls and lovely cheese. We can go and sit in Hyde Park, it's just around the corner, I drove straight past it!

HENRY: But how . . . ?

ANNE: I can't stay long though, I'm bloody busy, the play opens soon.

HENRY (*to himself*): Oh, God. (*Trevor stands, fascinated by Anne*) I wasn't expecting you.

ANNE: I found the address on your telephone table.

HENRY: You were snooping?

ANNE: It's not snooping.

HENRY: I don't believe you . . .

ANNE: Come on, let's eat quickly. I'm starving. (*Looks at Trevor*) Your friend can come too.

HENRY: Um, Anne, this is Trevor, he lives here. Trevor: Anne.

TREVOR: Hello, Anne. Hen's mentioned you.

ANNE (*instantly flirtatious*): Mmm, he's mentioned you too, once or twice.

TREVOR: You're an actress then?

ANNE (*all smiles*): An actor. Yes, I am. Sometimes.

TREVOR: And you're in a play, then?

ANNE: Yes.

TREVOR: Which one?

ANNE: It's called *Who's Afraid of Virginia Woolf?*

TREVOR: Edward Albee. Won the Pulitzer Prize.

ANNE: Do you know it?

TREVOR: Sure, sure. There's the film, i'n't there? Are you playing Honey?

ANNE (*impressed*): Yes. It's the role that Sandy—

TREVOR (*interrupts; excited*): Sandy Dennis played her, I know . . . I love that film. You'll be perfect. (*Trevor stares at Anne. They smile at each other. Henry looks uncomfortable. Anne sighs happily*) I'll 'ave to come and see it.

ANNE: Why don't you? Please.

TREVOR: I've done some acting.

ANNE: Have you? We all do at some stage, don't we . . . ?

TREVOR: Yeah . . . I was Hansel once, I sang a song called "I'm Your Big Brother I Must Take the Place of Dad and Mother."

ANNE: Did you steal the show?

TREVOR (*laughing*): I reckon I did! Mum's still waiting for me to crack Hollywood, though!

(*Anne laughs. Pause*)

ANNE: Well. You must come with us. Trevor.

TREVOR: No, no, I couldn't.

ANNE: Oh, please come.

TREVOR: No, I can't.

ANNE: Why not?

TREVOR: I'm goin' out later on.

HENRY: Are you?

TREVOR: Yeah.

HENRY: Where?

ANNE: Oh, what a shame.

HENRY: Where are you going?

TREVOR: Things on, you know. (*Beat*) I suppose I could cancel it.

ANNE: Try to. I should have met you ages ago, I want to get to know you better.

TREVOR: Yeah, likewise, smashing. (*He smiles. No one moves*) Wait then! I'll do it! One quick phone call and I'll be back.

ANNE: Good! (*Trevor exits into the flats slowly, looking back at Anne*) Fraps! What the dickens! So this is where he lives?

HENRY: You know full well.

ANNE: It was clever of me to discover it . . . admit it. He's fascinating.

HENRY: What are you doing here? I told you . . . this is pretty damn intrusive, Anne.

ANNE: Stop being ridiculous, I had to meet him—you were never going to introduce him to me. (*Looking after Trevor*) He's a strange boy. Low. A curious mixture. Very, very cute buns.

HENRY: Anne!

ANNE: Well?

HENRY: He's not all he appears.

ANNE: I don't doubt it.

(*Henry looks at her. Pause. Trevor returns with a bottle*)

TREVOR: I got out of it!

ANNE: Wonderful!

TREVOR: And I found a bottle of Bucks Fizz!

ANNE (*smiles*): Well . . . Hyde Park, it's so close, you lucky thing.

TREVOR: Yeah . . . it's blinding.

ANNE: I hope you like Gorgonzola.

TREVOR: I love them!

ANNE: Shall we go, then?!

HENRY: Snared.

ANNE: What?

HENRY (*angrily*): I said snared.

ANNE: Who?

HENRY: All of us.

ANNE: Take no notice of Henry, Trevor. He's a grump-pot.

(*Trevor and Anne walk off together, smiling. Music. Crossfade*)

Scene Ten

Henry's flat, Clapham. Bookcases. CDs. Henry and Trevor. Trevor is looking around.

TREVOR: I've never seen this place in the daylight.

HENRY (*laughing*): Don't say that, Trevor.

TREVOR: It's not that bad.

HENRY: It is—I don't like it much. Hang on, I'll make some coffee.

(*He does so throughout the following*)

TREVOR: White with three sugars. You shouldn't let it get you down.

HENRY: I can't help it. If I earned more money, I could afford somewhere nice, and I could live on my own—I'd prefer that.

TREVOR: You've got heaps of books.

HENRY: Some of them are Martin's. I've flipped through most of them.

TREVOR: Perhaps I should buy a few books like these. Here, I could borrow some.

HENRY: Why not. Fine.

TREVOR: It's nice stuff . . . all of this . . . I like it. Great CDs.

HENRY: Thanks.

TREVOR: The Beatles, Nine Simone, opera, opera. Opera. Bit of an opera queen, eh? Nothing really contemporary.

HENRY: No.

TREVOR: Judy Garland.

HENRY: Yeah.

TREVOR: *Lots* of Judy Garland: box sets!

HENRY: Yes.

TREVOR: You know what that means.

HENRY: Yes, Trevor, it's an old joke.

TREVOR: I like *Meet Me in St. Louis* best. Film stills. Cool.

HENRY: I got them for free.

TREVOR: No kidding?

HENRY: Anne gave them to me and they've just been sitting there for months . . .

TREVOR: Anne!

HENRY: Yeah.

TREVOR: Now, I meant to say to you a few weeks ago . . . she is something else . . . I like her.

HENRY: Yeah.

TREVOR: She's a top-notch bird, that one.

HENRY (*dismissive*)**:** I've known her for a long time . . . she's, she's an old friend.

TREVOR: I really like her, she's drop-dead. So she gives you free film pics and all? Industry contacts, I suppose.

HENRY: Sorry, did you say white?

TREVOR: Yeah. (*Pause*) How do you know her?

HENRY: Anne?

TREVOR: Yeah.

HENRY: Old friend. We met up a few years ago.

TREVOR: You bumped into 'er at the theatre, di'n'cha?

HENRY: How did you know that?

(*Beat*)

TREVOR: We've been out.

(*Beat*)

HENRY: Who?

TREVOR: Anne and me. I didn't mean to lie or anything.

HENRY: You've been out with her?

TREVOR: Yeah.

HENRY: Why?

TREVOR: Don't know why I didn't say anythin'. Just didn't. She's asked me out again too. She's asked me to the openin' night of her play.

HENRY: But how did you . . . find her?

TREVOR: She rang me up. (*Henry looks at him*) I . . . er . . . slipped 'er me phone number.

HENRY: Oh.

TREVOR: You don't mind? (*Henry doesn't answer*) We can talk for hours—she's got some wicked sense of humour you know. We talked about you. You two are pretty close, aren'tcha?

HENRY: Some of the time.

TREVOR: She's great.

(*Beat*)

HENRY: Where did you go?

TREVOR: Out and about. I don't think they're the sort of dives you'd normally get to.

HENRY: Meaning?

TREVOR: Not really your sport, see.

(*Pause. Henry is annoyed. He looks off*)

HENRY: She's pampered and out of touch. Her parents—they're not around any more—were very rich . . .

TREVOR: Lucky her.

HENRY: She has . . . a sugar daddy sort of figure. In her life.

TREVOR: A what?

HENRY: Sugar daddy.

TREVOR: A sugar daddy?

HENRY: Yes.

TREVOR: I need one of those.

HENRY: I see her . . . all the time.

TREVOR: Yeah, well I really liked 'er—we should all go out, together.

(*Pause*)

HENRY (*annoyed*): Here's your coffee.

TREVOR: Cheers.

HENRY: Sweet enough?

TREVOR (*smiles*): Perfect. (*Pause. Henry sits*) I'll just settle down here. (*He sits down next to Henry and drinks his coffee. He slowly goes to Henry and kisses him, tenderly, softly. Henry resists, then gives in. It lasts for a while*) We'll go out ourselves later, what do yer think?

HENRY: All right.

TREVOR: It's a good area this. We'll go to the Two Brewers, see what's on offer.

HENRY (*nodding*): Yeah.

TREVOR: I did well there the other night, you know.

HENRY: What night was that?

TREVOR: "The other night," you know, ages ago. You weren't around. He was a knockout. (*Henry looks into his coffee. Trevor kisses him again, shorter this time*) My writing's really coming along these past few weeks. I'm in the middle of this first-class cycle right now.

HENRY: Really?

TREVOR: Oh, yeah—you can read it soon. I'm a bit stuck on poem number four though. I've been trying to describe the inside of this bordello, this whorehouse, it's a place not far from here . . . though I don't s'pose you'd know it.

HENRY: What?

TREVOR: I know it's a bit seedy, but you know how it is . . . Anyway, this (*emphasizing it*) *den of iniquity*, as they say, is like brilliantly decorated in all this gold stuff, on the walls, you know what I mean?

HENRY: Does this make good poetry, Trevor? Really?

TREVOR: It's what all the great literature is about: Burroughs and the Beats, mate, even Shakespeare. Look: there's all this gold stuff on the walls, I need a word . . . to describe it . . . something . . . *decadent*.

HENRY: How about . . . "rococo?"

TREVOR: What?

HENRY: I don't know . . . it could be rococo, I suppose.

TREVOR: Rococo?

HENRY: Yah. Rococo. Is it?

TREVOR: What?

HENRY: Rococo?

TREVOR: I could make it.

HENRY: Well, there you go.

TREVOR: Rococo. Yeah. (*Henry smiles*) I bet every good writer in the land has used the word "rococo" at least once, what do you reckon?

HENRY: So I've heard.

TREVOR: Yeah. Thanks Hen. You're brilliant. Rococo. I bet it's just what I'm lookin' for.

HENRY: I hope it is.

TREVOR: Great stuff, wordsmith.

HENRY: Any time.

TREVOR: Hah! (*Sips*) Good coffee.

HENRY: I get it from Brixton Market.

TREVOR: Brixton! Now, have I had some go-through-the-motions-experiences there!

(*Beat*)

HENRY: Trevor, have you ever thought about . . . It doesn't matter.

TREVOR: No, go on.

(*Beat*)

HENRY: Well: repercussions.

TREVOR: Repercussions?

HENRY: You're so quickly obsessed with things. People. Then you drop them, and I was just thinking about . . .

TREVOR: It keeps me clean.

(*Beat*)

HENRY (*shaking his head; quizzically, upset*): Trevor.

TREVOR: What?

HENRY: Picking people up.

TREVOR: You do it.

HENRY: Yeah. But.

(*Beat*)

TREVOR (*gently*): You're different, you know.

HENRY: Strangers. It's almost as if you're . . . collecting strangers.

TREVOR: That's deep. That's poetry, that is. I'll 'ave to remember that. (*Sips. Softly*) You're not a stranger, Henry.

HENRY (*quickly; desperately, tearfully*): God. God.

TREVOR: What?

HENRY: You must know someone . . . somebody: who's died.

TREVOR: Nah, mate. No one. (*Beat*) Hen, baby. (*Finishes his coffee*) Let's go out.

(*Music. Crossfade*)

Scene Eleven

Anne's flat. Sunday evening, late. Anne and Henry. Bottle of wine, lit candles on the floor. Mozart. The floor is strewn with wrapping paper, cards, smart gifts—candlesticks, candles, teapots, picture frames, bottles and jars of fruit, etc. Anne busy, in her element, throughout.

ANNE: It's all confusion, look. Thank heavens you're here.

HENRY: You'll be all right.

ANNE: Henry, only one more performance to go before the bastards . . .

HENRY: You're amazingly nervous.

ANNE: I'm not nervous.

HENRY: You are.

ANNE: I'm not: just . . . fucking overwrought. Thank you, *thank* you—

HENRY: It's all right.

ANNE: —for coming, I needed you.

HENRY: I'm yours. Till you want me to go. (*Beat*) Here, I've brought this.

ANNE: What is it?

HENRY: A present.

ANNE: Oh dear, another one. Look around you. It's present city. First-night gifts, I won't get a chance to wrap them if I don't do it now. Put it over there, I'll open it later. No don't, I might give it to someone. Here . . . Or shall I wait till Tuesday?

HENRY (*gives it to her*): Break a leg.

(*Anne opens the present. It's a carriage clock*)

ANNE: Oh . . . oh, goodness. It's divine . . . (*Beat*) Golly. (*Kisses him on the cheek*) Thank you.

(*Beat*)

HENRY: You don't have one. Is it inappropriate?

ANNE: It's gorgeous, I love it. Thank you. (*Puts it down; bustles*) Are you drinking? There's wine open.

HENRY: I can't, I drove.

ANNE: Did you? Whose car?

HENRY: Martin's.

ANNE: Mine's playing up, otherwise I would have come and got you. It's very late . . .

HENRY: It's all right, Anne.

ANNE: Is it?

HENRY: Yes.

(*She smiles*)

ANNE: There's a thing in my stomach, right here. I spent the day pootling, and now it's hit me.

HENRY: I wouldn't worry about it, it's healthy.

ANNE: Are you sure you don't want to come tomorrow night?

HENRY: What?

ANNE: As well as the opening? Please, I need to know how it's looking.

HENRY: I'm sure it's brilliant. I won't make any difference.

ANNE: I think it's booked out anyway. I could squeeze you in. Please come.

HENRY: Let me enjoy the opening, Anne. Surprise me. I'll see you then. Tuesday.

ANNE (*gets to work; finishes wrapping something*): And you're coming to the party?

HENRY: Yes.

ANNE: It'll be very actory.

HENRY: I bet. Who else will I know—?

ANNE: Come here, come here. I need your help. Hold that while I cut. (*Cuts string, finishing present*) Wine?

HENRY: No. Thanks. Will Alec be there?

ANNE: Yes, he'll be there, Henry—he's always somewhere. Wine?

HENRY: No.

ANNE: I'll have some.

HENRY: This bottle?

ANNE: Yes. Any of them. (*Eats from a jar*)

HENRY: So tell me all about it . . .

ANNE: Excuse me, I'm eating a present. I'm starving hungry. What a day. The Sunday before and I go trotting off to Brighton, God knows why. Then I had to get back double quick for dinner at some self-important restaurant.

HENRY: Who with?

ANNE: Oh, the producer, who's too fat. I've only just got home. (*Offers*) Sun-dried tomatoes. Have some. Go on.

HENRY: Aren't they for someone?

ANNE: It's only some lighting technician who wants my babies. Eat.

HENRY: Yum.

ANNE: Indeed. Yum. (*Starts wrapping another present*) There's probably some balsamic vinegar amongst that lot if you want some . . .

HENRY: Looks like you've spent a fortune.

ANNE: On credit. I'm poor as a church mouse. (*Finishes wrapping*) Where's the raffia?

HENRY: This?

ANNE: Yes. Lovely. (*She ties the present with raffia*) Bum-di-bum-bum. Comfy?

HENRY: Yeah . . . fine.

ANNE: Here. Finger.

HENRY: What?

ANNE: Finger.

HENRY: Oh.

ANNE: And . . . hold . . . while I tie . . . yes . . yes . . . keep it there. Okay. Extract! Good. Thanks. Thank you. This is for her-who's-playing-the-lead.

HENRY: Oh right—I saw her in the paper.

ANNE: Damn. I wish it would curl. There. She looked haggard, yes?

HENRY: That's all right, isn't it? For the role.

ANNE: Yes. Could you pass me a card—over there . . .

HENRY: This?

ANNE (*looks up*): No, one of those Botticellis. (*As she works*) She's a real cow though. I would be too, I suppose. If it was my comeback role. How does that look? Pen?

HENRY: Here.

ANNE (*as she writes on card*): They're either going to come out saying, "That was the most gobsmackingly amazing thing I've ever seen" or, and this is looking more likely, "That. Was someone pulling my leg. And having a fucking good laugh about it." You look parched. I've got soft drinks. What do you want?

HENRY: Orange juice?

ANNE: Sorry, only prune. (*Attaches card*) There, how does that look?

HENRY: Lovely. Love the paper.

ANNE: Yes. It's what's on the outside that counts . . . as they say. Now this (*a candlestick*) . . . this is for my new friend, my very, very good-looking, very gay friend. He's playing my husband. Candlesticks like this are common as mud but never mind.

HENRY: Oh.

ANNE (*points*): Maroon tissue-paper I think. And Sellotape. Three pieces. You're tremendous. (*She works; he watches*) Change the music if you like.

HENRY: This is nice. Do you need a card?

ANNE: It's a rude one. That's what he's like. It's over there. (*He gets it, passes it to her; she works*) I had a dream—it's the tritest, most pathetic dream I've ever had. I was waterskiing. Down the King's Road. Everyone was applauding. And suddenly you were behind me, riding in my wake, eating a baguette from Prêt à Manger—I know—wearing bloomers. Orange bloomers. Everybody started laughing, and I thought I was going to die. So I grabbed you, rushed you into a shop and dressed you in the most divine olive-green Italian suit you've ever seen. Then we got back on our skis and everybody started applauding again.

HENRY: One ski or two?

ANNE: Henry . . . It was very peculiar.

HENRY: So you want to be adored . . .

ANNE: That's a sad, sad dream, a real indictment. Shows how shallow I can be, don't you think?

HENRY: You're not shallow.

ANNE: Some himbo star-gazer at the theatre told me it meant that I was desperate to leave all of you behind.

HENRY: What do you mean all of us?

ANNE: Everybody, all my friends. You included.

HENRY: What crap.

ANNE: Indeed.

(*Beat*)

HENRY: We're just about to publish a book on dreams.

ANNE: I hate all that stuff.

HENRY: The print run's enormous. Trevor's buying one of course.

ANNE: How typical. (*With the candlestick*) Ooops. This should be laid out in a box. Like me.

(*Beat*)

HENRY: So . . . you've seen him?

ANNE (*busy*): You're very lovely together.

HENRY: Come off it, Anne.

ANNE: You are. Seriously. It works in public as well.

HENRY: What?

ANNE: Nothing. There's no need to be embarrassed, that's all.

HENRY: What the hell do you mean by that exactly?

ANNE: Embarrassed by him.

HENRY (*cross*): I'm not.

ANNE: Okay, good. As I say, you look good.

HENRY: I don't need your approval.

ANNE: Don't get mad with me. Sellotape, please. One piece.

HENRY: Here.

ANNE: Thank you. Ha. I couldn't do this on my own. I'm glad you were home when I called. (*Works*) Oh, Jesus Frappy what if it transfers?

HENRY: Then you'll be made.

ANNE: It's not quite like that, actually.

(*Beat*)

HENRY: What would I know?

ANNE: Don't be cranky. I need you here. (*Goes to him; holds up present*) How does this look?

HENRY: Mighty fine, Miss Scarlet.

ANNE: Why thank you. Ashley. (*Looks at watch*) I'm running late. It's the morning! Would you mind wrapping that one? It'd be very helpful. It doesn't matter who the rest are for now. Could you?

HENRY: Of course.

ANNE: You're tremendous.

HENRY: Anne . . .

ANNE: You are . . . I'll do this one.

HENRY: Scissors.

ANNE: Here. (*Suddenly*) Shit. (*Looks at him*) Hell . . . Am I going to be all right?

HENRY: I know it. You are. You will be wonderful. You are, always. (*She smiles*) I can't wait. It'll be brilliant.

ANNE (*mock scream*): Aaaahhhh! I want somebody to describe me as vital. I want to be a *vital* presence. Frappy! (*She goes to him. Kisses him on lips. It lasts too long. She walks away. Smiles. Drinks. Eats*) More?

HENRY: No.

ANNE (*suddenly*): It's your birthday soon, isn't it!

HENRY: Yes.

ANNE: What are we going to do?

HENRY: Whatever. You'll be in the middle of your season.

ANNE: Lunch.

HENRY: Don't worry about it.

ANNE: Just the two of us. We'll go somewhere really nice.

(*Beat*)

HENRY: I'd love that.

(*Silence. They both wrap. As he works, sings; playful*) Good morning, good morning . . . It's great to stay up late. Good morning, good morning. To you.

(*Long pause*)

ANNE: I don't know what that's from.

HENRY: What?

ANNE: I don't know what it's from.

HENRY: Don't you?

ANNE: No. I don't.

(*Beat*)

HENRY: *Singin' in the Rain.*

ANNE: Oh. (*Beat, she works*) You're very camp, Henry.

HENRY: What? Don't say that. I am not.

ANNE: Yes you are. What's the matter?

HENRY: Bloody hell, Anne, I hate camp.

ANNE: Don't make me laugh. You drip it. (*Beat*) I'm still hungry. I'll get something else. Let's have tuna on toast.

HENRY: It's late . . .

ANNE: Oh don't go. Please. I'm really on the edge here. Two days! Only one more preview! Don't go yet.

(*Beat*)

HENRY: All right. If that's what you want.

ANNE: Yes. How hungry are you?

HENRY: Starved actually.

ANNE (*gets up; touches him*): I won't be a sec.

(*She kisses him on the forehead, goes out. Pause. Henry sighs, smiles, frowns, cups his nose and mouth with his hands for a moment, as if checking his breath, pauses, continues wrapping. Crossfade*)

Scene Twelve

A theatre foyer, Islington. The opening of Anne's play. The buzz of theatre-goers, etc. Henry looks smart, in a tie. He is reading the programme. Trevor enters, dressed up.

TREVOR (*holding his hand out*): Henry, great day, great evenin'!

HENRY: Hi, Trevor.

TREVOR: I'm glad I've made this. It was quite a journey, I can tell you, but I was early, I stopped off near the Angel for a quick bottle of Bud.

HENRY: Oh.

TREVOR: Not bad that place. Not very busy though.

HENRY: It's early.

TREVOR: Hen, Hen, Hen . . . we're finally here. I can't wait for this, I can't wait.

HENRY: She'll be . . . she'll be, pleased to see you.

TREVOR: Yeah, I saw 'er yesterday, and Sunday, come to that.

HENRY: Oh, really?

TREVOR: Yeah, she took me to Brighton, mate, never been before.

HENRY: Last Sunday?

TREVOR: Yeah.

HENRY: Two days ago?

TREVOR: We had a whale of a time—she showed me all the haunts you two used to go to.

HENRY: I can't remember our haunts. We haven't been to Brighton for a long time.

TREVOR (*looks around*): Wa'n't that long ago, she said—we did every-thin', ate rock, walked out on the pier, dodgem-cars, bookshops, the lot!

HENRY: She didn't tell me.

TREVOR: Been busy, I expect. Have you seen 'er today?

HENRY: Yeah, before.

TREVOR: And? How's she feelin'? How's it all goin'?

HENRY: She's fine.

TREVOR: This is an important one, yeah?

HENRY: Yes, it is.

TREVOR: She told me she needs it to lead on to other things, like. I know 'ow she feels.

(*Henry is uncomfortable, but smiles. Trevor smiles as well*)

HENRY: Come on, then, we'll get a drink.

TREVOR: Hey, hey, wait a mo. It was perfect! (*Privately; intense*) Courtesy of Mr Roget I got (*uses his fingers to make quote signs in the air*) "baroque" and "florid" and "ornamented." And then it came to me, I decided to use your word in a different context. Get this, what d'ya reckon? (*Gathers himself dramatically*) "Amy is the dominatrix, mark her magisterial frown / She is one of the most morally barren . . ." I like that, I like that, came to me in a flash "morally barren," brilliant . . . "In the whole of London town / Mark her ravishing torso / In her business it's the best / Lustrous, silky white, with a pair of rococo breasts." Yeah? Imaginative? Thought so.

HENRY: Well done.

TREVOR (*pleased as Punch*): Thanks, thanks a lot.

(*Alec makes his way through the crowd*)

HENRY: Oh, god. Here it comes.

TREVOR: What, mate . . . ?

ALEC: Excuse me, excuse me . . . excuse me . . . (*Reaches them*) Hello, Henry. How nice to see you here! I knew you would be. Of course. (*Holds out his hand*)

HENRY (*shaking it*): Hello, Alec.

ALEC: This is very exciting, is it not? Her first play in I don't know how long.

HENRY: Yes.

ALEC: I'm impressed by her commitment, Henry.

HENRY: She's been working hard.

ALEC: Yes. This is a significant opening night.

HENRY: Wouldn't have dreamed of missing it.

ALEC (*smiling; looking at Trevor*): No. (*Uncomfortable pause; Alex still looks at Trevor. To Henry*) I hear they've handled it like a banana.

HENRY: Excuse me?

ALEC: Peeled it. The skin, right off. To impart something fresh. Could be dated otherwise, I suppose. (*Beat*) Anne's wearing salmon.

HENRY: I know.

ALEC: An ambiguous inquiry into the sex part, so I understand. Who is attracted to whom? Anne's lucky, they mightn't have cast the women at all. (*Looks hard at Trevor; smiles*) A banana with the skin just ripped right off.

(*Beat*)

HENRY: Oh, I'm sorry, this is Trevor. Trevor McCowan: Alec . . . I'm sorry, I've forgotten your surname.

ALEC: Maybe you never knew it. Égon.

HENRY: Alec Égon.

ALEC: How do you do, Trevor, and are you Henry's friend or Anne's? (*Holds out his hand*)

TREVOR (*shaking it*): Both of theirs.

ALEC: Both. Fascinating. I'll ask her about you.

TREVOR: Anne's the best.

ALEC (*looking at them both; smiles*): I saw you both from afar. I wanted to come and have a chit-chat—there's nothing quite like a first night here, is there? But this isn't your side of London, is it? You don't live nearby, do you?

HENRY: No, miles from here.

ALEC: I thought so. The transport is satisfactory, I hope, across the river?

(*Beat*)

HENRY: Anne seems happy with everything.

ALEC: Did it seem that way to you? I'm glad, I was—concerned myself. Mentally, she's still developing, adjusting herself to these new circumstances. But you're right, she'll cope. She's a good actress, Anne, very good indeed. I mean it too.

TREVOR: I helped 'er with 'er lines.

ALEC: You did? You can take some of the credit then, if she's any good.

TREVOR: Oh, no, she'll be good, and it'll all be her doing.

ALEC: Would you like a drink, either of you?

(*Trevor is about to say yes*)

HENRY: No thanks.

ALEC (*looking around*): See her; the one so obviously on show; she's quite the young, bright, switched-on actress of the moment, isn't she, did you see her in the Shaffer?

HENRY: Oh. No.

TREVOR: She looks gaunt.

HENRY: Trevor . . .

TREVOR: I like some flesh . . .

ALEC (*takes this in*): Yes, me too. You're quite right, she looks gaunt. She's up in Stratford now . . . We must try and get Anne some work with the RSC, what do you think?

HENRY: We must.

(*Beat*)

ALEC: Oh, look who I've seen. Sorry gentlemen, I have to fly . . . We'll meet again soon, please.

HENRY: Okay.

ALEC (*looks at Henry, smiles*): I think you have a lot of untapped talent, Henry. Like Anne. (*Beat. To Trevor*) Goodbye.

TREVOR: Goodbye.

ALEC (*to Henry*): Goodbye

HENRY: Goodbye.

(*They shake hands. Alec leaves*)

TREVOR: What the hell? (*Henry is silent*) Who was that?

HENRY: He's a strange man.

TREVOR: You ain't kidding, weird science.

HENRY: I don't like him, I never have.

TREVOR: What's he got to do with Anne?

HENRY: Seemed like he owned her, didn't it?

TREVOR: You're not wrong.

(*Beat*)

HENRY: That's the one, Trevor. He's the sugar daddy.

TREVOR: Oh, so that's what it was all about. God, where did she find 'im?

HENRY: Silly old queen.

TREVOR: No, I don't think so. (*Henry looks at him. Looks off*) I know 'im—'e's on TV! I 'aven't been this excited in a long while . . . I wonder how she is? Hey, Hen what's she doing now?

HENRY: Who?

TREVOR: Anne.

HENRY: She's in her dressing-room, I suppose . . .

TREVOR: Right . . .

HENRY: Well not *her* dressing-room, I don't think this theatre's up to that . . .

TREVOR: That'd be it. Doing her make-up. When I was in the theatre I was always slapping on number nine!

HENRY: Me too dahrling!

TREVOR: She never normally wears much make-up, does she? I noticed.

HENRY: Don't think she needs to.

TREVOR: Nah, I don't suppose she does . . . she 'as perfect skin.

(*Beat*)

HENRY (*lyrical*): In her dressing-room, doing her make-up, *applying* her make-up; calm, but occupied, drinking from a bottle of Evian, dabbing her face with a powderpuff, maybe having a drag or two on someone else's cigarette.

TREVOR: Typical! (*Henry looks off*) Busy, i'n't it?

HENRY: Yeah.

TREVOR: Anne said it would be like this. Sticky. (*Trevor looks around*) What now?

HENRY: What?

TREVOR: Anne.

HENRY: Anne . . . Well . . . now she finishes her make-up and flicks at her eyelashes and swirls her tongue behind her lips. And she ignores everyone, everyone, everyone, and puts her headphones on and listens to Glenn Gould, turning the Preludes and Fugues up very loud . . .

TREVOR: Bach . . .

HENRY: Yeah . . . so that she can hear nothing else but the music.

TREVOR: She ignores everyone . . .

HENRY: . . . and she sits silently on a wooden chair in the wings long before she's called, confident it's going to be a hit. She stretches her arms up high above her head and smiles, breathes heavily and thinks of . . . of . . . (*Perhaps he's about to say "me"*)

TREVOR: Us! (*Triumphant*) She thinks of us!

(*Beat. Trevor smiles and looks around. Henry looks at him. Music. Blackout. If an interval is required, it should be taken here*)

Scene Thirteen

Henry's flat, late evening. His birthday. Henry, Anne and Trevor, sitting. They are drinking; Henry bottled beer. Anne is flicking through a magazine. Henry drinks. Trevor looks at Anne briefly, then looks at Henry, then smiles, then drinks.

ANNE (*after a while, sluggish*): This is the sort of rag that Henry gets, Trevor.

TREVOR: Very glossy . . .

ANNE: It's an opera magazine, look. Sometimes they have some excellent articles on . . . (*Trails off, flicks through the pages flirtatiously*)

HENRY: Opera?

ANNE: Yes. Opera.

TREVOR: I read the poetry magazines myself.

ANNE: Do you?

TREVOR: Yeah.

(*Silence*)

ANNE: Where's Martin?

HENRY: Out with Sally.

TREVOR: Or whatever 'er name is.

ANNE: Did they celebrate with you?

HENRY: No.

TREVOR: Oh, pity.

HENRY: We're not that close.

ANNE: It's just us then.

HENRY: Yes. The day's almost over, anyway.

TREVOR: Can't 'elp that though, can we? Anne here has these odd hours, she's got the London literati to keep 'appy now. Haven't you? (*Anne smiles at him*) And 'appy they are. (*Smiles, drinks*) Hate flatmates, me. (*Beat*) Another one bites the dust then, Henry?

HENRY: I suppose.

TREVOR: We're all getting older, eh? That's the one constant in life. God, we'll all be thirty soon. Come-on-Eileen, imagine that.

(*Beat*)

ANNE (*puts magazine down*): I'm sorry I couldn't come for lunch. Really.

HENRY: How was it this evening?

ANNE: Extremely good, the whole thing is such a buzz.

TREVOR: Yeah. Superb. Groundbreaking, I'd say. (*Trevor laughs a little, and toasts the air. He drinks*)

HENRY: More?

TREVOR: Nah, still going on this.

HENRY: Anne?

ANNE: I've had way too much to drink lately. It feels like I've been drinking hour after hour for days. Every night, we all go out afterwards: it's too much. (*Beat*) I'll say it myself, I've been getting lots of praise.

TREVOR: You deserve it, you're a star. (*Henry looks annoyed. Anne smiles*) Like a real star, you are, like W. Ryder, I'm telling you.

ANNE: He's seen it three times, Frappy.

HENRY: I know.

TREVOR: Four including tonight.

ANNE: Four times!

TREVOR: They know me there now; I always get the best seats. (*To Anne*) Caroline was saying today she thought you were terrif.

HENRY: Caroline?

TREVOR: Yeah. *Entre nous*, I've gone off Caroline a bit lately. She was sniffy that I knew someone in *Who's Afraid of Virginia Woolf?* (*Looks at Anne*) . . . Well it's the hit of the season, this, i'n't it, Hen. Still, I rose above it. The broccoli at the Safeways on the Edgware Road: I was very gallant when she dropped the shopping.

ANNE: Gallant?

TREVOR: Yeah, gallant. No one in Paddington as gallant as I. That's right, i'n't it, Hen?

HENRY: I hadn't thought about it.

TREVOR: Well there's you of course, when you're over my way. (*To Anne*) Whizzer with the ladies.

(*Beat*)

HENRY: I . . .

ANNE: Yes?

HENRY: I saw the reviews.

ANNE: Uhuh.

HENRY: Yours were very favourable.

ANNE: I like that. Very favourable. They were mind-boggling, Frappy. I couldn't have hoped for better.

(*Pause—they drink*)

TREVOR (*suddenly*): Oh, shit me! I forgot to get you a present.

HENRY: It doesn't matter.

TREVOR: It does. I can't believe it . . . I forgot to get him a present.

HENRY: I don't . . . make a big deal about . . . birthdays.

TREVOR: Damn . . . Wait! I might have something in me bag . . .

HENRY: Trevor, forget it.

TREVOR: I'll get you something.

HENRY: Don't worry.

TREVOR: No, I will . . . I'll get you a book or something. Hey, you got a copy of Anne's play?

HENRY: Somewhere.

TREVOR: I 'aven't seen it on your bookshelf. That's what I'll get for ya! It's only a paperback, but you've gotta have that one. You can't not have *that*. I'll get it for you. It's a Penguin paperback. (*Beat*) Anne has a copy that's signed and everything. (*Beat*) Damn, what's a birthday party without presents? (*Beat*) Or the video of the film with the lovely Liz T. Yeah.

(*Beat*)

HENRY: It's not a birthday party. (*They drink*) Why wasn't Alec at the cast party, afterwards?

ANNE: Who?

HENRY: Alec. He was at the theatre, at the opening: we saw him in the foyer. Why didn't we see him afterwards? (*Beat*) He came bursting through the crowd talking about you as if he was your agent or something, didn't he Trevor?

TREVOR (*after hesitating*): He was that protective of you, yeah.

ANNE: Why do you take any notice of the man? Don't.

HENRY: It's strange . . . why wasn't he at the party?

ANNE: I can't remember anything about that night—it's all a fantastic blur. (*Drinks*) I'm not seeing him a lot any more.

HENRY: No need I suppose, now that you're working . . . and earning.

(*Anne shoots Henry a look*)

ANNE: Trevor, Frappy was all set to live with me once.

TREVOR: Were you, Hen? I didn't know that.

ANNE: But he chose this place, what do you think?

TREVOR: I'd've chosen you.

HENRY: It suits me fine this way.

ANNE: I don't think so. Underneath it all, you need looking after.

HENRY: I don't.

TREVOR: He does! I look after 'im, for starters!

HENRY: Trevor . . .

TREVOR: He can't cook anythin', can he?!

HENRY (*patiently*): Once, Trevor brought over a curry.

TREVOR: I cooked it from a recipe left by this friend of mine, a student from Malaysia—no good for anythin' but the curry, mind. I brought everythin' over, didn't I, Hen?: tray, curry in an oven-dish wrapped in foil, plate, knife and fork, glass, and a bottle of Rolling Rock.

ANNE: Why?

TREVOR: Just to make it a complete catering service. Got some strange looks on the tube. It was worth it though, it's a fab curry, the best. I'll make some for you if you like.

ANNE: Why not!

TREVOR: It's hot stuff . . .

HENRY: It's the only time you've ever cooked for me; you're hardly meals-on-wheels.

TREVOR: Well, I'd love to do it again. Any time. You just give me a yell. There is nothing like this Malaysian curry.

ANNE: Really?

TREVOR: Straight from Kuala Lumpur! Bellisimo! (*Henry looks at Anne, she laughs*) Actually, we could do with some nosh now.

HENRY: I don't have anything.

TREVOR: What's a birthday party without food?

HENRY: It's not a birthday *party*. It's just my birthday.

TREVOR: We could call out for pizza, do you want that?

ANNE: Yuk.

TREVOR: Maybe not.

ANNE (*suddenly*): Oh, speaking of opera . . .

HENRY: What?

ANNE: I forgot to ask you, Trevor . . . damn. What are you doing tomorrow afternoon?

TREVOR: Working, I got an extra shift. Why?

ANNE: Oh . . . I meant to say something to you before . . . I have a ticket to the Coliseum, you could have come. I would have love to have known what you thought. Lesley Garrett in rehearsal.

TREVOR: Oh, I love her.

(*Beat*)

HENRY: Do you?

TREVOR: Very down-to-earth.

ANNE (*smiling, impressed*): She is.

TREVOR: Yeah.

ANNE (*avoiding Henry*): It's some dire French operetta they've set in the roaring forties, but it would have been fun.

TREVOR: Damn. Shame.

HENRY: *La Vie Parisienne.*

TREVOR: What was that, mate?

HENRY: Nothing.

(*Henry looks at Anne, hard. She drinks*)

ANNE: Call me if you change your shift. (*Finishes drink*) What about Sunday, are you free then?

TREVOR: Yeah (*Clocking Henry*) Are you free on Sunday, Henry?

HENRY: I don't know.

TREVOR: We could all go out, Sunday. All three of us if you like. Yeah?

ANNE: Yes.

TREVOR: Henry?

ANNE: Let's.

TREVOR: Henry?

ANNE: Oh, come on, why not, all of us. That's better. It'll be fun . . .

HENRY: Fine.

ANNE: Well don't look so down about it. Trevor, arrange it through me. (*Looks at her watch. To Henry*) Sorry. It's getting a bit late for me now.

TREVOR: I should get going myself.

ANNE: Oh.

TREVOR: You going out, mate? Early days, yet. Especially round 'ere.

HENRY: A quiet night in, that's all. Bed, in fact.

TREVOR: Oh well, don't let it get you down. (*To Anne*) We could catch a minicab back North together.

ANNE: Yes. It's on the way. We'll do that. Good.

TREVOR: I'll get you that birthday present mate, don't you worry.

(*Anne turns her face away, smiles in spite of herself*)

HENRY: What's so funny?

ANNE: Nothing. (*Beat*) Many happy returns.

TREVOR: As Shirley Maclaine said to her guru. (*Toasts*) Cheers, Henry the fourth.

(*Music. Crossfade*)

Scene Fourteen

Trevor's flat. Henry and Trevor are sitting. Trevor works on a model aeroplane.

TREVOR: What do you think of this? It's a World War Two bomber.

HENRY: Yeah. (*Trevor finishes the model, flies it through air*) I'll get going.

TREVOR: Why? (*Henry shrugs*) You don't have to be anywhere do you? Stay over then. Hen? Stay over, will you? Come on, mate.

(*Beat*)

HENRY: Okay.

TREVOR: Good. (*Trevor puts model down, jumps up, goes to Henry, ruffles his hair, smiles*) Rent payment's going up.

HENRY: Is it?

TREVOR: Bugger, i'n't it?

HENRY: Certainly is.

TREVOR: I'll put some music on.

HENRY: Fine. (*Trevor puts some music on. Trashy pop blares*) Turn it down a bit.

TREVOR: Yeah, we can't 'ear ourselves think, can we? (*Turns it down*) I'm going through a phase. Don't s'pose you really go in for this stuff.

HENRY: In small measures.

TREVOR: It's better than all that shit you 'ave over your place. Hey! Do you want to hear my latest poem?

HENRY: Of course.

TREVOR: It's imprudent of me to show you. Imprudent. Good word that. I saw it the other day. In some novel. (*There is a knock on the door*) Who's that? Damn. Hold on. (*He goes out. Off*) Caroline!

CAROLINE (*off*): Hi, Trevor.

TREVOR (*off*): Come in.

CAROLINE (*off*): No, I only came to get that . . .

(*Trevor enters, ushering in Caroline*)

TREVOR: Look who's here: Caroline.

HENRY: Hi, Caroline.

CAROLINE: Hello. (*Beat*) Look: Trevor

TREVOR: Hey! You can listen to it too. It's that ready, I'm telling you.

CAROLINE: What?

TREVOR: The latest poem.

CAROLINE: Trevor, I just came to get the book.

TREVOR: Yeah, I've got it. Here, sit down.

CAROLINE: No, I can't stay . . .

TREVOR: Please . . .

CAROLINE: All right, briefly.

HENRY: How are you?

CAROLINE: I'm, fine. Thank you.

TREVOR: I've just got to get it. Hold on. (*As he goes*) Get a drink, why don't you, Caroline—plenty in the fridge.

(*He exits. Pause. Caroline sits*)

CAROLINE: So how is it with you and your friend Trevor? He's been very busy lately, if my dear old aunt's lorgnette is anything to go by.

HENRY: He's not my friend Trevor.

CAROLINE: He tried to ask me out the other day.

HENRY: I know.

CAROLINE (*without malice*): There have to be restrictions in my life now. And he tends to park himself well and truly on the double yellow line.

HENRY: Why do you lend him books?

CAROLINE (*smiling*): He doesn't so much borrow them as steal them. You're cute, really, you are. (*Beat*) What's taking him so long?

HENRY (*calling*): Trevor.

TREVOR (*off*): Hold on! Adjustments!

CAROLINE: Have you noticed how he leers all the time?

HENRY: I know.

CAROLINE: The first time I met him, when he moved in here, too long ago, he leered.

HENRY: He leered when I met him, too.

CAROLINE: Do you like him?

HENRY: He's a show-off.

CAROLINE: He walks down the front there sometimes, on his way to the gym, or wherever it is that he gets to, springing on his toes, and his arse sticks up in the air, high and inviting . . . virile. He crosses the road, all postured, with his arms away from his torso . . .

HENRY: He's a show-off.

CAROLINE: . . . sometimes I'm absolutely disgusted and other times I'm so turned on I could die. (*Pause*) Once—before I made him out of bounds—we went out, I can't remember what for, miles and miles, East, and this man came up to us and asked us where a Turkish sauna was. And Trevor knew. "It's a tenner to get in," he said.

HENRY: Strange.

CAROLINE: It's all in the poetry, everything you want to know.

HENRY (*surprised*): You've read it before this?

CAROLINE: Some.

HENRY: The stuff about you?

CAROLINE: It's not about me . . . *specifically*. Just my friends. He hates my friends.

HENRY: Yes.

CAROLINE: It's terrible, isn't it?

HENRY: Atrocious.

(*Trevor enters*)

TREVOR: Sorry, I discovered there were one or two last minute changes . . .

CAROLINE: Never mind.

TREVOR: Hen, I forgot to tell you: my parents are comin'.

HENRY: From Dorset?

TREVOR: Yep.

CAROLINE: This should be fun.

HENRY: Are they staying with you?

TREVOR: Oh, no, couldn't 'ave that—they're goin' round the corner to one of those bed breakfast places. Henry, they want to meet you.

HENRY: Me?

TREVOR: Yeah. Well, not just you . . . they want to meet some of my friends. But you you 'ave to meet. With a friend like you I can show them I'm gettin' somewhere with the poetry.

CAROLINE: Oh, please.

HENRY: Why? What do you mean?

TREVOR: Well, you're the wordsmith, aren't you, you've been to university and you're in publishing and all that . . . they'll see I'm getting somewhere. Yeah. So, come over and see them.

HENRY: Errr, when?

TREVOR: Few weeks.

HENRY: Okay . . . thank you . . . that will be . . . nice.

TREVOR: Mum's cooking. This is brill.

CAROLINE: Simply brill.

TREVOR (*turns off the music*): Okay, everybody. Ready?

CAROLINE: Ready.

TREVOR (*stands, declaims dramatically*): "I'm in love with Soho: with Frith Street / With the smelly and dark 'Fast Bar' / Where, every night, the shades are down / And there's the smell of incense all around . . . / I'm in love with Alice Hollowbrook / Who comes into the room, snarling / 'I've just done a show, darling!'" . . . that's a messy rhyme there, I'll fix that rhyme . . . "I'm in love with her voice as it barks / In the dark / Its tone as sharp / As the teeth of a shark . . ." I like that bit.

CAROLINE: The wonders of a rhyming dictionary.

TREVOR: Hey! How did you know? I couldn't do without it.

CAROLINE: Do you know what a malapropism is?

TREVOR: Yes. Do you? Anyway . . . (*continues*) "As rough as tree bark / I'm in love with Alice / She of the 'Fast Bar'" (*Recites with frenzied passion*) "I'll buy her a fast car / To take her away, I will by gaddy / From her life of artifice and loneliness / And her evil Sugar Daddy."

(*Pause*)

CAROLINE: Well. What's it all about!

HENRY: Trevor, I don't think you can do that.

TREVOR: What?

HENRY: I know what that's about . . . I know who that is . . .

TREVOR: You do as a matter of fact. Remember that prozzie we saw down the road after we first met? It's 'er. I've given 'er a history, turned her into a second-rate actress, relocated 'er to Soho. Clever, huh?

CAROLINE: Her name is Alice!

TREVOR: Yeah, d'ya like it? It gives it a bit of a, sort of, Lewis Carroll flavour. Bit Wonderlandy.

HENRY: It seems . . . a bit close to the bone, actually.

TREVOR: What do you mean?

HENRY: You're not . . . all that stuff about— (*Stops*)

TREVOR: What?

HENRY: Have you spoken to Anne lately, Trevor?

TREVOR: Of course I 'ave, all the time, mate.

HENRY: It's not Anne you've relocated to Soho, by any chance, is it?

TREVOR: Knock it off, mate.

HENRY: You know: you can't. Do that. She's not one of your cheap . . .

TREVOR: What? It's out of my hands, this, it's poetry, I use everybody for that. Everybody.

HENRY: Well you can't use Anne.

TREVOR: I'm not using Anne, I haven't. (*Beat*) You don't like it.

HENRY: I didn't say that.

TREVOR: Why can't I write about whatever I like, anyway? She's not yours.

HENRY: No . . . she's not.

CAROLINE: Trevor, do you think I could get the book, and then I'll leave. (*Beat*) For what it's worth, I enjoyed it.

HENRY (*quickly*): Yeah, it's a beauty, Trevor. I'm sorry, though, I have to go, really, I have to go. Bye. Caroline.

CAROLINE: Bye-bye.

HENRY: Bye, Trevor.

TREVOR: Bye, Hen. I'll write some new stuff, I'll make it a bit less contentious, hey? But you've gotta take the bull by the loins, yeah, if you want to write poetry.

HENRY: Yeah.

TREVOR: Cheers, then.

HENRY: Bye.

TREVOR: Oy! Hen. Don't forget about my parents. In a few weeks. I'll let you know.

HENRY: Fine.

TREVOR: Ciao!

(*Henry looks back at Trevor. Music. Crossfade*)

Scene Fifteen

Trevor's flat. Henry, Anne, and Trevor, after a dinner party with Trevor's parents. All a bit drunk.

TREVOR (*calling at the door*)**:** Bye! Bye-bye! Yes . . . Mum, all right!! (*Pokes his head back into the room*) I better see them down to the cab. (*He exits*)

HENRY (*to himself*)**:** Don't leave your heterosexual friends up there for too long, Trevor.

ANNE (*arch*)**:** Interesting.

(*Beat*)

HENRY: He even writes poetry about you, now.

ANNE: Yes I know that.

HENRY: I heard one. It's a pitiful *roman-à-clef*. You work in Frith Street in something called the "Fast Bar."

ANNE: That's old, Frappy. There have been many since then.

HENRY: He makes you cheap.

ANNE: I've never had anyone write poetry about me before.

HENRY: That's pathetic.

ANNE: Fuck off Frappy, I haven't. (*Beat*) He's desperate to sleep with me. (*Beat*) I haven't allowed it to happen. Yet. (*She smiles, he looks at her*) But he likes men too.

HENRY: Yes . . . well . . . not according to his parents.

ANNE: You've slept with him, naturally?

(*Beat*)

HENRY: Not exactly.

ANNE: Of course you have.

HENRY: No, really, not exactly. Yes I have. But . . . well, not . . .

ANNE: Not penetration?

HENRY: Well . . . no . . . not really.

ANNE: I don't know what that means: "Well . . . no . . . not really." I suppose it's all perverse and messed-up for you isn't it?

HENRY: What?

ANNE: Your sort.

HENRY (*very shocked*): Anne!

(*Beat*)

ANNE: I'm sorry. I didn't mean that. (*Beat*) It's all over him, he *loves* men.

HENRY: I can tell you he brings plenty of women home as well. And there's Caroline, upstairs. He's in love with her.

ANNE: Other men too?

HENRY: Yes.

ANNE: Aside from you. (*Beat*) Yes. As I thought.

HENRY: Anne. You should . . . you should keep your wits about you.

(*Trevor enters*)

ANNE (*mocking*): "We did well to bring him into this world."

TREVOR (*brightly*): Get away.

ANNE: They're lovely people, Trev, so nice and friendly. It's sweet—you walk just like your dad.

TREVOR: They both love you.

ANNE: Oh, good! I am glad.

TREVOR: And you too, Hen, they thought you were capital.

ANNE: The food was wonderful.

TREVOR: She did it all for you. She's not a bad cuisine-maker, my mum. (*Looks at Anne affectionately*) Make yourself comfy, Anne, I've gotta pop to the men's room. Back in a mo. (*Trevor exits*)

HENRY: You were obviously a hit.

ANNE: Yes, I was.

(*Beat*)

HENRY: I haven't seen you for ages.

ANNE: No, Frappy darling, it's been a while.

HENRY: How's Alec?

ANNE: Why?

HENRY: I didn't know you were going to be here tonight.

ANNE: I was only invited this afternoon.

HENRY: Really?

ANNE: Trevor thought he'd make it a real party.

HENRY: Well, for that we need you.

(*Beat*)

ANNE: Do you like my fingernails?

HENRY: Yes. You keep them well.

ANNE: My long, spidery fingernails, unpolished for a Saturday. Poor fingernails. It was exciting having no idea where that wine came from.

HENRY: Anne . . .

ANNE: No, it was exciting. It could have come from *anywhere*. It could've come from Newcastle. (*Pause. Quietly*) You have a problem, don't you?

HENRY: Have you been seeing him?

ANNE: You know I have.

HENRY: "Yes, Mrs. McCowan," you were saying . . .

ANNE: What . . . ?

HENRY: You were saying it . . . your whole body was saying it, the way you went on about your . . . everything . . . your career: you do *not* know Bruce Forsyth. "Yes Mrs. McCowan. I'm with Trevor. We have a future together. We are going to get married, I'm going to stop him writing lewd poetry and I am going to have your grandchildren . . ."

ANNE: Oh . . . you . . . that's disgusting . . . you're disgusting.

HENRY: No, you're disgusting. I've never seen such a performance. You should try acting. (*Beat*) Neither of you give a fig for each other, really.

ANNE: He's a pillock.

(*Pause*)

HENRY: Do you know what's amazing? Look at this place: he hasn't even censored the smut. For their visit. (*Points to posters on the walls*) *Taxi Driver*, fine, Kim Basinger with her tits out, fine, but look (*points*): his bedroom door wide open so we can all see a huge blow-up of "Moana de la Miner"—of the Vauxhall Tavern de la Miners? Never heard of her? It's so corny, Anne, she's the eleven o'clock act there every Friday. She lip-synchs to Liza Minnelli. She's quite talented, if you're off your head. Liza with an E. God, I hate gay anthems. In case you didn't know, she's one of Trevor's good friends. And there she is above his bed, with red sequins and stubble, trying to look impish. Pretty obvious she's a bloke, huh? But do the parentals, Mr and Mrs thick-woollen-jumper-McCowan, even think to ask questions? Why should they? Thanks to your behaviour and his obscene lies it's much nicer, much more convenient to presume that you two are an item . . . that you'll become their sodding daughter-in-law.

ANNE: I'm not going to listen . . . to . . . *this* (*Trevor enters*) Oh, good. My turn.

TREVOR: Right you are. Actually, get me some floss while you're in there wouldja? Mum's meals are a bit stringy between the teeth.

(*Anne exits*)

ANNE (*off*): Oh, Trevor how too divine, I hadn't noticed. Marilyn Monroe on your shower curtain. And it's like a hologram!

HENRY: Great, she rates the bathroom.

TREVOR: Yeah. (*Beat*) Thanks for everything. The evening was a poem.

HENRY: Yeah, can I have another drink?

TREVOR (*over this*): You'll leave now, won't you?

HENRY: Pardon?

TREVOR (*charmingly*): Thanks for coming around. But I think you might like to go now though, if you know what I mean.

HENRY: Uum, no.

TREVOR: Great friends, the greatest.

HENRY: Right.

TREVOR: I feel it now, though, Hen. The time is right, you know? You wouldn't want to spoil my plum, wouldja, mate?

HENRY: What?

TREVOR: Spoil my plum.

HENRY: Oh, oh, no . . . no . . .

TREVOR: You know how it is. (*Henry guffaws wryly and slowly gets his coat*) Do y'wanna cab?

HENRY: No. Thank you. I'll walk for a while.

TREVOR: Still early.

HENRY: Yes. Very. Always.

TREVOR: Never know what might be out there. (*Pause*) It was the best, this evening. (*Henry looks hard at Trevor*)

HENRY: I can't believe this . . .

TREVOR: I'll be in touch. (*Smiles*)

(*Beat*)

HENRY (*calls*): Goodnight, Anne. (*Pause. Louder*) Goodnight, Anne.

ANNE (*off*): Goodnight, Frappy darling. See you soon. We should do lunch, sometime. Hold on. (*She enters*) Bye, Frappy. (*Kisses him*)

TREVOR (*offering hand*): Bye, wordsmith.

HENRY: Bye. (*He half moves to peck Trevor on the cheek. Trevor puts his hand on Henry's shoulder to stop that happening*)

TREVOR: See ya.

HENRY: Thanks, Trevor.

TREVOR: Thank you. Rococo. Great word.

(*He punches Henry on the arm and whisks him towards the door. Music. The lights begin to fade as Henry walks slowly out, then turns to look. Music louder, as Anne and Trevor embrace and lower themselves to the ground, kissing passionately. Lights fade, pooling Henry, who looks at them, mortified. The music gets very loud. Crossfade*)

Scene Sixteen

Alec's London flat, Holland Park. Henry and Alec.

ALEC: Why are you here?

HENRY: Because I didn't know, all the time I've known you, what you really are to Anne and I feel sick, betrayed about that.

ALEC: There's no need. It isn't relevant. Why now?

HENRY: I want you to keep away from her.

ALEC: How melodramatic of you.

(*Beat*)

HENRY: A couple of months ago we were watching *The Magnificent Ambersons* at the Everyman . . .

ALEC: Ah, yes. One of her favourites, I recall.

HENRY: We've watched it together a few times. She was in good form. We had lots of giggles about Agnes Moorehead. "All that spite!" Anne kept saying. "All that hysteria! Madly over the top! Oooh, Frappy, I can't wait to see her again! Dear Agnes!" But my head just throbbed, Alec. All I could do was think of you. Halfway through the film I was . . . repelled by Anne's merriment, the cinema seemed ridiculous, Agnes Moorehead was tedious, and I found it hard to believe that I was ever taken in by that actressy turn of hers.

ALEC: What was the problem? Henry.

HENRY: It suddenly occurred to me that . . . that . . .

ALEC: Yes?

HENRY: That you'd . . . abused her.

(*Beat*)

ALEC (*brightly*): I've always considered myself a bit of a cross-generationalist. My good friends are my good friends' children. (*Beat*) When Anne was five, she asked her mother—she-what-was-done-in-by-too-much-gin—what DNA was! That slip-up convinced she-what-was-done-in-by-too-much-gin that she had a prodigy, a child-genius, on her hands. But it came to pass that Anne was decidedly average. (*Beat*) Did you know that I bought most of the furniture in Anne's house? I suppose you gathered that. A lot of restoration was done on that Georgian mahogany sideboard in the hall. *That* cost me a fortune. (*Beat. Soft, grave*) You think she's *yours*, don't you?

HENRY: Pardon me?

ALEC: You like strutting about with her, don't you?

HENRY: I know she doesn't need me, any more, never did.

ALEC: We are all vile little men, you know. All men are vile. I think you understand me, don't you. Think of all the things you've done. They're vile, aren't they? Do you think she's yours?

HENRY: No.

ALEC: Good.

HENRY: I'm sorry, Alec. I shouldn't be here.

ALEC: You don't know why you're here, do you?

HENRY: I've been worried. I'm just so worried.

ALEC: You feel like she's been unfaithful, Henry?

HENRY: What?

ALEC: Because she fucked your boyfriend?

(*Beat*)

HENRY: He's not my boyf . . .

ALEC: No. And I'm not your therapist. So.

(*Beat*)

HENRY: All along I've wanted to say—it's just that she has to be . . . well, she has to be careful with Trevor. Safe.

ALEC: No more careful than she needs to be with anybody.

HENRY: No, maybe not.

ALEC: Stop kidding me around, Henry.

HENRY: He's a lout you know. He writes bad, bad poetry and he comes all the way to Clapham just to show it off and I'm too kind to tell him the truth. It's pretentious and shallow. And he has sex with more people than I know. He doesn't care who they are, he just goes out and picks them up from these seedy places he goes to. He spends half his time in front of the mirror, and he listens to rotten music and well, Jesus Alec, he's just a bloody drip.

ALEC: But you like him a lot, don't you?

HENRY: Yes.

ALEC: Your visit here is pointless. (*Beat*) She knows what she's doing, let her be.

HENRY: Did you do that to her?

ALEC: What?

HENRY: Why don't I know? Anything. Did you abuse her?

(*Beat. Alec starts laughing*)

ALEC: You're serious, aren't you?

HENRY: I just want . . . information. Anything . . . please . . .

ALEC: Yes. You're brave to ask me. Something. That's impressive. You don't ask enough questions, Henry, I've noticed. You don't *do* enough. You think you're on the watch but you never *see*. See? Scrutinize, Henry. (*Pause*) I have never abused her, she has never been made to do anything she didn't want to do. In the end our relationship, such that it was, was all about dosh.

HENRY: You can stop doing that now—you can stop giving her money.

ALEC: Oh, give it up. It is a long time since you've seen her. It's already been arranged that I stop, Henry. She's done it herself. (*Pause. Alec smiles and reaches into his jacket. Henry reacts a little fearfully. As charming as can be*) Here is my card.

HENRY: Pardon me?

ALEC: This is my card, Henry, with my New York number. I'm going back for a while. To my apartment, you should see it. On the Upper West Side. It's surrounded by actors and writers and painters. You'd fit in very well.

HENRY: Why would I want your number? Put it away.

ALEC: My secretary will put you through to me, when I'm there. For whenever you want to talk.

HENRY: I won't ever want to talk to you.

ALEC: One day, when Anne—she-what-drinks-too-much-gin, mark two—has disappeared off the face of the earth, just like her parents did, or, if fate plays a different hand, and she becomes so famous that you won't be worth the dirt that her Sloaney feet tread upon, you may want a piece of her. And I am giving you my address so that you can come and talk to me. I know more about that girl than you'll ever know. Come see me. Sometime. We'll share memories. And I'll have more than you. Here's my card.

HENRY: I don't know whether you're some twisted, fucked-up sicko or not.

ALEC: You make me want to retch, Henry, certainly. Don't you ever come here unannounced again—no more of these mysterioso arrivals, all right, I don't like them. (*Smiling*) Call me first. (*Beat. He stuffs the card in Henry's shirt pocket and holds out his hand*) Goodbye, Henry. Take care.

(*Pause*)

HENRY: I really want to hurt you.

(*Pause. Alec smiles. Suddenly, Henry punches Alec, an almighty wallop in the stomach that makes Alec double over and cry out in pain. Henry stares at him. Crossfade*)

Scene Seventeen

Near Trevor's flat, late at night. Henry loiters. Trevor enters singing; seems drunk.

HENRY: Trevor . . . ?

(*Trevor sees Henry and sobers in an instant*)

TREVOR: Henry, mate.

HENRY (*smiles*): Hi.

TREVOR: Look at you out this hour, and all on your own.

HENRY: Sorry, it's a bit late, I shouldn't have . . . I thought you were up-stairs. The light's on.

TREVOR: Oh, right. No, I 'ad to whip down to that Indian twenty-four hour gaff for a few vitals. (*Looks up to his window*) Um . . . Hen. Yeah. It's been too long. (*Beat*) I was reading a grippin' article in *The Independent*, that *is* my chosen organ, yesterday, all about the diminishin' interest in London as the settin' for contemporary novels. Didja see it?

HENRY: No, I didn't I'm afraid. Look . . . I don't want to interrupt any-thing Trevor, just passing.

TREVOR: Just passin' through Paddington, eh, aren't they all? Very eru-dite it was, this piece, I showed it to Caroline who ignored it with a huff, but it's true you know, the place doesn't universally pulsate, does it? . . . You know, like New York *pulsates* . . . (*Pause. Softly*) Henry, mate . . .

HENRY: I'll get going.

TREVOR: Did you come 'ere to see me?

HENRY: Umm . . .

TREVOR: You should have rung, yeah? I'm sorry, I've got Andromeda up there tonight.

HENRY: Mm. I'll go. Sorry, Trevor . . .

TREVOR (*quickly*): No, no, don't go. Look, look, stay a bit. Sit. It's all right, I'm not going to talk to you all night about the decline of the Lon-don novel am I?

HENRY: Well . . .

TREVOR: Got something I wanna show you 'ere, anyway. It's a new poem.

HENRY: Oh.

TREVOR: It's about you, actually.

HENRY: Is it?

TREVOR: Don't panic. I 'ad this . . . this picture in my head, and I just 'ad to get it out. It's really weird. I reckon you're a muse or something. I've been writing some great stuff since I've known you—this is one of me best.

HENRY: How strange.

TREVOR: It's just a matter of time before I'm published now, I reckon.

HENRY: That's what your mum and dad think, anyway.

TREVOR: Sure, sure. (*Grabs some crumpled paper out of his back pocket*) Take this, read it wouldja? Let me know whatcha think.

HENRY: Okay, I will.

TREVOR: I really want your opinion, you know, your advice. Let me know . . . read it soon . . .

HENRY: I will. Thanks. (*Puts the paper in his pocket*)

TREVOR: No, no, thank *you* . . . wordsmith.

(*Henry smiles. They sit back and look at the sky*)

HENRY: Nice night.

TREVOR: Bit cold.

HENRY: There have been so many calm nights lately. I walk around all the time now, at night.

TREVOR: Yeah. (*Lights a cigarette*) Drag?

HENRY: Thanks. (*He has a drag then hands the cigarette back to Trevor*)

TREVOR: Yeah, yep, yep, yep, yep, yep.

(*Long pause*)

HENRY: So, how's Caroline?

TREVOR: Huh? Aah, she's preparing for an exhibition at that stupid art gallery in Notting Hill.

HENRY: I haven't been there for a while.

TREVOR: She'll never be ready, you know.

HENRY: Why not?

TREVOR: She has, like, plaster everywhere.

HENRY: What's new?

TREVOR: This is worse. She's workin' on four or five things at once.

HENRY: What is it? A series?

TREVOR: Somethin' like that. Somethin' to do with women's insides— creation or procreation or menstruation or something. I can't see it though. She won't let me 'ave a look.

HENRY: Well, I suppose she's flat out.

TREVOR: Yeah, always too busy with that bloody gallery. (*Beat*) She doesn't give a shit for me anyway.

HENRY: She does like you, I think.

TREVOR: She's a cow.

HENRY: Yeah.

TREVOR (*laughs*): Yeah. (*Trevor smokes, they look upwards*)

HENRY: That's the fattest cat I've seen in Paddington, Trevor. You've been feeding that one haven't you?

TREVOR: Rotten thing. (*Beat*) I 'aven't seen Anne, you know, not for a long time. (*Henry looks at him*) She's great, right, I like her, but she's gotta few problems, that one; latched 'erself on to me for a bit, then she was gone. I feel a bit rotten about it, left you for dead.

HENRY: It's all right.

TREVOR: Yep, she annihilates reality, that one.

HENRY: Excuse me?

TREVOR: She annihilates reality.

HENRY: Where did you read that?

TREVOR: Fuck off.

HENRY: Sorry. (*Beat*) We all deny things, if that's what you're talking about.

TREVOR: That's what I *am* talkin' about. She does it all the time, you noticed? She either gets on stage, or she walks tall with you or she puts away the gin and snorts god-knows-what or she criticizes everyone around her, or she goes all King's Roady or she has sex—all these things are 'er drugs—and she just annihilates . . . *reality* . . . in the process. (*Beat*) Makes life easier, I s'pose. (*Takes a long drag on his cigarette*) Gave her some advice, though.

HENRY: What?

TREVOR: Alec, the Americano. That guy we saw at *Who's Afraid of Virginia Woolf?* Sugar daddy. She 'as to dump 'im.

HENRY: Yeah.

TREVOR: She talked about 'im a lot.

HENRY: Did she?

TREVOR: She was drunk. Don't think many people know much about 'im. Actually, I think she was telling me so that I'd tell you. (*Beat, he*

smokes) He keeps her, yeah. We all know that. And they've . . . you know
. . . (*Indicates with his fingers*)

HENRY (*to himself, very quietly*): Fuck . . .

TREVOR: I thought you'd know. It's obvious, i'n't it?

(*Beat*)

HENRY (*resigned*): What did you do?

TREVOR: Huh?

HENRY: What did you do when you found out? What did you do?

TREVOR: I didn't do anything, mate. I'm not gonna do anything. What's
to do? I seen 'im a few times, to be honest, I quite like the guy. Henry.
There's nothing against fucking some sucker who gives you money, now,
is there? That ain't illegal.

(*Beat*)

HENRY: The whole thing . . . it's all . . . awful.

TREVOR: Leave it, she's working it out, I reckon. I told 'er she 'as to.
Move on, you know? (*Beat*) Have you ever 'eard of Sally Bowles?

HENRY: Yes.

TREVOR: Anne is just like 'er. And Sally Bowles was a bitch.

HENRY: I liked Sally Bowles.

TREVOR: God, mate, yeah. The perfect woman. (*Beat*) Look, I um, 'ave to
go in a minute.

HENRY: Yes.

TREVOR: You're all right.

HENRY: Is this what you do? Every night.

TREVOR: As long as it doesn't affect anyone else.

(*Beat*)

HENRY: But it has. It does. Me.

(*Beat*)

TREVOR: I've written a poem about this. I'm never guilty . . . I never get into trouble. (*Henry grabs Trevor's hand. Jokingly*) Not 'ere mate. Decorum. Impressionable kids about! (*Smiles. Pause*) How about coming out with me tomorra night? I mean it. I want to.

HENRY: Okay, I will.

TREVOR: Great. Excellent. I'll call for you. (*Pause*) Look, mate, I've got to go inside. Andromeda. (*Pause*) It's nothin'.

HENRY: Yeah. I understand. I'll give you a call.

TREVOR: Let me know what you think of that poetry. I can't wait to hear your critical opinion, serious.

HENRY: I will.

TREVOR: See ya then.

HENRY: Bye.

(*Trevor stands, then quickly bends and kisses Henry on the head. Henry tries to kiss him on the mouth. Trevor pulls back*)

HENRY: Trevor?

TREVOR: It's a sad world, i'n't it? So much crap.

(*He exits. Beat. Henry sits and laughs ruefully to himself*)

HENRY: Wanker. (*Looks out front*)

(*Music. Crossfade*)

Scene Eighteen

A pub, Neal's Yard. Henry sits on his own. Eventually, Anne appears, in a long coat, scarf.

ANNE: Henry?

(*Henry looks around and sees her*)

HENRY: Hi. I didn't know if you'd come.

ANNE: Usually, I go straight home, Henry. Usually I don't read messages given to me by the stage door. I never took you for a stage door Johnny.

HENRY: You never used to call me that, Henry. (*Beat*) How're things?

ANNE: I'm all right. (*Smiles*)

(*Pause*)

HENRY: I saw a review.

ANNE: Which one?

HENRY: Don't remember. I saw your name . . . thought I'd come to see it.

ANNE: Poor you.

HENRY: It's all right.

ANNE (*sighs*): It's terrible. Not my thing and not yours either.

HENRY: I liked it. What can I get you?

ANNE: I'm not having anything. I can't stay.

HENRY: Not much of a pub, this.

ANNE: I know you've been before, Henry. It's a bit hard to sneak out before curtain call in that theatre. That was really silly. (*Beat*) Not letting me know.

(*Beat*)

HENRY: Are you okay?

ANNE: Stop asking me that. Why wouldn't I be?

HENRY: I worry . . . everything. I miss you. I want to know why you didn't tell me you were in a new play. I want to know . . . what's . . . happened . . .

ANNE: I've got some film work.

HENRY: Oh. Anne! That's wonderful. Congratulations.

(*She looks away*)

ANNE: When this has finished you won't see me on stage for a while, I hope. Or in London. It's been too cold for me here, lately.

HENRY: This is what you've wanted for ages.

ANNE: Yes.

HENRY: I suppose Alec's pleased.

ANNE: Why do you bring him up? (*He makes no answer*) I know that you know that I've dumped him.

HENRY: What do you mean?

ANNE: What do I mean? What do you mean, asking me? Don't ask me questions.

(*Beat*)

HENRY: This is almost the West End, Anne. You're almost acting in the West End.

ANNE: I don't give a brass razoo about that.

(*Pause*)

HENRY: I didn't know what to think . . . I thought . . . I knew it was coming. Shit. He's a funny guy, Trevor.

(*Anne looks upwards*)

ANNE: Really, Frappy, I haven't seen Trevor for a long time.

HENRY: I'm worried. Scared. You don't know all about him. (*Rubs his temple*) If you only knew what was going on up here.

ANNE: It's in France. I'm going away for a good while. Yes. I'm going to France. The pay's good. Better than ever. I'm going to France! Maybe I'll meet a Frenchman and turn into the next . . . (*Stops*) Maybe not. I feel calm. Everything is just so. (*Beat*) Trevor, Frappy, is stupid. Not stupid, pointless. Yes. One of those pointless . . . (*searches for word; angry*) pervs. But, he can . . . at least he can . . . articulate, can't he?, he can talk. Sense, amazingly. (*Beat*) Poor Henry.

HENRY: I was so jealous. He was mine. You were mine.

ANNE: That was selfish of you.

HENRY: I felt betrayed. Still do. (*Looks away*)

ANNE: No one betrayed you. I never lied. Don't come at me with all this crap now. It's too *late*. Who cares now?

(*Long, long pause. She looks at him. She looks away. Eventually, he faces her*)

HENRY: What's your part?

ANNE: It's a tiny, weeny, minuscule thing.

HENRY: A love interest?

ANNE: Sort of. It's a bit hard to explain. Very Merchant Ivory!

HENRY: Gordon's for lunch tomorrow?

ANNE: I can't.

HENRY: No, I can't, either.

ANNE: You see him, right? Trevor.

HENRY (*nods*): Whenever I can.

ANNE: Really?

(*Henry nods*)

ANNE: Send him my love, then.

HENRY: Maybe. Yes. (*Pause*) I think we might move in together.

ANNE (*surprised*): What?

HENRY: I think I might ask him to move in with me.

ANNE: Why?

HENRY: I . . . I . . . like him. I think.

ANNE: Do you really?

HENRY: Yes. (*Beat*) I think.

ANNE: I don't know why.

HENRY: I don't either.

ANNE: Can you trust him?

HENRY: It's not the same, for him.

ANNE: *You're* stupid. I can't believe you, saying that, "It's not the same for him." Trust is trust. Someone like . . . *that* . . . he's . . . You're dumb.

HENRY: I've never denied that. Aren't we all.

(*Beat*)

ANNE (*blasé*): He was a bit of a lecher. (*Long pause. He is not looking at her*) I want to carefully turn your head, so that you're looking into my eyes. Stare into my face, Frappy. (*Beat*) You've got such gorgeous hair, I've always loved it. (*Beat*) I won't miss London. Fresh fields!

HENRY (*turns to her*): Shall I wish you good luck?

ANNE: If you want to.

(*They look at each other. Music. Crossfade*)

Scene Nineteen

Outside Trevor's flat. Late at night. Trevor sits on the steps to the main entrance. He has been drinking and has a whisky bottle. Henry walks up.

HENRY (*to a cat*): Pppsstt, you little fucker!

(*Pause*)

TREVOR: Hey, Hen.

HENRY: Trevor! What are you doing outside? It's freezing. (*Sits down next to him*)

TREVOR (*offers bottle*): Have a drink?

HENRY: Thanks, I will.

TREVOR: A fag?

HENRY: Yeah, that too. (*Beat*) Are you all right? (*Trevor nods. Beat*) I went to see Anne.

TREVOR: Did you? Get it sorted?

HENRY: I think.

TREVOR: I hope so. (*Beat*) I reckon our troubles are just beginning, mate.

(*Beat*)

HENRY: I'm here to tell you something. Anne's gone away. Martin's moving out of the flat. He's going to live with Sally, or whatever her name is.

TREVOR: Really?

HENRY: Yeah.

TREVOR: He's doing the right thing.

HENRY: Is he?

TREVOR: Oh, yeah. Shouldn't stay in a dump like that for too long.

HENRY: So you do think it's a dump?

TREVOR: It's the worst, mate, your place is the worst. (*Henry laughs*) Bad for someone like that guy.

(*Pause*)

HENRY (*shyly*): I'll be looking for someone . . . When does your lease expire?

TREVOR: Dunno, mate.

HENRY: Would you consider . . . leaving here?

TREVOR: Just right for me, 'ere, wordsmith. (*Beat*) I could check, though, think about it . . . we could . . . (*Looks away*)

(*Pause*)

HENRY: I thought you'd be out tonight.

TREVOR: No, not tonight.

HENRY: I've borrowed a friend's car. Thought I'd check to see if you were in.

TREVOR: I'm in.

(*Pause*)

HENRY: I haven't heard any of your poems for a while.

TREVOR: I gave you that one . . .

HENRY: Oh, yeah. Sorry. I haven't read it yet.

TREVOR: Paahh! I 'aven't written anythin' for a long time. Too busy. It's bullshit.

(*Caroline enters*)

CAROLINE: Well, hello boys.

HENRY: Hello, Caroline.

CAROLINE: How are you both?

HENRY: All right. Thanks.

CAROLINE (*to Trevor*): Not out tonight? (*No answer*) Are you waiting for something? Someone?

HENRY: Just talking.

CAROLINE: It's cold.

HENRY: Yeah.

(*Beat*)

CAROLINE (*to Trevor*): You're quiet. (*Pause*) Isn't he quiet? I've never heard anything like it. Hello? (*Pause*) Are you mute? Did a trick get your tongue?

HENRY: Caroline . . .

CAROLINE (*over this*): What have you done to him?

(*Pause, she looks at Trevor*)

TREVOR: Where've you been?

CAROLINE: That's more like it. Out. With friends. Somewhere you've never been. (*Trevor looks away. Caroline is uncomfortable. To Henry*) I can't work it out, what you see in him.

HENRY: What do you mean?

CAROLINE: Nothing.

HENRY: No, what do you mean?

(*Caroline looks hard at Trevor*)

CAROLINE: Are you all right? Trevor? (*Beat*) Trevor? (*He says nothing. Makes her way upstairs*) Apart from me, but I don't count, you're the only person I've ever known who's put up with him for more than six months.

TREVOR (*quietly, looking at Henry*): It's getting on to a year now, i'n't it, mate?

HENRY: Yeah, almost a year.

(*Beat, Trevor looks away*)

CAROLINE: Most people I know . . . (*She trails off*)

HENRY: Yes?

(*Beat*)

CAROLINE: Most people I know just end up telling him to fuck off. Well, good night.

(*She exits. Long pause; Henry smokes, puts his cigarette out, has a swig of whisky*)

TREVOR (*quietly*): I had a bad day today.

(*Pause*)

HENRY: Why?

TREVOR: I went to give blood.

HENRY: Oh . . . really?

TREVOR: I 'aven't given blood for ages. I always used to when I was a bit younger. Mum used to do it as well. She'd take me to the blood bank in Dorchester and we'd do it together. I remember once I said I'd eaten but I 'adn't and when I came out afterwards, I was on cloud five 'undred and fifty-nine. I 'aven't been as 'igh since.

(*Henry laughs. Pause*)

HENRY: I haven't given blood.

TREVOR: No, mate, well . . . (*Beat*) You should have. (*Beat*) It's something really worthwhile.

HENRY: So did you give blood today?

(*Trevor looks at Henry long and hard; pained, innocent*)

TREVOR (*stammers*): Nah, I . . . I couldn't . . . could I?

HENRY: What do you mean?

TREVOR: I couldn't mate. They wouldn't let me. Well, it's not that they wouldn't let me. But I couldn't fill out the form.

(*Beat*)

HENRY: Trevor— (*Stops*)

(*Beat. Henry moves to comfort him, Trevor backs away*)

TREVOR: I couldn't fill it out, you know? Not without lying. And I couldn't lie, this time, I just couldn't.

HENRY: Trevor . . .

TREVOR: I'm a risk. I couldn't give blood. I'm a risk . . .

(*He shakes his head and begins to cry. He knocks over the whisky bottle and begins to grope for it, but the tears pour from his eyes and he loses his sight. Henry takes him in his arms. Trevor sobbing*) I couldn't give blood . . . I couldn't give blood. . . .

HENRY: Oh, Trevor . . .

TREVOR: . . . they wouldn't let me give blood . . .

HENRY: Shhhhh. Ssshhh. Oh, Trevor . . . ssshhhhh . . .

(*Henry holds Trevor tight and rocks him. Music. Crossfade*)

Scene Twenty

Trevor's flat. Henry sits on his own, writing in his diary. Trevor enters and watches.

TREVOR: Look at you, writin' away. You're like me, I'm like that; head down, don't let anyone disturb me, get everythin' on paper, then I re-work it. Saw a Burroughs film once, apparently you shouldn't do that, not if you've got real talent, that's censorin' yourself. (*Henry doesn't look up*) What's that?

HENRY: What?

TREVOR: That.

HENRY: It's a letter.

TREVOR: Who from?

HENRY: Anne.

TREVOR: In France?

HENRY: Yeah.

TREVOR: She still there?

HENRY: Yes.

TREVOR: You 'aven't opened it.

HENRY: No, I will, later.

TREVOR: That's bad luck, that is. Rotten omen if you leave it for too long. I wonder what she's up to? France. Wow. I wonder when the film'll be out.

HENRY: I read that it might not get a release here.

TREVOR: Oh. Shame. We'll 'ave to go and see it over there, eh? Maybe not. Whatcha think of this hair?

HENRY: It looks fine.

TREVOR: Shall I cut it a bit more? The scissors are blunt, though. Do you wanna cup of tea?

HENRY (*smiling*): No.

(*Trevor exits, smiling. Caroline knocks on the door and enters*)

CAROLINE: Hello . . . ?

HENRY: Come in.

CAROLINE: Oh, hello.

HENRY: Hello.

CAROLINE: I've only come to . . .

TREVOR (*off*): Who's that?

CAROLINE: Caroline.

(*Trevor bounds in*)

TREVOR: Caroline! Caz! You're here to get what was it?

CAROLINE: My book.

TREVOR: Yeah, got it. While you're 'ere, I've got some news. I've just bought a cappuccino maker and Henry's bought a rather special new telly with all the trimmings.

CAROLINE: So?

TREVOR: I'm getting out *Natural Born Killers* tonight, and *Victor/Victoria* tomorrow night.

CAROLINE: I haven't seen either one of those.

TREVOR: Seen both, ten times apiece.

CAROLINE: There's something different about you.

TREVOR: Is there? No, there isn't. I'm the same, same old me. Hey, Caroline, I'm moving to Clapham.

CAROLINE: Clapham?

TREVOR: Yep, Clapham, way down South.

CAROLINE: Trevor?

TREVOR: It's all arranged.

CAROLINE: What are you talking about?

TREVOR: I'm moving.

CAROLINE: You're kidding . . .

TREVOR: Nup! I'm off!

CAROLINE: What about your lease?

TREVOR: Fuck 'im.

CAROLINE: But you can't just . . . leave.

TREVOR: Why not?

CAROLINE: There are . . . commitments . . . aren't there? Here . . .

TREVOR: Who to?! To whom?! I'm getting out ! My new poem is called "Paddington Snare."

CAROLINE: The lease . . .

TREVOR: Come on! Sod it! I given him enough dosh over the past few years, I'm out of 'ere! We're both out of 'ere!

CAROLINE: Are you two . . . (*indicates with her hands*)?

HENRY (*looking up*): Yes, Caroline, he's moving in with me.

CAROLINE: It won't last.

(*Beat. They all look at each other. Trevor bursts out laughing. Henry laughs too*)

TREVOR: Nothing does, Caroline . . . ! Whatever lasts!?

CAROLINE: When are you going?

TREVOR: Sunday. Or the following one.

CAROLINE: I can't believe it.

TREVOR: Getting away! You should try it.

CAROLINE: I give it a week.

TREVOR: You'll miss me, won't you?

CAROLINE: No, Trevor, I won't.

TREVOR: Liar. (*Still looking at Caroline*) Nothing else for it, I suppose, is there Hen?

(*Trevor smiles as Caroline stares. Henry looks up from his diary as the lights fade around him; he stares out front*)

HENRY: No. Nothing else for it.

(*We can only see Henry. Silence. Blackout. End*)

RESCUE AND RECOVERY

by Steve Murray

Rescue and Recovery was first produced at Actor's Express in Atlanta in July, 1999. The production was directed by Chris Coleman and featured the following cast:

Cameron	Brad Sherrill
Janie	Kathleen Wattis
Mark	Rob Beams
Jay	Jeff Feldman
Timothy and other parts	Jeff McKerley

Characters

Cameron—A physician in his 30s
Janie—His ex-wife, an attorney, 30s
Timothy—An actor, 30s
(also plays Therapist, Contractor, Waiter, the three
dates, Trick, Alcoholic, Clerk)
Jay—A businessman, 30s
Mark—A bank teller, 20s

Setting

Atlanta, the present and recent past. One set suggesting multiple locations.

AUTHOR'S INTRODUCTION

Many of my plays investigate the shifting nature of "truth." I put truth in quotation marks, because facts and actions, seen from a distance, may seem unequivocal. But once you factor the minds and the hearts of the characters into the equation, the nature of what's *really* going on can be a matter of multiple interpretations. Especially when it comes to love.

With *Rescue and Recovery*, I wanted to use two separate narrators, bound together by history and emotion, but perhaps very different in how they see things. At the start of the play, they agree to "tell the story together . . . jam the puzzle pieces together and see if they fit." By the end of the evening, at least two things happen. First, the audience may believe they know exactly where the plot is going, only to discover that much of what they've been watching is not what it may seem. Second (and more interesting to me) was to watch as our two narrators come to realize that the story they believe they are telling—about their friends, lovers and acquaintances—is really about something else entirely: themselves.

Though gay characters and themes are usually a part, in some way, in my scripts, "R&R" is possibly the most "out" there of them all—in its humor, its pain, its lust, its longing. At the same time, it might also be my most universal, because these are not exactly the exclusive property of those of us who are gay.

STEVE MURRAY
Atlanta, 2000

ACT ONE

The audience enters to find the stage floor strewn with a man's change of clothing: shirt, pants, socks, underwear.

If there's any stationary furniture, it's a doctor's examining table.

The lights come up on Cameron standing among the clothes, naked.

CAMERON (*to us*): I thought I'd get it out of the way, since, metaphorically what I'm doing—it's the same. Make the metaphor manifest. It's how I felt for a long time: walking around naked. (*Looks down at his dick*) So. Not the biggest. Not the smallest—I hope. Not a six-pack stomach, but not a keg either. So. Just normal. (*He begins to dress*) You're like that, right? Want people to think you're just normal, but extra-special at the same time. Normal/special—pulled in opposite directions.

Like sex. You want to make an impression. But not such a big impression that the guy you're with thinks, *Where did he learn that?* - thinks, *What sort of den of iniquity did he learn* that *in, from what sort of,* you know, *fluid-dripping leatheroid sex monster?* But I was never just a sixtynine'll-do-me-fine, suck-and-cuddle kind of guy. I mean, sex should be, it should go beyond routine . . . That's how my wife found out. I'm not proud of it. Cheating on her. I'm not proud of getting married, for that matter. I mean, it was the '90s. Post gay rights, Stonewall, all that. It was something men my father's age did. But propriety and passion, those are two other things that split you apart. I loved Janie. I did. Still do.

(*Janie appears*)

JANIE (*to us*): But not, as they say, in that way. (*She watches Cameron dress*) Cameron can play show-and-tell all he wants with his—*you-know.* But don't expect a striptease from me. There's a reason for clothes. Especially after 30. I didn't suspect about Cameron. Not for the longest time. I felt so dumb, after the fact. But he was such a good lover. It's not like I caught him with his eyes closed, fantasizing about Jeff Stryker—is that his name?

CAMERON: But it wasn't fair.

JANIE: It wasn't fair to either of us.

CAMERON: But since when is fairness a factor in the love equation?

JANIE (*to us*): The way I found out—it's ironic. I figured it out because he became a better lover. More imaginative. Till it occurred to me that imagination is all well and good, but some things you do in bed you need hands-on practice for. Or if not hands . . . you know what I mean.

CAMERON: Sorry I'm late.

JANIE: You mean late again.

CAMERON: Late again.

JANIE: Who is she? One of your nurses? Doing it in the hospital linen closet—that's a cliché, but clichés are clichés because they're true.

CAMERON: What are you talking about?

JANIE: You're different, Cam. Okay, maybe I'm making it up. But tell me. Or if it's some fling—we can work through it.

CAMERON: I don't know what to say.

JANIE (*pause*): Start with her name.

CAMERON: Kyle.

JANIE: Kyle. Nurse Kyle.

CAMERON: Yes. He's an RN.

JANIE: *He* is.

CAMERON: Yes.

JANIE (*to us*): I was expecting a Kathy or a Candy, but it was a Kyle. I look back on it now. What if I hadn't forced the issue? *Ambushed* him? He would experiment, get it out of his system. Then stay with me and Brian. I don't know when to keep my mouth shut. And when there's a Nurse Kyle, RN, hanging in the air between you, there's no turning back.

CAMERON (*to us*): All things considered she was great about it.

JANIE: I puked for fifteen days.

CAMERON: But all things considered—

JANIE: Fifteen days solid. The upside was, I lost an inch in my hips.

CAMERON: All things considered—

JANIE: I was great, I was flawless. Did he mention our son?

CAMERON: We sat him down with that book, *Daddy's Roommate*.

JANIE: Brian.

CAMERON: Our son Brian. He was only five at the time, so he couldn't actually *read* the book—

JANIE: But a picture's worth a thousand words. My mother was so worried, "What about Brian, do you think *he's* one?"

CAMERON: They say it skips a generation. The gene, or whatever.

JANIE: But this is about Mark. That's what this is really about.

CAMERON: Yes, Mark.

JANIE: This is about Mark and Jay. And Timothy. I introduced them. Thank God *after* the divorce, when we were doing the supportive nurturing '90s ex-spouses thing, you know? Wait, it wasn't Mark I introduced you to, it was Jay.

CAMERON: Well yes, but I'd already sort of met Jay. *Seen* him. (*To us*) You know what it's like, you're in a bathroom. And a guy steps up to the urinal next to you. The kind of guy who unzips, puts his hands on his hips and lets it flop out, because it's that big, a mind of its own, like letting an animal stop for a drink . . . only the opposite. Hands on his hips, and for a moment, the only thing in the world is this big dick hosing down the porcelain. "Okay, Tiger, you done?" Tuck, zip, and the world breathes a sigh of relief, 'cause Tiger came out, did his business and nobody got hurt. That's how I met Jay. Well, didn't meet him. Except out of the corner of my eye.

JANIE (*to us*): Thus, appropriately enough, our story begins at a urinal.

CAMERON: It's a story we tell now.

JANIE: Separately.

CAMERON: At cocktail parties.

JANIE: Therapist's offices.

CAMERON: We try to hit all the right notes: Funny, elegant—

JANIE: —Dirty.

CAMERON: Tonight we'll tell it together.

JANIE: Jam the puzzle pieces together, see if they fit.

CAMERON: The urinal was in the bathroom of a theater.

JANIE: I was on their board. Theaters love lawyers, ever since the NEA. It was opening night. Some Ionesco something, they were very avant-garde-old-hat-French. They're bankrupt now. But at the time . . .

CAMERON: I was Janie's date.

JANIE: Two years after the divorce, but you see how liberal I am? Was?

CAMERON: There was a reception. Wine and cheese.

JANIE: Prosciutto roulades.

CAMERON: Asparagus spears.

JANIE (*a diversion*): Oh! Now not everybody smells it, when they pee. Asparagus? You know what I mean? Cameron can explain to you the physiological details, but—

CAMERON: Are we doing this?

JANIE (*reluctantly*): Yes . . . *Rhinoceros*, that's what the play was, and there was a reception.

(The scene begins: The Reception. Timothy appears. Janie leads him to Cameron. She's drinking champagne)

JANIE: Cam, this is—

CAMERON (*to Timothy*): You were really good.

TIMOTHY: Thanks!

JANIE: Timothy Johnson. This is Cameron, my ex-husband.

(Jay enters with a wine glass and a bottled water; gives the water to Timothy)

JAY: Baby Bear.

TIMOTHY: What is this?

JAY: Pelligrino.

TIMOTHY: It's opening night. Champagne!

JAY: Honey . . .

JANIE: Cam, this is (*Forgets*) . . . oh shit.

JAY: Jay, hi.

JANIE: *Jay*, Timothy's—wait, how do you say it—?

TIMOTHY: Boyfriend.

JAY: Lover.

JANIE: —Because everybody has their own word for it.

TIMOTHY (*sings*): "Let's call the whole thing off."

JAY (*shaking hands with Cameron*): Hi.

CAMERON: We met.

JAY: Oh, I'm sorry, I don't—

CAMERON (*embarrassed*): I mean, I *saw* you earlier. Nothing.

JAY: So you two—?

CAMERON: We were married.

JANIE: Till he earned his letter jacket for the other team. (*To us*) You see, I was continental, I was cosmopolitan, I was an idiot.

CAMERON (*to Janie*): You were very kind.

JANIE (*to us*): Kindness schmindness. I'm Jewish, does it matter?

TIMOTHY: A little champagne won't kill me. It's opening night!

JANIE (*to us*): *Half* Jewish. My mother, oh she laughed! A goy, *and* gay! One letter's difference, it meant the same to her.

TIMOTHY (*to Cameron*): Are you gay?

CAMERON (*on the spot*): I, uh—

JANIE: Yes, he is.

TIMOTHY: The wife would know.

JANIE: Ex-wife.

TIMOTHY: Bingo. Honey, one glass.

JAY: Remember what your doctor said?

TIMOTHY (*to Cameron and Janie*): I'm dying, you know.

JANIE: No. I didn't. I'm just on the board.

TIMOTHY: Everybody knows. This is my swan song. The dying swan.

JAY: Timothy.

TIMOTHY: A soothing glass of champagne would stop me saying outrageous things. (*Jay exits*) He is the best man in the world. For a corporate industrialist pig.

JANIE: You've been together—?

TIMOTHY: Six years. He's not sick, just me. He knew from our first date. Most people you say "positive" and they're, "Please, let me get the check, I'd love to see you again, just have to consult my daytimer." Then the phone never rings. They buy off their guilt with the cilantro-pesto-chicken-breast special and a bottle of so-so Merlot. Coffee, if you're lucky. But my Jay—

CAMERON: He works for—?

TIMOTHY: Exxon. It's our dirty secret. He pisses me off, I do my oil-slick Exxon Valdez swan-dance for him. Oh, it's all about dying swans tonight, isn't it?

(*Jay returns with two glasses of champagne, hands one to Timothy*)

JAY: Baby Bear.

TIMOTHY: Big Boy.

JAY (*offering Cameron the second glass*): Champagne?

CAMERON: No thanks, I'm in recovery.

TIMOTHY: What from?

CAMERON: Champagne.

JANIE (*to us*): And Demerol.

CAMERON: Thank you, honey.

JANIE (*to us*): A teensy bit of cocaine.

CAMERON: I had a problem.

JAY: A lot of people do.

TIMOTHY: Temptation.

JAY: Sure, the stress.

CAMERON (*to Timothy*): You know about the new AIDS therapies. What they call cocktails?

TIMOTHY: Oh, yum!

(*He takes Cameron by the hand, pulls him a step away from the others*)

CAMERON (*to us*): He took me by the hand. That's when I knew—how thin his wrist was, how frail.

TIMOTHY: So what is it that *you* do?

CAMERON: I'm a doctor.

TIMOTHY: Oh, my mother would swoon. Don't be jealous, Jay! Not Ph.D., not some academic philosophy bullshit, when you say doctor you mean—

CAMERON: M.D. I'm an internist.

TIMOTHY: I have seriously got the vapors now. And unattached?

CAMERON: Well—

TIMOTHY: Other than your wife?

JANIE and CAMERON: Ex-wife—

TIMOTHY (*to Jay*): Honey, a doctor! Hold tight to me, I might float off into his arms! (*To Cameron*) Child, you are prime real estate. You are Boardwalk and three hotels! Turn your head left and right, survey your domain. The gay landscape spreads itself flat at your feet, chico.

CAMERON: Well, I haven't met the right—

TIMOTHY: Yes you have.

CAMERON: I'm sorry.

TIMOTHY: You *have* met the right man.

JAY: Honey . . .

CAMERON: What therapies does your doctor have you on?

TIMOTHY: Everything. Yes, the lovely cocktails. Protease whatchamacallits, but they're inhibiting nothing. I have a very good doctor, and nothing works. I'm the overachieving student that screws the curve.

JAY: Timothy . . .

(*Mark comes out with a tray of asparagus, wearing only bikini briefs*)

TIMOTHY: Do you know our friend Mark? Mark, this is Cameron and Janie Trace.

(*Cameron and Mark shake hands*)

CAMERON (*absorbed*): How do you do.

JANIE (*to us*): He wasn't really in his underwear—but the way Cam looked at him, he might as well be.

MARK: Hi. Mark Frank.

CAMERON: Oh, like German dollar, French dollar.

MARK: Sorry?

CAMERON: Your name.

MARK: My name?

CAMERON: Two different currencies. Never mind.

MARK: Oh. Right. Asparagus spear?

(*He picks up a hefty stalk from the tray and slides it suggestively into Cameron's mouth*)

JANIE (*to us*): Actually, he had a suit on, not Armani, but a nice Italian knockoff.

TIMOTHY: Mark volunteers.

CAMERON: For what?

TIMOTHY: For the theater, silly.

MARK (*Consulting Janie and Cameron, breaking out of convention*): Can I put my clothes on?

JANIE: If the novelty won't send you into shock.

(*Mark turns and exits. Janie watches him go. She takes Timothy's champagne and has a good swig. Timothy hands Cameron a card*)

TIMOTHY: Call us sometime. We should all have dinner.

(*Timothy and Jay exit. Cameron takes the champagne away from Janie*)

CAMERON (*to her*): We don't have to do this.

JANIE: No, you can't start a story and just stop. (*To us*) Am I right? It's like telling a joke without the punch line. Ready when you are.

CAMERON: Okay . . .

(*The scene shifts: The Car: Cameron and Janie drive home*)

JANIE: Thanks for picking me up tonight.

CAMERON: Thanks for the invitation.

JANIE: If you want to come in and see Brian—

CAMERON: It's almost midnight.

JANIE: Right. He'd never get back to sleep . . . Nice couple. Jay and Timothy.

CAMERON: A bit flamboyant.

JANIE: Timothy? You can see why Jay loves him, though. I mean, by comparison, Jay is sort of a mouse.

CAMERON: Not all of him.

JANIE: What?

CAMERON: Nothing . . .

JANIE: I mean, Timothy's the handsome one. Jay is nice-enough looking. Balding a little—not that there's anything wrong with it—

CAMERON: Except when people say things like that . . .

JANIE: Timothy's the looker though. Have you noticed?

CAMERON (*at a driver*): Speed up, asshole! Noticed what?

JANIE: Couples you meet. One of them's the pretty one, and one is—I mean, by comparison, plain. There's some dynamic there.

CAMERON: I know lots of good-looking couples.

JANIE: But one of them is always the star, and the other one—well, I guess they're the satellite around him. Or her.

CAMERON: Get off the road!

JANIE: One is the loud one, the other one's quiet. One of them loves the other more than they're loved.

CAMERON (*pause*): That's not necessarily true.

JANIE: Nothing wrong with it, it's just a dynamic you see.

CAMERON: Is it that obvious?

JANIE: What?

CAMERON: I'm balding.

JANIE: You're not balding . . .

CAMERON (*pause*): Are you seeing anybody?

JANIE: No.

CAMERON: You should.

JANIE: You mean therapist or date?

CAMERON: I mean therapist.

JANIE: Ha ha. You seeing anybody?

CAMERON: No.

JANIE: Whither Kyle?

CAMERON: Next subject.

JANIE: You should call Jay and Timothy. Let them introduce you to some nice men.

CAMERON: Oh, like that Gen-X caterer?

JANIE: He had a nice suit.

CAMERON: I didn't notice.

JANIE: You *seemed* to notice. Brian keeps asking, "When does Daddy get a roommate, like in the book?"

CAMERON: I'm too busy to date.

JANIE: Oh, so just the occasional backroom tryst in some cruise bar?

CAMERON (*appalled*): How do you know about back rooms?

JANIE: I read the manual: *You and Your Gay Husband*. Watch the road.

CAMERON: You take an unhealthy interest in my sex life. Or lack thereof.

JANIE: Honey, two people with our history—people would kill for a relationship like ours. No screaming arguments, no broken glass, the tiniest bit of child support, and you get Brian every other weekend.

CAMERON: I know.

JANIE: Whenever you want him. Count our blessings, that's what I say.

CAMERON: I know. We're lucky . . . I love you, old girl.

JANIE: "Old girl," that's nice.

CAMERON: You're the one who said I was balding.

(*They break out of the driving scene*)

JANIE (*to us*): I never did! You heard me. I never said he was balding. I know how vain he is, I would *never* point it out. Okay, so maybe I was "all up in his bidness," as my pro bono clients would say. But I mean, he didn't *see* anybody, not after that business with Nurse Kyle.

CAMERON (*to us*): Kyle and I got caught. Indirectly. Stains on the sheets.

JANIE: It *was* the linen closet, I knew it!

CAMERON: Not caught outright. But a close call. Suspicious glances from the nurses' station, etcetera. Kyle wanted to carry on outside the hospital. Only, I just couldn't see him in my apartment, the apartment I moved into after Janie and I. . . . Plus, I found out, *he* still lived with his mother. So. It just sort of died out. A failure of nerve.

JANIE: Or a relapse of taste.

(*Cameron alone*)

CAMERON (*to us*): I dropped Janie home. Life went on, I never thought twice about that night at the theater. But a few months later, at the hospital. I do intake twice a week. New patients. I didn't recognize his name when I picked up his history.

(*The hospital: Timothy is sitting, waiting. Cameron enters reading his chart*)

CAMERON: Hello, Mr. Johnson.

TIMOTHY: Oh, we're well beyond that now, aren't we Herr Doctor?

CAMERON: Oh, hi—

TIMOTHY: *Timothy*. How soon they forget.

CAMERON: How are you?

TIMOTHY: Still dying! Lawsie! Is it hot in here, or are my night sweats going daytime?

CAMERON: We have a ventilation problem.

TIMOTHY: Me too, you should see what I hack up.

CAMERON (*to us*): It was repellent to me, if I can be honest here. This sort of—*showmanship*. I never could stand a drag queen. Not that he was a drag queen. But. You know?

TIMOTHY: Is that a reflex hammer in your pocket, or are you just happy to see me?

CAMERON (*to us*): I was a quarterback in high school. I dated the home-coming queen, that's the sort of queen I knew.

TIMOTHY: I think my prostate needs a checkup, but I bet all the boys tell you that.

CAMERON (*to us*): At the same time, I have to admit . . . there was something liberating about him.

TIMOTHY: Shall I slip into something more comfortable, like an open grave?

CAMERON: Timothy, please.

TIMOTHY: Call me Tim. Nobody does. Oh, can you give me steroids?

CAMERON: Steroids?

TIMOTHY: Friends of mine, their doctor gives them steroids. Seriously, people are seroconverting just so they can get the shit legally and build the body they always wanted. Downside is, people take one look at their bulky beefcake selves and think: Steroids, AIDS, pass. So they get even fewer dates than ever. Gay life in a nutshell.

CAMERON: I don't prescribe steroids.

TIMOTHY: Just as well, they shrink your thingy.

CAMERON: Why have you come here? You're Ellis Wainwright's patient.

TIMOTHY: Why do doctors all have such pissy names? Ellis Wainwright, Cameron Trace—I think you make them all up, like—

CAMERON: Drag queens?

TIMOTHY: *Actors.* Drag queen, please! You won't catch me in a dress, I'm much, much, much too butch. . . . All right. Sorry. Kaput with the clinical cabaret.

CAMERON: It's good to see you.

TIMOTHY: You never called, sigh, that was summer, it's already fall.

CAMERON: And see, you're still alive.

TIMOTHY: I hold a mirror to my lips each morning. But no, this isn't a social visit . . . I want you.

CAMERON: I uh—

TIMOTHY: As my doctor, you big vain poof!

CAMERON: But Dr. Wainwright—

TIMOTHY: Has the coldest hands this side of Nome. Killed a man with emphysema last week, touched the guy's chest and freeze-dried his lungs.

CAMERON: I went to school with Ellis. There's a code of professional ethics.

TIMOTHY: It's not like you're seducing me away from some longtime lover. *I'm* coming to *you.*

CAMERON: Oh, so you're breaking up with your steady.

TIMOTHY: It's not a crime. I like you better. It's not always about competency. It's about feelings.

CAMERON: Well, in medical terms—

TIMOTHY: The doctor-patient *je ne sais quoi.* The mind and the heart are part of the full-health equation, too.

CAMERON: Yes. All right. I'd love to be your primary caregiver. But it's up to you to have your records transferred.

TIMOTHY: My records?

CAMERON: Your medical history.

TIMOTHY: Thank God, I thought you were requisitioning my Donna Summers. That's fine. I'll call my favorite nurse.

CAMERON: His name's not Kyle I hope.

TIMOTHY: No. Christina. Why?

CAMERON: Never mind.

(*They disappear. Janie steps forward. Janie's law office*)

JANIE: He came to see me too. At my firm.

(*Timothy joins her. Janie examines some papers*)

JANIE: It's a generous insurance policy.

TIMOTHY: Did you think I just acted? Who can live on that, or even gracefully die? No, I work for the historic preservation society. They're very considerate when it comes to death. Where would they be without it? Plus I've been there forever, the same insurance. So none of that pre-existing-condition crap. AIDS or a car crash, they still have to pay.

JANIE: My assistant Claire can witness the signing . . . I hate to bring it up. But with wills. Given the nature of your illness.

TIMOTHY: You mean dementia? Oh, your husband examined me.

JANIE: He did?

TIMOTHY: He's my doctor now. I can't get enough of you two. Adopt me!

JANIE: And you have the paperwork?

TIMOTHY (*hands it to her*): I am totally compis, or whatever the word is. Maybe he said "compost," which I'll be soon enough . . . So what are you doing Thanksgiving?

JANIE: Thanksgiving?

TIMOTHY: That little day next week where people slaughter turkeys and try not to slaughter their families? Of course you don't *have* family now.

JANIE (*buzzing her intercom*): Claire, can you come in?

TIMOTHY: That came out wrong, blame the little diamond-shaped pills. By family I meant, you know, Cameron. *He's* coming.

JANIE: Coming where?

TIMOTHY: Chez nous, Jay and moi.

JANIE: I think you're mistaken, we're having dinner. Cam and I, and Brian.

TIMOTHY: He said *you* were eating three-ish. *We* start late. Let's say seven. Come with. Bring Brian. Two Thanksgiving dinners, why not? It's America.

JANIE (*to us*): The strange thing was, I said yes.

(*Blackout. Timothy exits. Cameron steps forward and joins Janie. How they met—*)

CAMERON (*to us*): People ask us how we met.

JANIE (*to us*): Do you know how we met? Typical for Cameron. I had a flat. I needed rescuing.

CAMERON: Where's your jack?

JANIE (*to us*): We were sophomores. It was on frat row.

CAMERON: Where's your jack?

JANIE: What's a jack?

CAMERON (*to us*): She was helpless. She was perfect.

JANIE (*to us*): The eyes on the man. And meeting cute like that. Discovered. I felt like Lana Turner in the soda shop.

CAMERON (*to us*): We went to a soda shop.

JANIE (*to him*): Coffee shop.

CAMERON (*to her*): Did they have coffee shops then?

JANIE: Not *coffee* coffee shops, not latte. But they had coffee shops. How come I'm the only one who remembers?

CAMERON: I remember.

JANIE (*to us*): It's that Maurice Chevalier-Hermione Gingold bullshit.

CAMERON: I *remember!* We had . . .

JANIE and CAMERON: Coffee!

JANIE (*to us*): He's so sentimental!

CAMERON: And muffins, you had a blueberry muffin.

JANIE (*ready to refute him, then . . .*): Yes, he's right. I did.

CAMERON: Thank you.

JANIE: Thank *you!*

CAMERON (*to us*): She was so lovely. So smart and driven and—

JANIE: I like the lovely part.

CAMERON: I remember the blueberries. I tasted them on your lips when I kissed you.

JANIE (*to us*): He kissed me. Eyes like that, he fixed my tire, and he kissed me. Maybe that doesn't excuse twelve years of cluelessness on both sides, but it was a good start!

CAMERON: We saw each other the next weekend.

JANIE: I gave my roommate tickets to the Eurythmics so she'd be out of the room. Washed the sheets, shook the mothballs off my IUD.

CAMERON: I didn't expect it. Only our first real date.

JANIE: Oh, so I trapped him?!

CAMERON: I didn't say—

JANIE: I wasn't imagining the bulge in your pants.

CAMERON (*to us*): Is that a reflex hammer or—

JANIE: What?

CAMERON: Nothing. (*To us*) She was like carving into butter.

JANIE (*to us*): He was like opening a book, and it's your favorite poem.

CAMERON: I mean, I'd never ever been with a man. Sure I'd had *feelings* for men. But you can control your feelings. Right?

JANIE: From then on, we were inseparable.

CAMERON: All through undergrad—

JANIE: Med school for him, law school for me.

CAMERON: The perfect couple.

JANIE: Maybe we got intoxicated by it.

CAMERON: The rightness.

JANIE: The convenience.

CAMERON: Drunk on it.

JANIE: And you don't think twice about the headache in the morning.

(*Blackout*)

(*Thanksgiving: Timothy and Jay's. Lights up on Timothy, Cameron, Janie, and Jay*)

TIMOTHY: He's in mourning. Be sweet.

JANIE: Who?

JAY: Mark.

CAMERON: *Who?*

(*Mark comes in, this time dressed in a black suit*)

MARK: Hi. Happy Thanksgiving.

CAMERON: Oh, hi.

(*The others freeze as Cameron digresses*)

CAMERON (*to us*): Truth is, I didn't know how to date, after Janie. No time for it. My patients, the hospital. The only thing you could call social was my AA meetings. I go to a gay and lesbian clubhouse, but the guys there, too busy giving it up to a higher power to put out a little lower pleasure. And bars? (*A burst of the latest, loud dance music. Cameron shouts*) How do you even *talk* to somebody? (*Music out*) Or bathhouses. I can't in good conscience go to one, as a physician. To tacitly endorse that behavior, it'd be hypocritical, *and* un-Hippocratic. Though I wouldn't mind *watching*. In the interests of public health. (*Pulls out a whistle, blows*) "Hey, pal, wrap that puppy up in latex!" But I've never been to one. I'm shy. Part of me is shy. *This* part (*pointing to head*) not *this* part (*pointing to his crotch*) but this part (*the head*) usually wins out.

JANIE (*to us*): Usually. (*To Cameron*) Can we get on with this?

CAMERON: Right. Thanksgiving.

(*Mark, Timothy, and Jay start to resume the interrupted scene*)

MARK (*to Cameron*): Hi. Happy Thanksgiving.

(*Janie holds up a hand and freezes them*)

JANIE (*to us*): What's funny—to backtrack a little, before our divorce. If I had done a little detective work I would have known. Even before Nurse Kyle. I mean, Cameron's gym, the gym he goes to?

Oh, I don't do gyms. I jog. If you're stranded on a desert island, you don't have Nautilus. Physical fitness should be something you can do on your own. Not free weights. And aerobics? High-kicking to Gloria Estefan, lycra shorts crammed up your crack, no thank you. So I didn't go to his gym. I never inspected his gym. And if I had? (*Looks around*) "Where's all the women?" The lycra getting jammed up cracks—*those* cracks were very hairy cracks, not to mention the balls. Which were shaved, not hairy. And it wasn't Gloria Estefan, it was Gloria Gaynor. "Had I but known." Emphasis on "butt."

CAMERON: Janie . . .

JANIE: I'm sorry, get on with it, right. Thanksgiving:

(*Thanksgiving resumes*)

CAMERON (*to Mark*): Oh, hi.

(*Janie joins them. She's tipsy*)

JANIE: Hi, we never met. Janie Trace.

MARK: Mark Frank.

JANIE: Oh, like—

MARK: German dollar, French dollar. (*To Cameron*) See, I got it.

JANIE: Nice suit. Somebody die?

MARK: What?

TIMOTHY: Might as well. Poor baby, he's in recovery.

JANIE: From what?

TIMOTHY: L'amour, l'amour.

JAY: Timothy . . .

MARK: It's okay. I broke up with Robert, my boyfriend.

JANIE: Oh, sorry.

MARK: Yeah, were together nearly a year. He was a financial analyst. *Is*, I mean.

JAY: He did my portfolio, that's how we met Mark.

TIMOTHY: Dinner!

MARK: Anyway. He just—the last few months, Robert was like, "I don't feel comfortable being sexual, you know?"

TIMOTHY: Can you imagine?!

JAY: Timothy . . .

TIMOTHY: Not everyone's a martyr, honey. You and me, there's a reason. My Jay is a saint! But Mark and Robert, they're perfectly healthy, beautiful men in their twenties, which I vaguely remember. Look at Mark, I ask you, would you *not* want to have sex with *that?*

JAY: Who needs wine?

TIMOTHY: Make the Guests Blush, it's in my job description.

JAY: Janie?

(*He pours a glass for Janie*)

JANIE: I'd have sex with you, Mark—if I had a Y chromosome. (*To us*) Oh, wasn't I a goddamn witty liberal?

MARK: It's just sad, is all.

JANIE: *You'd* have sex with him, wouldn't you, Cam?

JAY: Cameron?

CAMERON (*distracted by Mark*): What?

JAY: Wine?

CAMERON: I don't drink.

JAY: Oh. Forgot.

JANIE: Let's all have sex with Mark right now!

CAMERON (*to us*): At our first Thanksgiving dinner that afternoon, Brian and I drank grape juice. So did Janie, the fermented kind.

JANIE (*to Cameron*): Admit it, I was fun! Every party needs a party girl.

(*They proceed with dinner*)

MARK: I dated girls. When I was fourteen.

JANIE: Girls, or a girl?

MARK: Janice. I lost my virginity under the bleachers. Varsity soccer match. Only Coach found us under there.

JANIE: Oops . . .

MARK: No, it was cool, 'cause he took me to the locker room, gave me a rubdown, then I hooked up with *him*. So I mean, both virginities, same night.

TIMOTHY: Is it hot in here?

JANIE: This is like a Hallmark Hall of Fame special, this is like "a very special episode of *The Wonder Years*."

MARK: Yeah, I still *wonder* how I got home.

JAY: Gravy?

CAMERON: I'm sorry, Jay—I forgot. What is it you do?

TIMOTHY: I'm a swan, I'm a swan, my lungs are full of crude!

JAY: Exxon.

TIMOTHY: He loves it when I do this.

JAY: I pay no attention.

TIMOTHY: I'm the albatross around his neck, only I'm a swan!

JAY: Site inspection, that's what I do. A lot of travel. All the offshore—

TIMOTHY: Drilling, goodness!

JAY: Yeah yeah, the environmental stuff. It's bad. It happens. But to get what you want, some things have to go. Anyway, I'm corporate. It's a business like any other. It's all just business in the end. Strategy, patience, and coming out on top. No great mystery. Like chess. You know what you want, and you get it.

(*Cameron is staring at Mark*)

JANIE: *I* want more potatoes!

TIMOTHY: That's my girl. I mean, we couldn't be more unalike, professionally. These oil people smell a whiff of crude, they'll tear down anything to get it. And I work for the preservation society, for God's sake.

JAY: That's buildings, though. We don't plant wells in the middle of cities.

TIMOTHY: You would if you could.

JAY: Sit back, enjoy, he's performing.

TIMOTHY: I'm not! It's important. And this isn't about Exxon. This is about America. Atlanta! The problem with this city—they tear everything down, there's no history. A culture, a civilization is built on what it *was*. But people prefer to knock things down, start fresh. American amnesia! It's disrespectful to everyone who came before.

MARK: It's like New Orleans. That's where I'm from.

TIMOTHY: Exactly! One of the few places in this country where there's still a sense of history.

MARK: Yeah it's cool. All the old stuff.

TIMOTHY: San Francisco, Santa Fe to some extent, New York, and Boston—considering what a young country we still are, what we think of as "history" is there. And at least they don't flatten everything on some whim.

JAY: We have the Margaret Mitchell house.

TIMOTHY: "The Dump?" Please! It's not even the original house, it burned down. Twice!

JAY: I thought you'd appreciate the effort.

TIMOTHY: It wasn't even her house, she rented an apartment in it, she *hated* it. That place is a tacky museum built by some bored Dunwoody debutante.

MARK: And the Mercedes people, right?

TIMOTHY: Right, Mercedes. Too bad Miss Mitchell's not around to appreciate the irony. Run over by a car, *hello?*

JAY: Timothy . . .

TIMOTHY: The Margaret Mitchell house isn't history. It's a tourist trap.

MARK: So is New Orleans, though. The French Quarter. That's the only thing that keeps the city going. Tourism.

JANIE: What do you do, Mark?

MARK: I work at NationsBank. I'm a teller.

JANIE (*nothing to say to that*): Oh.

TIMOTHY: But New Orleans isn't just tourism. People *live* in the French Quarter.

MARK: Yeah, and screw in the streets.

TIMOTHY: Well, Mardi Gras, sure.

MARK (*to Janie*): Excuse me.

JANIE: I've been to Mardi Gras.

TIMOTHY (*to Janie*): Screwing in the streets?

JAY: All those circuit-party gym boys.

CAMERON (*to Janie*): When did you go to Mardi Gras?

JANIE: With my sorority sisters.

TIMOTHY: So, no screwing in the streets.

CAMERON: Anyway.

TIMOTHY (*to Jay*): What do you have against circuit parties?

JAY: Screwing in the streets.

TIMOTHY: My baby, such an innocent!

JAY: But it should be *about* something. Shouldn't it? Sex?

MARK: I think so. You know, commitment and communication and trust.

TIMOTHY: It *should* be about coming, too.

JAY: I'm with Mark.

TIMOTHY: We're all with Mark. We're all with *you*. I'm just fiddly-diddling!

MARK: Because without love and trust—

TIMOTHY: Right, it's just stains on the linen.

(*Janie looks at Cameron. Pause*)

MARK (*to Cameron*): So you two. You have a little boy?

CAMERON (*to us*): It was the worst segue I ever heard in my life.

JANIE (*to us*): Don't mind me, I'm just a stray pillowcase, some of Cam's love-juice splattered me by accident—and, presto!

CAMERON (*to her*): He didn't mean it like that.

JANIE: He never meant anything, that was his special charm. (*To us*) But *my* contribution to the dinner table.

CAMERON: I forgot.

JANIE (*to the others*): Am I the only one concerned about this worldwide web thing?

CAMERON: I never use it.

JANIE: Your son does.

TIMOTHY: Let me guess: He's addicted to kiddy porn.

CAMERON: Brian is seven, what's he doing on the internet?

JANIE: Cam—this is the '90s, *three*-year-olds are designing their own web pages. They're going public with the browsers they invented. (*To Timothy*) And no, not porn. But the problem is—he gets e-mail.

MARK: E-mail's not the web, that's basic online service.

JANIE: I stand corrected. *Anyway*—some little friend of his sends him this e-mail. "A Glossary for the Proper Grammatical Usage of"—pardon me—"the Word *Fuck*."

JAY: He's seven?

JANIE: It was actually kinda funny. Usage as an insult, "Fuck you." Or disgust, "Fuck me!" They had these little historic examples like, oh—Marie Antoinette: "What the fuck is wrong with cake?" And the captain of the Titanic, "The fuck was that thump?"

TIMOTHY: How 'bout the Trojan army—"What's up with that fucking wooden horse?"

JANIE: Exactly!

CAMERON: Prometheus, chained to the side of a mountain—"Here comes that fuckin' eagle."

JANIE: And as Jocasta said to Oedipus—

JANIE, CAMERON, TIMOTHY, and JAY: "Motherfucker!"

MARK: Who's Oedipus?

JANIE: It was enlightening. "Fuck" as an adjective, an adverb, a noun. Everything but "fuck as a verb," thank God, because *then* I would have had to explain to Brian exactly what that means.

TIMOTHY: You're never too young.

JANIE: Seven?!?!

JAY: That's the thing about it. Everybody uses the word so much now, you know, movies, rap songs. It's lost its meaning. Its original meaning.

CAMERON: As a verb?

JAY: Yeah, because you can say "fuck this," "fuck that," "that fuckin' so-and-so." But to actually say, you know.

JANIE: "Let's fuck."

JAY: Or "I want to fuck you."

TIMOTHY: No, there's no ambiguity there.

JAY: That's what I'm saying.

CAMERON: It's a statement of intent.

(*Awkward pause*)

JANIE: They also had some other examples. Not just historic. There was an O.J. one—

JAY: "Shut the fuck up you stupid dog."

JANIE: Right!

TIMOTHY: "Here's your fucking glasses."

CAMERON: "Why's that dumbfuck wearing a ski mask?"

JANIE: "Whose fucking glove is this?"

MARK: I think he did it.

TIMOTHY: What?

MARK: O.J.

JAY: Of course he did it.

JANIE: Crime of passion.

CAMERON: What I don't get about O.J.—I don't understand how some-body could let his feelings get away with him like that.

MARK: You think he was high on something?

TIMOTHY: *L'amour, l'amour.*

JANIE: Hollywood, everybody's high on something. (*To Cameron*) Is it the kind of thing you'd do on cocaine?

CAMERON: What?

JANIE: Cocaine. Kill somebody? Jealous rage?

CAMERON: Why are you looking at me?

JANIE (*laughing*): Oh honey.

CAMERON (*drop it*): Janie . . .

JANIE: We're all friends here. Cam had a little (sniff-sniff) problem.

JAY: I've never done cocaine.

TIMOTHY: He's pure as the unsnorted snow.

CAMERON: I had a little . . . *flirtation* with the drug.

JANIE: More like a full-time affair. When he was a resident, having to stay up all hours.

CAMERON: It was stupid.

JANIE: Then came home so wired, took half a bottle of scotch to get to sleep.

CAMERON: Janie!

JANIE: It's history, it's in the past!

MARK: But I thought, you know, a doctor—you'd be—what's the word?

TIMOTHY: *Vigilant.*

CAMERON: You don't know it's a problem till, well, it's a problem.

JANIE: I had no idea. Miss Clueless. Another thing I was clueless about.

TIMOTHY: Don't you miss it? The drinking? The drugs?

JANIE: Of course he doesn't.

CAMERON: Yes. A lot.

JANIE: You do *not*.

JAY: I used to smoke.

CAMERON: You miss it?

JAY: No.

TIMOTHY (*to Jay*): I see you staring at people during intermission, like a starving puppy.

JAY: Well sure, but I don't *do* it.

CAMERON: It never goes away. Wanting it. The thing about drugs, alcohol—any addiction. It's like—I know it's a false sensation, but they give you a sense of beginning, middle, end. It's like an art form. Any kind of drug. It creates a sense of drama where there is no drama, a feeling that you're *part* of something. Very seductive.

JANIE: Navel-gazing as a global event.

CAMERON: That's the danger of addiction. I can imagine looking back over a year, five years, twenty, having this drug-fueled sense that you've lived a vivacious, fascinating, scintillating life. But nothing to show for it. You can't justify all the time you dribbled away. It's just a scrambled string of momentary sensations.

MARK: Like coming over and over?

CAMERON: Uh, kind of.

JAY: Masturbation.

CAMERON: That's it. But it makes you feel like you're not alone.

JANIE: Oh, then I need to do a line. . . . Joke, it's a joke.

TIMOTHY: But it's a fake feeling—like you said.

CAMERON: Absolutely. But it's like—*you're* an actor. When you audition, right? They only give you a little piece of the script.

TIMOTHY: Sides, they call it.

CAMERON: So suddenly your life feels like a series of these *sides* they hand you at an audition: vibrant, compelling, lucid—and yet, they don't connect to a bigger picture.

TIMOTHY: Doesn't sound like drugs, that sounds like life. Who gets to read the whole script? We all get it one scene at a time.

JAY: I used to have a drinking problem.

TIMOTHY: Here we go! Full disclosure.

JAY: I'd drink a couple more beers than I should, this bar I used to go to.

TIMOTHY: Before he met yours truly, natch.

JAY: I was friends with the owner and his boyfriend.

TIMOTHY: That means he *did* the owner and his boyfriend. (*To Janie*) Gay lingo, baby, "friends" can mean a whole lot more than a handshake.

JAY: Can I tell this?

TIMOTHY: I'm all ears.

JAY: Not since I've known you.

TIMOTHY: Ouch . . .

JANIE: So this bar . . . ?

JAY: They had a patio out back, a tree in the middle of it. And one night late, Darren and Clint and I were out there—

TIMOTHY: The owner and his beau.

JAY: Clint was really drunk and climbed up the tree till we couldn't see him. We yelled at him, he didn't answer. Darren got freaked, he said, "Jay, make him come down." So I climbed up the tree after him.

TIMOTHY: That makes a lot of sense.

JAY: You do things like that, fucked up. Try to rescue somebody when you yourself, you're in no condition. Don't ask me how we got back on solid ground. Stupid as it was, sometimes I miss those fucked-up days. It's like the smoking. I quit. But now that I've done it, I'm never gonna *not* want to smoke. I miss it. It's in my system.

CAMERON: Experience leads us to loss.

MARK: Who said that?

CAMERON: Um, I did.

MARK: Oh . . .

JANIE: *Cheers!*

CAMERON (*to us*): Then our plates were empty so we cleared the table—

JANIE: I can't believe I ate two turkey dinners!

CAMERON (*to us*): And theirs was better.

JANIE: Theirs was *better* goddamnit, and I slaved!

CAMERON: After dinner, Timothy said he needed to talk, he led me to the den.

JANIE: I helped Jay and Mark clean up—oh, just like one of the girls.

CAMERON: Give her a drink, it all comes to the surface.

JANIE: No, it took me a long time to get there.

CAMERON: Anyway. The den . . .

(*The den: Cameron and Timothy*)

TIMOTHY: That's Jay and me in Constantinople. The dust! Jay was on his see-the-world-boil-your-drinking-water-wipe-your-ass-with-wood-chips phase. But the pictures came out nice.

CAMERON: Oh, remember: You need to come to the hospital next Tuesday, we'll do up your blood work.

TIMOTHY: I'm sure I wrote it down . . . You know when I met you. When I said you'd meet the right man?

CAMERON: Yes?

TIMOTHY: Oh don't blush. I don't mean me, I'm history. But my Jay.

CAMERON: Timothy . . . whatever you think you're doing—

TIMOTHY: The timing couldn't be better. You're unattached—

CAMERON: Jay is your boyfriend.

TIMOTHY: You're a man of science. Why act naive? You've seen my charts.

CAMERON: This is very morbid of you.

TIMOTHY: I don't want your bedside manner. Do you know how wonderful Jay is? Six years together. And the past three, with me really sick. Sex has been a non-issue. Still, Jay stuck with me. Is that a saint, or what? I owe him. And *you*. You've got it together. You're a together kind of guy. And a doctor, mercy! If you find him attractive, if you find him at all attractive . . . Would you just consider it?

CAMERON: Timothy . . . Yes I find him attractive. (*To us*) I lied. (*To Timothy*) He's an attractive guy.

TIMOTHY: Big dick, did I mention.

CAMERON: But the regimen of treatments we have you on—

TIMOTHY: Is the same as that Wainwright prick prescribed!

CAMERON: Besides which—I don't even know Jay. He doesn't know me.

You can't just strategize putting people together like that, we're not chess pieces.

TIMOTHY: He finds you attractive. I can tell.

CAMERON: This is a moot point. This is the definition of moot point.

TIMOTHY: You think I do this with everybody? I see the people he could end up with. Gym bunnies. Even the sweet ones, like Mark. I adore Mark, but he's twenty-seven, he's a twinkie with a good dry cleaner. Jay needs a *man*.

CAMERON: Timothy, I appreciate—but you know, this whole dating thing is new to me, I was married.

TIMOTHY: You've been with men.

CAMERON: Well yes.

TIMOTHY: Fucked men.

CAMERON: Sure, but—

TIMOTHY: *Been* fucked.

CAMERON: Actually, no.

TIMOTHY: Some people just run from pleasure, don't they? My point is, there's a difference between your garden-variety sex, and somebody you would actually *want* to be with. Like Jay.

CAMERON: We should join the others.

TIMOTHY: You should take it as a compliment, you know. I want you to rescue him, Cameron.

CAMERON: Rescue?

TIMOTHY: Jay. I thought I could. I was arrogant enough to think I could. You're a doctor, you should be plenty arrogant enough.

CAMERON: For what?

TIMOTHY: I'm a fool. I'm an actor. Everybody's playing a role. I just wish somebody else could pin it down: This dream that keeps sliding out of reach.

CAMERON: Timothy?

TIMOTHY: This dream I have of rightness, where the people who *should* be together would be together. Never mind . . .

CAMERON: I like Jay, Timothy, but—

TIMOTHY: Chess pieces. Right. But there's a reason chess has been around so long.

CAMERON: You're going to be fine. (*To us*) It was embarrassing. Flattering but embarrassing.

TIMOTHY: Cameron. About our situation. Jay and me . . . there's something I need to explain.

CAMERON (*to us*): But I was already opening the door. We should get back to the others.

TIMOTHY: Right. Right. I have to walk the dogs.

CAMERON: You have dogs?

TIMOTHY: We pen them up when company comes. They're vicious. Basenjis.

CAMERON (*to us*): We joined the others. I poured Janie off the couch—

JANIE (*to us*): I did not pass out, I was resting my eyes. It was the tryptophan in the turkey!

CAMERON (*to us*): I took her home. A few days later, at the hospital . . . *His* name I recognized.

(*The hospital: Mark appears. Cameron joins him*)

MARK: It's good to see you again.

CAMERON: Same here. So what seems to be the problem?

MARK: You came highly recommended by Timothy, so.

CAMERON (*pause; he digests this*): I see. Are you on any current treatments?

MARK: Treatments?

CAMERON: Protease inhibitors or—

MARK: Oh, no, no—no, I'm negative. I just—I need a physical. I thought your nurse told you.

CAMERON (*relieved*): No. No. So then. When was your last physical? Sit up here.

MARK: The last was—well it was probably back in college.

CAMERON: Oh, a whole two years ago.

MARK: Five.

CAMERON: Your body's probably falling apart.

MARK: It's good to keep tabs on things.

CAMERON: I couldn't agree more. Uh, let's start with your temperature.

MARK: The nurse already did it.

CAMERON: And blood pressure, right, we pay her to do that. Um, what's your type?

MARK: I dunno. Smart, funny, athletic—

CAMERON: *Blood* type.

MARK: Oh. O-positive.

CAMERON (*writes it on the chart*): My uh, my nurse—she should have told you to strip to your underwear.

MARK: She did. It was cold. I was waiting for you.

CAMERON (*to us*): There was that prickly feeling in the air. Like you get before a storm.

MARK: Do you want me to strip?

CAMERON: Not yet. We'll do the ears and the uh—

MARK: The popsicle stick?

CAMERON: Yes, I uh . . . (*To us*) I forgot the names of everything. Fumbled for something to say. Then I noticed he wasn't wearing black any more so I said— (*To Mark*) I hope you're feeling better.

MARK: Better how?

CAMERON: Your, uh—

MARK: Oh, you mean my ex. Robert. I'm fine. Anyway, that's the only suit I have. *Not* because of Robert.

CAMERON: His loss.

MARK: That's sweet. Thank God for Timothy and Jay. Thanksgiving. It would have been, you know, a turkey sandwich at Arby's.

CAMERON: Oh, I bet you have a lot of friends.

MARK: Sure. But Timothy and Jay, they're like family. God, it's awful. Timothy. I hear all these like miracle cures. And he's just . . .

CAMERON: Say "ah." (*Mark does*) It's different for everybody. The therapies.

(*He finishes inspecting Mark's mouth*)

MARK: But everybody else seems to be getting—

CAMERON: Part of it is the right mindset. There's a very tricky, powerful relationship between the mind and body. Timothy has a good attitude.

MARK: A good attitude about dying gracefully.

CAMERON: I'm working on that.

(He palpates the glands at the base of Mark's neck)

MARK: So you can help him?

CAMERON: I can do what I can do.

MARK: I mean, what would Jay do without him?

CAMERON: It's nice you're so worried about your friends, when you're still getting over—

MARK: Robert.

CAMERON: Robert. Right. Because— *(To us)* And I was amazed I said it, I was so new to this whole flirting thing, I said— *(to Mark)* Because you must be trying to make sense of the world.

MARK: The world?

CAMERON: Trying to figure it out. Knowing you were living with a lunatic.

MARK: What?

CAMERON: Robert *had* to be a lunatic, not to want to . . . *be* with you.

MARK: You mean fuck me?

CAMERON: I mean—uh—your glands are fine.

MARK: Or "make love" or whatever people say. Everybody wants to fuck me. I'm not even bragging. I don't get it. I mean, would you be attracted to me? Hypothetically?

CAMERON: Hypothetically?

MARK: Or maybe I'm asking. Are you?

CAMERON: Mark, I'm a physician, I'm not coming onto you.

MARK: Why not?

CAMERON: You want me to?

MARK: Why not?

CAMERON: Because we're in a hospital and you've sought me out as a doctor.

MARK: But outside the hospital?

CAMERON: Maybe.

MARK: Maybe you want to?

CAMERON: Do you *want* me to?

MARK: If *you* want to.

CAMERON: I want to.

MARK: So say it.

CAMERON: I want to come onto you.

MARK: You're already doing that.

CAMERON: I want to—yes, hypothetically, I wouldn't mind making love to you.

MARK: And the other thing?

CAMERON: What other thing?

MARK: That thing that starts with F.

CAMERON: Mark . . . In the room next door there's a 70-year-old woman with an enlarged pancreas, and on the other side is a guy with a twisted intestine. This isn't the place to talk like that. PS., your ears are fine.

MARK: So what about the rest of the exam?

CAMERON: Oh, right, uh. If you could uh undress.

MARK: Help me?

(*He stands*)

CAMERON: Uh well no, actually—

MARK: This is probably run-of-the-mill for you.

CAMERON: I wouldn't say that.

MARK: You see people naked all the time.

(*Pause. Cameron unbuttons Mark's shirt*)

CAMERON: Of course. The human body. I see it every day. Naked, dressed. Fat and thin, alive and dead, or somewhere in between. I touch two, three dozen patients a day, my fingers on their breasts and up their rectums. It's what I do. But that's professional. And this is . . . this is very strange, is what this is. (*He peels Mark's shirt off, unlaces Mark's shoes*)
I can tell you how things work when two people come together. The heart accelerates up to two-and-a-half times the normal rhythm, the veins dilate. The lungs quicken—fast but shallow. And certain tissue expands. (*He pulls of Mark's shoes. Mark holds his feet up, and Cameron pulls his socks off*) The adrenal glands, I can tell you all about 'em. And the effect sustained rhythmic pressure has on specific parts of the anatomy. (*He undoes Mark's belt, unbuttons his fly*) The way perspiration coats and cools a body, the heart like an engine running hot. The way the testes tighten and draw close to the perineum at just the last second. No turning back. The muscles around the urethra contract, then—release. (*He unzips Mark's fly*) On the molecular level—glandular, muscular, neurological, I can explain the whole thing to you. The body isn't a mystery. (*He pulls Mark's pants down; Mark steps out of them, and stands there in his underwear*)
But the animating spark—the thing that causes those reactions, the erotic stimulus, the match that turns the body into an explosion waiting to

happen—that's not science. Some say it's pheromones, chemicals we smell that we don't know we smell, wafting to us off that other person's body.

But it's really a mystery. You won't find it in the PDR. They don't teach you that. (*He kneels and pulls Mark's underwear down; Mark steps out of them. Cameron stands and circles him. He pulls on plastic gloves*)

A glance, a smile, the way the sun plays through a certain shade of hair. The elegance of a wrist, or that rim of ankle where the hair stops growing. Physical beauty, yeah, there's that response. Just glands. But then there's something else. A laugh, a turn of phrase. It's perception. It's poetry, a thing that happens in the air between two people, an invisible tug that translates into—

MARK: Fuck me.

CAMERON: Or words to that effect.

(*Mark kisses him. It lasts a while*)

MARK: Who was that guy you were talking about, chained on the side of a mountain?

CAMERON: Prometheus. He was a god. He brought the gift of fire to mankind.

MARK: I like that.

CAMERON: He got his liver ripped out for it—or was it his heart?

(*Cameron kisses Mark*)

MARK: I'm an orphan, you know.

CAMERON: Not any more.

(*End of Act I*)

ACT TWO

When the audience returns, the stage floor is again covered with a man's clothes.
The lights come up on Jay. He's dressed, kneeling among the clothes, picking up the items, folding them.
If there is a doctor's examination table, it is now a bed.
Cameron appears, apart.

CAMERON (*to us*): I pride myself on diagnosis. I'm known for it. Patients come to me when other physicians fail, when other physicians throw up their hands and say, "It's all in your mind." But I have a gift. I can run a symptom down.

Like those—what are they, Scotties? Dogs that can hear a mole burrowing underground. Something the highest calibrated audio device can't detect. That's me. Not to brag, but. . . . Sometimes I can even—it's scary, I can lay my hand on a person's skin and feel the virus, the bacteria, the cancer, wherever it's hiding in that person's body. I'm very seldom wrong. Very seldom. Very seldom surprised. I read a person's history . . . and then it's simple. I thought I could handle anything. . . . If that's what Timothy meant by arrogance, then he was right. I was arrogant.

(*He goes. Janie enters and joins Jay*)

JANIE: Everybody's gone. Cameron and Mark just left. I put the dishes in the dishwasher. Do you have a broom?

JAY: I'll do it tomorrow.

JANIE: But there's cracker crumbs, somebody spilled some quiche—

JAY: It's okay.

JANIE: You should eat. You didn't eat all night.

JAY: There's calories in vodka. Potatoes, carbohydrates. I could run the Peachtree Road Race. If it was July.

JANIE (*to us*): It was only May. The end of May. Six months later.

JAY: Really, I'm fine. You should get home. Your sitter.

JANIE: Oh, I told her I might be late.

JAY: Is it late?

JANIE: Quarter of twelve.

JAY: Go home.

JANIE (*about the clothes*): What are you doing?

JAY: They're Timothy's. It's a waste, you know? Salvation Army. Homeless people in Tommy Hilfiger.

JANIE: Jay. You don't have to do that right now.

JAY (*a buried anger; we haven't seen this*): What else am I supposed to do? Go bowling? Go to a bar? See a nice Kevin Costner movie? What?!

JANIE (*beat*): Well, we could—we could sweep the floor.

JAY (*calm again*): I have a cleaning woman.

JANIE: Jay. (*She kneels beside him; then doesn't know what to do*) It was a really nice service.

JAY: Friends in the theater, you can count on a nice service.

JANIE: The *Gypsy* medley was really very moving . . . I let the Basenjis out, is that okay?

JAY: I ought to just burn his clothes.

JANIE: Oh no.

JAY: Why not? I'm walking down the street one day, there's some fucking crackhead in Timothy's Perry Ellis?

JANIE (*to us*): He had a point.

JAY: To get *ambushed* like that . . .

JANIE: You have a point.

JAY: Fuck the homeless.

JANIE: Oh, fuck everybody.

JAY: I wish I could. What did you do with Cameron's clothes?

JANIE: His clothes?

JAY: When he left you.

JANIE: He *took* his clothes.

JAY: Oh, right. But he must have left something.

JANIE: Sure, aftershave. You know. Toiletries.

JAY: Did you give *them* to the Salvation Army?

JANIE: Of course not, I threw them away. (*To us*) That was a lie. Cameron left a bottle of Obsession for Men, sometimes, I would dab a little on my wrist—but—but this isn't *about* me. (*To Jay*) I threw it all away.

JAY: See? Have to make a fresh start. You can't be sentimental. (*Suddenly emotional*) I miss him so much . . .

JANIE: Oh Jay . . .

(*Janie puts her arms around him. He puts his around her. Lights down on them, and up on Cameron*)

CAMERON: It was May. Six months later. The night of the funeral, Mark fell asleep beside me, crying. I stroked the small of his back till he was quiet. I felt so guilty. Guilty, because all the therapies I'd prescribed, none of them rescued Timothy. I also felt guilty because, God help me, I was so happy. Happy, because in those six months—

(*Mark's apartment: Mark appears leading Cameron in*)

MARK: It's not much—

CAMERON: But it's home.

MARK: What?

CAMERON (*to us*): This was a few days after his physical. Our first date.

MARK: I like it okay. Original hardwood floors. Not a lot of space but—

CAMERON (*to us*): And almost no furniture. His bed in the middle of the floor, plaster statues of saints and candles everywhere. (*To Mark*) Catholic I presume?

MARK: Well, no, my parents were. I guess.

CAMERON: You guess?

MARK: My *adoptive* parents were Methodist. But I was left on the doorstep of St. Philip's in New Orleans, so I guess my real parents, or my mother anyway . . .

CAMERON: Catholic. So you converted?

MARK: No. But I love the candles.

CAMERON (*to us*): When he lit them all, the place smelled of sulfur.

MARK: And the saints are cool. I mean, if you're gonna collect something—

CAMERON: Might as well be St.—?

MARK: That's a Bartholomew.

CAMERON: What's his specialty?

MARK: Um, maybe shipwrecks? I'll look him up.

CAMERON: Who's the patron saint of lust? (*To us*) I thought I was being, what's the word, "hot."

MARK: Lust? Well, Catholics, they're pretty frigid, you'd have to move on to Santeria.

CAMERON (*to us*): Getting colder. (*To Mark*) Still . . . a lot of these saints—like Saint Francis—they led wild lives before God tapped 'em on the shoulder—

MARK: But then they put on their robes.

CAMERON: And sometimes got *inside* each others' robes.

MARK: That's kind of disrespectful.

CAMERON: You said you weren't Catholic.

MARK: Well you can't be. And suck dick.

CAMERON (*to us*): Getting warmer. (*To Mark*) I don't know, from what I hear about priests and choirboys—

MARK: Really, I think that's disrespectful.

CAMERON (*to us*): He had this wild mix. One minute very herbal-tea, sensitive-schoolboy prudish, and the next—

MARK: Let's play "John and Hustler." You're the john, what do you want me to do? And make it *dirty*.

CAMERON: (*to us*): But I'm jumping ahead. That *first* night . . . He lit his candles. Turned the saints' faces to the wall.

(*They approach each other. . . .*)

MARK: So . . .

CAMERON: So . . .

CAMERON (*to us*): Then we were on the floor. Our clothes were someplace else, maybe the bed, where *we* should have been.

(*They both sit on the floor*)

MARK: I like it down here. I'm a down-to-earth kind of guy. Got my feet on the ground.

CAMERON (*to us*): Two minutes later, I had 'em in the air. He always liked the floor. Hardwood. When we finished, I checked his back for splinters.

MARK: Wow.

CAMERON: Wow.

MARK: Times like this, I wished I smoked.

CAMERON: Filthy habit.

MARK: Like that isn't?

CAMERON: That's not a habit, that's—that's— (*To us*) The sort of thing you build a habit *around*.

MARK: Will you stay?

CAMERON: It's late—

MARK: Will you stay tonight?

CAMERON: I've got rounds—

MARK: I want you to stay.

CAMERON (*to us*): I stayed. I had to get up at 4:30, and it was already one, but I stayed. I fell asleep beneath a statue of St. Theresa or St. Debbie, some insipid smiling martyr holding roses in her hands. And at approximately 2:45 I woke up and felt Mark's mouth on me. And at 2:46 his thighs were around my neck. And at 2:48 his legs were over my shoulders, again. And again at 4:15. I had to go directly to the hospital without a shower and the nurses looked at me like they smelled something, and they did. Two days later it was his birthday.

(*Cameron, Mark, and Jay celebrate. Janie watches, aside*)

JANIE (*to us*): I wasn't invited.

MARK: My *approximate* birthday. They had to approximate, from the day they found me at the church. It could have been anytime, from today through the last two weeks.

JAY: No matter what, you're a Sagittarius!

JANIE (*to us*): Stubborn, fickle, and also bluntly honest, though I don't think that applies in his case.

CAMERON: Where's Timothy?

JAY: He's tired. Turned in early. He says happy birthday, Boo-Boo.

CAMERON: Boo-Boo?

MARK: That's what he calls me.

JAY: *Timothy* does.

CAMERON: Happy birthday, Boo-Boo.

JANIE (*to us*): The next week, if I have my chronology right, the very next week Mark moved in with Cameron.

MARK: I love my apartment, but my upstairs neighbor is a deejay.

CAMERON: Plenty of room here. Sorry I dropped your saint.

MARK: That was just a Lucy, I've got a spare. So. You wanna play "Bank Teller?"

CAMERON: That's what you do all day.

MARK: But I don't get to *play* it.

CAMERON (*getting it*): Okay . . . I want to make a deposit.

MARK: Penalty for premature withdrawal.

JANIE (*to us*): He didn't call me. He usually called me. Every couple of days, Cameron called me.

CAMERON (*to us*): He liked to play games. He'd insist, these games—call me at the hospital, give me my coordinates. Ten o'clock, corner of Cypress and Seventh. I'd pull up, he'd be waiting. Knock on my window . . .

MARK: Hey mister, lookin' for a tour guide?

CAMERON: Uh, yeah, I'm new around these parts.

MARK: Yeah, you look pretty touristy. I can take you south of the belt, there's always a party goin' on.

CAMERON (*to us*): We'd do it in the front seat, middle of the street. Insane.

JANIE (*to us*): Cameron and I, *our* sense of sexual adventure, we'd maybe light a candle on the bedside table. . . .

(*A restaurant*)

CAMERON (*to us*): Public places. He dared me to. Dinner at Indigo, he'd say:

MARK: Reach under the table.

CAMERON (*to us*): He'd be ready, his fly unzipped. I took my time, slow and easy. Started during the salad, ate with one hand, the other under the tablecloth on him, until—

(*A waiter enters*)

WAITER: And for dessert there's chocolate rum bread pudding, flan with kiwi glaze, or bananas flambee and clotted cream.

MARK (*he comes*): *Aaaaah!*

WAITER: Bananas and cream it is.

CAMERON (*to us*): He'd say things like—

MARK: This is very special to me, you know. Sex is a very sacred tender act, a communion of souls.

CAMERON (*to us*): And twenty minutes later—

MARK: Harder, doctor, harder! *Yes!*

CAMERON (*to us*): Mark was ripe, like a delectable fruit, something you dig into with your eyes, mouth, fingers, teeth, lips. And it never changes, you always hunger for it. Although fruit, God bless it, doesn't talk.

MARK: It's hard, not being wanted.

CAMERON: You're wanted.

MARK: But from the very first second of your life, not wanted. An orphan. I think they must have been French, my parents. Creole maybe. I always liked beignets and croissants. And maybe they abandoned me because they knew they wouldn't be together long, because relationships never work out, mine never have, so why should they bother. Or maybe they knew about me. They knew I was gay. They knew even when I was just a baby, maybe I liked my blanket too much or my mother's necklace, and they couldn't stand the thought of it, just left me there in the middle of the street because I was perverted.

CAMERON: You're not perverted, you're beautiful.

MARK: If you didn't think it was perverted, how come you got married? Why didn't you just come out?

CAMERON: That's different.

MARK: I hate myself sometimes. I ought to be a monk.

CAMERON (*to us*): And the next minute—

MARK: I simply cannot get enough of your dick.

(*Mark exits. Janie appears*)

CAMERON (*to us*): He was a walking contradiction, he made no sense.

JANIE (*to us*): But instead of raising Cam's red flag, Mark's behavior excited him. I know. When he finally did call me, it's all he talked about.

CAMERON: There's something so innocent about him, something unexamined.

JANIE (*to us*): You ask me, every square inch of Mark had been thoroughly examined by any number of, pardon me, tools.

CAMERON: He's so innocent.

JANIE (*to us*): Cameron was the innocent. The myth of science. Thought human nature was as easy to predict as blood through a vein.

CAMERON: He's so sweet, he's like a lost boy.

JANIE (*brisk*): I'm sure he's very sweet.

CAMERON: I thought you wanted me to meet people.

JANIE: A bank teller?

CAMERON: Snob!

JANIE: You don't need to adopt a lost boy. You have a son of your own. Not that you see much of him these days, *he* might as well be adopted.

CAMERON: Things at the hospital have been really—

JANIE: Maggie Bryers saw you in the park last Sunday. Rollerblading. With Deutchmark, or whatever his name is. You said you were on-call. Don't lie to me, Cam, okay?

CAMERON: I'm sorry, it was a last second . . . thing.

JANIE: At your age. You're a doctor, you better be careful.

CAMERON: We use condoms.

JANIE: Rollerblading! Jesus! I'm talking about rollerblading!

CAMERON: I'm sorry.

JANIE: It's not about me. It's about Brian.

CAMERON: So. What about you?

JANIE: What about me?

CAMERON: Seeing anybody?

JANIE: Oh, plenty. (*To us*) And I was. Though quantity sure ain't quality.

(*Split scene: Janie dates / Cameron cuddles. Janie and a date. Mark returns in pajamas and cuddles with Cameron*)

DATE: I invested twenty dollars per share, two years later I've got a 500-percent profit.

JANIE (*already bored*): Golly.

DATE: The land I bought twelve years ago—ever heard of a sweet little spot called Gwinnett?

JANIE: Heard of it.

DATE: Largest retail mall in the state, that's what they want, but I'm holding out.

JANIE: Aren't you Mr. Strategy.

DATE: Two thousand dollars an acre I paid for it then, guess what it's worth now?

JANIE: The mind somersaults.

DATE: Five hundred thousand, that's what I'm asking, that's what I'll get.

JANIE: Have you read any poetry?

DATE: What?

JANIE: Poetry.

DATE: What, like Hallmark Cards?

JANIE: Exactly: "Oh what fun, don't call me a bimbo, but dinner with you is like being in limbo."

DATE: Hey—I've danced the limbo.

JANIE: Excuse me, I have to change my colostomy bag.

(*Cameron and Mark, lying together*)

MARK: How's Janie?

CAMERON: Fine. I guess. Why?

MARK: It must be hard. Being a straight woman.

CAMERON: Yeah. She's not lucky like us.

(*Janie and second date. He's showing her photos*)

JANIE: Oh, he's really cute.

SECOND DATE: That's Jake, he's five. And this is—

JANIE: Ellen, right? You told me about her.

SECOND DATE: She was so proud, made ten dollars off her lemonade stand.

JANIE: Ahhhh. . . .

SECOND DATE: Here's both of them together.

JANIE: Oh, and is that—behind them? Your ex-wife?

SECOND DATE: Yeah. That's Yvonne.

JANIE: What happened, she break her arm?

SECOND DATE: No, just a sprain, from where I threw her down the cellar.

JANIE: Well. I have a really early case tomorrow.

SECOND DATE: Where you going?

JANIE: Bye!

SECOND DATE: Get back here you prick-tease bitch!

(*Cameron and Mark*)

MARK: I feel sorry for her.

CAMERON: Who, Janie?

MARK: Well, company excepted, men are pigs.

(*Janie and third date*)

THIRD DATE: Do you know what I mean when I use the term "three-way?"

JANIE: Check!

THIRD DATE: He's a Lhasa apso, but we're close.

JANIE: Check! Waiter! Check!

(*Cameron and Mark*)

CAMERON: Good night.

MARK: Good night . . . I love you.

CAMERON: What?

MARK: I love you.

CAMERON: I love you too. Night, Boo-Boo.

MARK (*pause*)**:** Don't call me that.

(*Lights down on them. Janie steps forward. The Rose Garden*)

JANIE (*to us*)**:** A long time before all this started, I got a call at my office.

A contractor we'd talked to. A wing we wanted to add to the house. This was the week after Cameron moved out. Neither of us thought to call him. The contractor. Cancel. He phoned me at the office and—I wasn't thinking, I was ambushed. I said, "Sure, three o'clock—Claire, hold my calls!"

(*The contractor appears*)

CONTRACTOR: Shame to tear up your garden.

JANIE (*to us*): I met him outside the house, walked him around the yard.

CONTRACTOR: My wife grows roses, too.

JANIE: Oh, what kind?

CONTRACTOR: Shit, I should know, it's her pride and joy . . . Excuse me for the "shit."

JANIE (*to us*): At least he didn't say "fuck." (*Showing him roses*) These are called Emerald Mist, see, slightly green. Very fussy. And these are Moonshadows and those are Monets. The first two years, nothing. But I didn't give up on 'em, and voila.

CONTRACTOR: So, you planning on more kids?

JANIE: What?

CONTRACTOR: That what the wing's for?

JANIE: Oh, yes. Three, four, seven, kids, who knows.

CONTRACTOR: Catholic?

JANIE: Careless.

CONTRACTOR: Good for you. Family values.

JANIE: Though if I'm gonna have all those kids, I'm gonna need a husband.

CONTRACTOR: Wait, I thought you and Dr. Trace—

JANIE: We're getting divorced—don't worry, I'm fine about it, he's downright gay.

CONTRACTOR: So maybe you don't really want this extra wing.

JANIE: Oh, I'm not gonna back out on you. I for one, I honor my commitments. (*To us*) And I did. Paid for it all myself. It was a nice distraction, with Cameron gone—all these strange men wandering around, measuring, sawing, hammering. I had sex with one of them. He laid the concrete, then me.

(*Cameron appears*)

CAMERON: You never told me that.

JANIE: Oh, he was gone before the foundation even dried. But he was the first man I'd been with. Since you. You had Nurse Kyle, I had Mr. Concrete.

CAMERON: Why didn't you tell me that?

JANIE: Because we no longer told each other everything. Besides, this isn't about me, or Mr. Concrete. This is about Mark and Jay. And Timothy.

CAMERON: Right. (*To us*) Timothy died at home. Very sudden. There was a reception after the funeral, at his and Jay's house. Janie stayed late, helped clean up.

(*Janie and Jay on the floor again, as before, hugging*)

JAY: He just—he said goodnight. I was in the den reading Forbes. Pecked me on the cheek. Nothing unusual about it. Only he said—I should have known—he said, "Good night, my Swan Prince."

JANIE: So you think he knew he—he was . . . ?

JAY: He had pills.

JANIE: What?

JAY: He had some pills.

JANIE: Pills.

JAY: He saved them up. I didn't know. I threw 'em away, what was left. And the note. Before the police.

JANIE: Shhhhh.

JAY: He just went to the bedroom, closed the door. . . .

JANIE: Shhhhhh.

(*She kisses his cheek. Lights out on them. Up on Cameron*)

CAMERON (*to us*): I was the happiest I've ever been. Isn't that pathetic? A bank teller. But you know what Woody Allen said about what the heart wants. And if you don't, you're in the wrong place (*Mark appears*) I told him—"You're my personal Prometheus."

MARK: The fire guy?

CAMERON: Exactly. You brought it into my life, I was living in a cave.

MARK: That's good, I guess.

CAMERON (*to us*): He was so blue that week. After Timothy. I tried to cheer him up, took him out. You know, Bacchanalia, Terra Cotta—

MARK: You trying to make me fat?

CAMERON (*to us*): So I thought, Okay, a show. "Les Miz" was playing at the Fox. So we get our tickets, we're walking in— (*To Mark*) Are you okay?

MARK: I'm fine.

(*Cameron runs his hand through Mark's hair. Mark pulls back*)

MARK: People are looking.

CAMERON: *Now* you're shy?

MARK: They're blinking the lights.

CAMERON (*to us*): Then, at intermission:

MARK: I have to tell you something.

CAMERON: Anything, honey.

MARK: I have feelings.

CAMERON: Feelings?

MARK: Feelings for Jay.

CAMERON: I know. He's having a bad time. You're such a good friend.

MARK: Not *friendly* feelings.

CAMERON: What do you mean?

MARK: Like boyfriend feelings.

CAMERON: For Jay? Now when you say Jay, you mean *Jay?* (*To us*) Really, I had to think twice. Him? The balding mouse? who I'd heard speak maybe twenty sentences since I'd known him.

MARK: Yes. Jay.

CAMERON: So what are you saying?

MARK: I'm saying I have feelings for Jay. And I want to explore those feelings.

CAMERON: Do you want to explore those feelings or do you want to explore Jay?

MARK: Don't make it sound dirty. They're blinking the lights.

CAMERON: Who cares, they all die. Fantine, Jean Valjean, and Toto too. Fuck the singing frogs and talk to me.

MARK: I don't know what to say.

CAMERON: Say you love me.

MARK: I do love you.

CAMERON: Say you drank too much wine at dinner.

MARK: I didn't have wine at dinner.

CAMERON: Trick question: We didn't *have* dinner. You're starving. You're lightheaded. You're dizzy from that turntable they've got onstage, you don't know what you're saying.

MARK: I'll stay with my friend Patrick till I figure this out.

CAMERON: What about us? I thought everything was great.

MARK: Well, it is. But I don't think you love me for me. You just want to have sex all the time.

CAMERON: *I* do? (*To us*) I couldn't believe my ears.

MARK (*moving away*): Taxi!

CAMERON (*to us*): This friend Patrick—I'd never heard of him before either. Next day when I get home some of Mark's clothes are gone, and there's a note on the coffee table.

MARK: "I love you with all my heart, Cameron, but a relationship is built on trust, and openness—

CAMERON (*to us*): He spelled "openness" with one "n."

MARK: "—and to be fair to us both, I need some time apart to sort out my feelings—

CAMERON: That word again, "feelings!"

MARK: "—so I am going to take this time and look deep within myself and understand my true needs and wants so that I can know completely the way I really feel."

CAMERON: Longest goddamn run-on sentence I ever saw. And he still didn't leave me Patrick's number, I don't think this Patrick existed.

JANIE (*to us*): So then, after long silence, I finally hear from Cam.

(*Janie and Cameron*)

CAMERON: I called Jay's house. No answer. I drove by. Nobody home. Not even the Basenjis. The only thing was a big heap of ashes in the backyard.

JANIE: Timothy's clothes.

CAMERON: Jay burned Timothy's clothes?

JANIE: Well, he couldn't stand the thought—

CAMERON: Of having 'em around cause he was sleeping with some twinkie less than a week after he buried Timothy.

JANIE: He burned them because he couldn't stand the memory—

CAMERON: 'Cause he was sleeping with this twinkie.

JANIE: Two days ago he was the love of your life, now Mark's a twinkie?

CAMERON: If he's sleeping with Jay, he is.

JANIE: Who says he is?

CAMERON (*to us*): Three days later, I come home and—

(*Mark appears*)

MARK: Hi.

CAMERON: Hi. I got your voicemail. Were the mountains nice?

MARK: Fine.

CAMERON: Did you sleep with Jay?

MARK: No! We talked.

CAMERON: You went together to a cabin in the mountains for three days and—

MARK: We talked. I missed you.

CAMERON: You just talked. Really?

MARK: I love you. And I realized I love Jay as a friend. Only, I had to figure that out. He was so needy, so heartbroken. So my feelings for him got all mixed up.

CAMERON: So you didn't sleep with him.

MARK: No! I told you. I love you.

CAMERON (*to us*): I was so happy. I was shaking. Don't ask me why, 'cause Mark *was* just a twinkie with a few nice ties, but . . . To tell you the truth, before "Les Miz," I was getting pretty tired of him. All he could talk about was numbers—interest rates, loans, mortgages, CD's. Or the poor-pitiful-me-ness of being an orphan. And he liked to go *antiquing*. We didn't have anything in common. Except the sex.

MARK: Rikki-Tikki Tavi wants to bite the head off big bad Mr. Cobra!

CAMERON: And the sex was—

MARK: Baby Jessica fell down the well! Send a probe down to find her!

CAMERON: If he'd channeled that energy into art, he coulda been a Picasso.

MARK: I'll be in France, and you be the Chunnel!

CAMERON (*to us*): To prove that everything was okay, Mark asked me to go with him to his therapist.

(*Cameron, Mark, and therapist*)

THERAPIST: So you're having issues of trust?

MARK: I was stupid—

THERAPIST: Don't hate yourself.

MARK: But I was. I'm in love with Cameron. I love Jay, but that's a friend thing. And I gave Cameron such a bad time, because I didn't know.

THERAPIST: Cameron, do you have anything to say to Mark?

MARK: I was an idiot, tell him.

CAMERON: I love Mark. That's all I know.

THERAPIST: Mark, do you have anything to say to Cameron?

MARK: I want to spend every second of the rest of my life with you.

THERAPIST: Group hug!

CAMERON (*to us*): Then, to prove it was really okay, Jay invited us over for drinks one night.

JAY: You're such a great couple. You're great together.

CAMERON (*to us*): We talked stupid shit. The Braves. I don't remember. But I caught Mark watching Jay play with the Basenjis. Like he was watching somebody very, very brave: Sidney Carton climbing the gallows—"a far, far better thing." Or Rick making Ilsa get on that plane. So I wasn't surprised a few days later when—

MARK: I still have feelings for Jay.

CAMERON: But does he have them for you?

MARK: He's in mourning.

CAMERON: You just feel bad for him, you're in love with his tragedy.

MARK: I just wish I could rescue him.

CAMERON: Him? You can't rescue yourself!

MARK: What?

CAMERON: Jesus, be realistic.

MARK: I'm gonna stay with Eddie.

CAMERON: Who is Eddie?! Jesus!

JANIE (*to us*): And then, Cam called me again.

CAMERON: I'm glad it's over, good riddance.

JANIE: I'll say.

CAMERON: Asshole!

JANIE: Why are your hands shaking?

CAMERON: They're not.

JANIE: I wonder what Jay's doing with the money?

CAMERON: What money?

JANIE: Timothy's life insurance. Three hundred thousand.

CAMERON (*to us*): That night, Mark was packing. Wearing a new suit.

MARK: I'm sorry.

CAMERON: How can you just go? We have a history.

MARK: Seven months.

CAMERON: That's marriage in gay years! That's commitment! Seven months—that's a ring, a house, that's a Jack Russell terrier!

MARK: I'm sorry.

CAMERON: So you're going over to their house.

MARK: *Their* house?

CAMERON: Timothy and Jay's house.

MARK: No. I've got a sublet. A friend of mine.

CAMERON: Eddie?

MARK: Steven.

CAMERON: Who's *Steven*?

MARK: I need to figure things out with Jay.

CAMERON: You're not even my *type*, for God's sake. But I love you.

MARK: I love you too.

CAMERON: But not that way.

MARK: I knew Jay before I knew you. I have a history with Jay.

CAMERON: History! The history you have is waiting around for his boyfriend to die.

MARK (*pause*): I can't believe you said that.

CAMERON: I take it back.

MARK: You can't!

CAMERON: I'm a professional, I'm a doctor for fuck's sake, a physician! You're a bank teller, you're a goddamn male stewardess, only you crunch numbers instead of hand out peanuts. How dare you leave me! It's sick psychology, it's bad Freud, you're looking for a father figure!

MARK: Don't talk to me about "father." If you know what you want, how come you married Janie?

CAMERON: Don't change the subject!

MARK: Jay and I know each other.

CAMERON: So you did sleep with him.

MARK: Of course I slept with him.

CAMERON: When you went to the mountains. I knew it!

MARK: No, I told you, we talked.

CAMERON: Then when?

MARK: What do you mean when? We've been sleeping together for two years.

CAMERON: Two years?

MARK: Well not exactly *sleeping*.

CAMERON: What? *What?* While Timothy was alive?

MARK: Of course. We had a, you know, an arrangement. Timothy said he told you. Didn't he? We'd have dinner, the three of us. Then Timothy went to the bedroom, closed the door. Monks are one thing. Celibacy. But Jay isn't even Catholic. Timothy *wanted* me to.

CAMERON: To?

MARK: Comfort Jay.

CAMERON: Comfort him? With your dick?

MARK: Why are you so crude?

CAMERON: Two? Years?

MARK: Anyway, if you'd saved Timothy, you and me could still be together.

CAMERON: Only with you fucking Jay on the side?

MARK: I stopped when I started seeing you. Mostly.

CAMERON: "Mostly?" Get out of my house! Get the hell out of my house!

(*Mark exits. Pause*)

CAMERON: Come back! Where are you going? Mark, come back!

JANIE (*to us*): Physician, heal thyself. Ha!

CAMERON (*to us*): I tried to. I went out that night. I—what do you call it—*tricked?*

JANIE (*to us*): Nurse Kyle, Mr. Concrete, same principle.

CAMERON (*to us*): The Armory. I even danced. The way my knees popped, they thought something was wrong with the speakers. This guy, though, he bought me a drink. Evian, I mean. I don't remember his name. Took him back to my place, only problem was, I couldn't stop crying.

(*Cameron and trick*)

TRICK: We gonna fuck or what? . . . (*Cameron sobs*) Ah jeez, I know that sound. What's his name?

CAMERON: Mark.

TRICK: He dead?

CAMERON: No! Don't say that!

TRICK: Sorry. Mark what?

CAMERON: Mark Frank.

TRICK (*pause*): That twinkie!?

CAMERON: What?

TRICK: God, he wanted to marry me. Had to be in a relationship, you know? Serial monogamy. Some guys! Either it's no breakfast and bon voyage, or it's a U-haul in your driveway. Honorary lesbians. Me and Mark were together four, five months? He moved in and all. So I go home to Baton Rouge one weekend, run into my ex. We have dinner. And I call Mark from there. You know, guess who I ran into, honey? And Mark is all—you mean you're with him now? And I say yeah. He says, get rid of him! I mean, I'm calling from a Denny's in Baton Rouge at eight o'clock at night! And Mark's all, get rid of him, or I'm going out tonight! I just laughed. It was adorable. But I drive home Sunday and sure enough, Mark went out. Backstreet. Met some accountant. Monday he's moved in. They were together maybe a year. Next thing I hear, Mark's living with somebody else. You gotta laugh. But one sweet ass, I give Mark that. And his hustler-john routine, that always got me going.

CAMERON: That's a good idea.

TRICK: What?

CAMERON: You. Going. Now.

(*Cameron and Janie. Her house*)

JANIE: It's not the end of the world. You said you were getting tired of him.

CAMERON: But *he* dumped *me!*

JANIE: Men . . .

CAMERON: I got dumped! A doctor and I got dumped by a bank teller!

JANIE: Well, it never would have happened if . . .

CAMERON: What?

JANIE: If you hadn't been *schtupping* a bank teller.

CAMERON: You're a big help.

JANIE: I'm trying to make you see the bigger picture.

CAMERON: I *saw* the bigger picture. Standing at that urinal.

JANIE: What are you talking about?

CAMERON: Do you think my penis is inordinately small?

JANIE: Not inordinately.

CAMERON: What's inordinate?

JANIE: It's your damn word, not mine. Your son is waiting. He wants to go to the zoo.

CAMERON: I feel like I'm *in* the zoo. I feel like everyone's staring at me through the bars going, "Oh look at the monkey's little penis!"

JANIE: Why is it always dick size with you guys? There's more to it. Okay, sure, Jay has a nice-sized penis, so what?

(*Pause*)

CAMERON: How do you know he has a nice-sized penis?

JANIE: What?

CAMERON: How do you know Jay's got an enormous schlong?

JANIE: It isn't enormous.

CAMERON: How do you know that? How do you know I was even talking about Jay?

JANIE (*to us*): I told you, I don't know when to keep my mouth shut. (*To Cameron*) I heard it somewhere.

CAMERON: I never told you.

JANIE: Brian, Daddy's waiting!

CAMERON: Janie?

JANIE: What is the deal with big dicks anyway? Once it's inside you it doesn't make any difference. (*To us*) I was trying to change the subject, but when he heard those words.

CAMERON: "Inside you?"

JANIE: Speaking theoretically.

CAMERON: Janie . . .

(*Jay appears at the side*)

JAY: I was in the den reading Forbes. Pecked me on the cheek. Nothing unusual about it. Only he said—I should have known—he said, "Good
night, my Swan Prince."

CAMERON (*to Janie*): Talk to me.

JANIE (*to Jay*): Shhhhh.

JAY: He went to the bedroom, closed the door . . .

CAMERON: Janie?

JANIE (*to Cameron*): Shhhhhh. Cameron. It just happened. He was crying.
I kissed him on the cheek. And then he was kissing me.

CAMERON: And then?

JANIE: The bedroom.

CAMERON: Jesus!

JANIE: I was just trying to comfort him.

CAMERON: Why does everybody want to comfort that asshole?!?!

JANIE: I guess I was sort of in love with his grief. By the way he was dev-
astated, how committed he was to Timothy, what a, what a *husband* he was.

CAMERON: Some husband—fucking a friend before the wind can scatter
the ashes! Did you use a condom?

JANIE: Of course I used a condom. I'm a single woman. I always carry condoms. Sort of an act of blind faith. I don't have to explain myself to you.

CAMERON: Jesus, I can't believe . . . Was he good?

JANIE: You can have the video for $19.95, available on the internet.

CAMERON: Was he better than me?

JANIE: What right do you have to ask that? It never would have happened if you'd been there—instead of home in bed with that ridiculous twinkie—this never would have happened if we were married!

CAMERON: Don't turn this around!

JANIE (*pause*): I'll take Brian to the zoo. I don't want him seeing you like this.

(*Janie exits. Cameron alone*)

CAMERON (*to us*): That night, I dreamed about Timothy.

(*Timothy appears*)

TIMOTHY: Okay, so I didn't offer full disclosure. So we looked like the perfect monogamous loving couple to you? Well that was my job, I was an actor. I wanted a husband.

(*Jay appears*)

JAY: When we met, Timothy told me he was positive. He said—

TIMOTHY: But I want a husband, and a nice life, and the picket fence.

JAY: So did I.

CAMERON: Even if it was a lie?

TIMOTHY: Actor, liar, where's the boundary? Tell me what you mean by lie?

JAY: Your life with Janie, was that a lie?

CAMERON: No, that was—

JAY: Okay then.

CAMERON: That's apples and oranges.

TIMOTHY: It's all still fruit.

(*Mark approaches Timothy and Jay, naked*)

MARK: Can I speak?

CAMERON: No, this is my dream.

MARK: Can I speak? I'm, like, the villain here or the idiot or something.

TIMOTHY: Let him.

CAMERON: No.

MARK: I want to speak.

CAMERON: Okay already! Speak!

MARK (*floundering*): I . . . I . . . I'm an orphan.

JAY: Is that it?

TIMOTHY: Speak!

JAY: Sit!

TIMOTHY: Lie down!

JAY: Roll over!

(*They vanish, leaving Cameron alone*)

CAMERON (*to us*): I woke up every night. It's true what they say: three A.M. Then I got a book in my mailbox. Somerset Maugham, *Of Human Bondage*. Next week day it was a copy of *Death in Venice*. No return address, but I knew it was Janie, gloating.

JANIE: I wasn't gloating.

CAMERON: Next, a video in my mailbox, *The Blue Angel*.

JANIE: I don't know what he's talking about.

(*Timothy appears*)

TIMOTHY (*sings like Dietrich*): "Falling in love again, never wanted to, what am I to do, cahn't help it."

CAMERON (*to us*): I'm not proud of this. I'd call Mark at work. Hang up. Drive by Jay's house, late. But Mark's Honda was never there. So I could hope it wasn't working out. . . . Then one night, I found myself on Jay's doorstep.

(*Jay appears, greeting him*)

JAY: Come in if you're coming in.

CAMERON: I don't want to come in.

JAY: It's raining.

CAMERON (*to us*): I came in. (*To Jay*) Is Mark here?

JAY: No. He sublet an apartment. Want a drink? I was gonna have a scotch. Oh, sorry, I forgot.

CAMERON: Straight up, please. (*To us*) We went to his kitchen.

JAY: Do you want to talk?

CAMERON: Not really.

JAY: Do you want to hit me?

CAMERON: Yes.

JAY: Okay. But just to warn you, I know karate.

CAMERON: Just to warn you, I know a lawyer.

JAY (*handing him a drink*): Here. It's a double. Look, Cameron, things happen. Some people are meant to be together. Others . . .

CAMERON: It isn't fair.

JAY: What's fair got to do with it? It's just math. Not everybody can be with everybody. You and Mark, you had a good six months.

CAMERON: Seven.

JAY: That's good for Mark. I mean, you can't be too surprised how things turned out. The arrangement we had.

CAMERON: You and Mark in the den and Timothy alone in the bedroom?

JAY: Well, sometimes he stayed and watched.

CAMERON: I never knew that.

JAY: Timothy introduced me to Mark. He knew. Me and Timothy, we didn't have sex. Not for years. So I went to bars a lot. He worried about me, wanted me to be safe and with somebody he trusted.

CAMERON: So he wasn't just your husband, he was your pimp?

JAY: You're very judgmental, I never knew that. You're the doctor. You diagnose. You know how—what?—*organisms*, how they work together. And we worked. The three of us. We called Mark Boo-Boo because, well, the first time we were together he uh—well, it took a professional cleaner to get that stain off the love seat. Look, I thought the two of you would work out. I did. But I guess I'm what you'd call a—what is it? Pre-existing condition.

CAMERON: So who did Timothy fix you up with while Mark was with me?

JAY: Oh, Robert.

CAMERON: Mark's ex? Mark's Robert? Who didn't want to have sex?

JAY: Him? He was a minus in the sack, I think the celibacy thing was just his way of covering up a lousy technique.

CAMERON: I just don't understand this way of living!

JAY: Cameron, you're a doctor. It's bodies, glands. No biggie. This is just Mark we're talking about.

CAMERON: We're talking about Janie too.

JAY: Oh . . . She was very sweet to me the night of the funeral.

CAMERON: Yeah, well some people send flowers and leave it at that.

JAY: Hey, a little sportfucking. No hard feelings, Cameron, it just happened.

CAMERON: You people live in a world where things just HAPPEN!

JAY: That's the world most people live in.

CAMERON: No, you plan your life, things have meaning, you strategize and make decisions and know what to expect.

JAY: And then you fuck a male nurse—

CAMERON: Hey!

JAY: Or get wrung out by some kid like Mark. Look at you! Where's your well-ordered structured life now? You gotta roll with the punches.

CAMERON: Roll with this—

(*He tries to hit Jay; Jay catches his fist, draws him close—and kisses him, seriously. Cameron resists, then responds. Jay vanishes*)

CAMERON (*to us*): And then Jay fucked me. I let him. I wanted him to. There on the kitchen floor. I didn't hesitate. Didn't resist. Hell, I ripped my favorite pair of Calvins, kicking them off. I mean, he was doing it to me every other way, why not make the metaphor . . . manifest. And boy did it ever manifest. I'd never actually been, you know—*done* to like that. And by him? I thought I was gonna die. I wanted to die because it felt so awful and so good. I wanted to buy every linoleum square of that kitchen floor from him and hang 'em on my living room wall. I was Blanche to his Stanley, and now I know what made the old girl crazy, cause she knew she'd only get it like that once.

(*Jay returns buttoning his shirt*)

JAY: Wow.

CAMERON: Wow.

(*They roughhouse for a moment, like kids on a playground*)

CAMERON (*to us*): I thought, hey, isn't it funny how things work out? After all this craziness. Me and Jay. Timothy wanted us together. And all of a sudden, I saw that Jay was actually handsome. I couldn't wait to find out what he was like in a real bed, not just on the floor.

JAY: The mistake you made with Mark—you forced the issue. You made it black-or-white, me or you. Mark, he's just a kid. You say, "Don't do that," and it's the first thing he does.

CAMERON: Yeah, I have a seven-year-old.

JAY: Bingo.

CAMERON: But Mark is twenty-seven.

JAY: He's an orphan. Anyway, look, this was fun. I'd ask you to stay—

CAMERON: No, it's late.

JAY: But I told Mark I'd come over. Help him pack.

(*Pause*)

CAMERON: Oh.

JAY: End of the month. Steven needs his apartment back.

CAMERON: I see.

JAY: He's moving in.

CAMERON: Oh, right.

JAY: It's just business, Cameron. Chess. No hard feelings.

CAMERON: Um, did you know, this is funny. Timothy, before he died. He wanted us to get together.

JAY: And we did.

CAMERON: I mean, *together* together.

JAY: Yeah. He figured we'd make the perfect couple. Truth is, Cam, you're not really my type.

(*Jay disappears*)

CAMERON (*to us*): It was still raining. So I went to a bar. Just to stay dry. Only I didn't stay dry. My throat didn't. And then the rain turned to snow, straight up my nose. And some time later Janie was standing over me— my bed I thought, though it proved to be the coffee table I was sleeping on.

(*Janie appears. Cameron on the floor*)

JANIE: Your nurse called me. You've been missing for two days. Have you been drinking?

CAMERON: Yes.

JANIE: Much?

CAMERON: Yes.

JANIE: They can suspend your license. Any Demerol?

CAMERON: No.

JANIE: Cocaine?

CAMERON: A mountain.

JANIE: Get up.

CAMERON (*he doesn't*): Oh Janie. They tricked me.

JANIE: Male duplicity? I could've taught you a few lessons.

CAMERON: You don't know what it feels like.

JANIE (*with an edge*): Oh yeah, how could I?

CAMERON: I loved him and he—

JANIE: I know.

CAMERON: You don't. You don't have a clue.

JANIE: I've been there, Cameron.

CAMERON: The hell you have—when?

JANIE (*laughing bitterly*)**:** Jesus . . .

CAMERON: When did you ever—?

JANIE (*almost losing it*)**:** You were *there*, Cameron, you *know* when! (*Calms herself*) Come on, I'm taking you to a meeting.

(*She struggles to lift him up. He doesn't help*)

CAMERON: No.

JANIE: Come on. Upsies.

CAMERON: You're not my mother.

JANIE: I know.

CAMERON: You're not my wife.

JANIE: I know. Get up.

CAMERON: Go away!

JANIE: Get up, Cameron. Now!

CAMERON: Go the fuck away!

JANIE: Damnit, help me!

CAMERON: Stop it! I don't want you here! *I don't want you!*

(*He pushes her off. This is enough, finally. She loses it*)

JANIE: I know that! You—you fag! You stupid fag!

CAMERON: Fag hag!

JANIE: Cocksucker!

CAMERON: Slut!

(*They ineffectually try to slap each other, but he's too wasted and she's too tired. They both end up collapsed on the floor. They have to laugh*)

CAMERON (*laughing*): I hope there's a hidden camera somewhere. (*Sobbing*) Oh Janie, I'm so alone!

JANIE (*to us*): He kept circling around it. This open wound. And I know I was supposed to help him in his . . . recovery. But it never occurred to him what it cost *me*. You have to decide, do you climb up that tree after them? Or wait it out. I didn't climb the tree. It was the first time I didn't.

CAMERON: I love him.

JANIE (*to us*): And that is when your heart breaks. When you know, finally know, that this is not your story. (*She looks at him. To us*) He had stubble, his eyes were red, a fleck of spit or snot or coke on his lower lip, and he smelled. I had never loved him so much in my life. I couldn't wait to get away from him. (*She gets up. To Cameron*) You're a handsome man, Cameron. You're smart. You're rich. You save lives. And your penis is an inch or so more than adequate. I can't waste any more sympathy on you. I need to get on with my life; you need to stop fucking yours up.

(*She exits. Cameron stands*)

CAMERON (*to us*): So I went to a meeting.

(*AA Meeting: Alcoholic appears, raises his hand*)

ALCOHOLIC: Hello, my name is Randall, I'm an alcoholic.

CAMERON and (*offstage*) **MARK, and JAY:** Hi, Randall!

ALCOHOLIC: So I'm trying to make amends to that lady that I burned down her house when I was drunk, but I think she has a grudge still on account of the scars and prosthesis. I took her a cake but she hit me with her wooden leg, so she's still processing. My brother-in-law wants to prosecute me for the hundred thou I embezzled—that's when I was cross-addicted on crystal. I'm paying him back quick as I can, but working at Wendy's, it's hard. So I feel his frustration. So anyway. One day at a time, right?

MARK and JAY (*off*): Thanks, Randall!

(*Cameron raises his hand*)

CAMERON: Hi, my name is Cameron, I'm an alcoholic—

MARK, JAY, and ALCOHOLIC (*off*): Hi, Cameron—

CAMERON: —Cross-addicted, cocaine—

MARK, JAY, and ALCOHOLIC (*off*): Hi, Cameron!

CAMERON: And, uh, Demerol.

MARK, JAY, and ALCOHOLIC (*off*): Tell us your story, Cameron!

(*Janie appears to the side, observing in the shadows*)

CAMERON: Well, compared to Randall, my story, it's . . . a broken heart. Feeling like an idiot. Big deal. It's not a new story. It's an old silly one. Till it happens to you. Then it's the only story.

JANIE (*to us*): Tell me about it.

CAMERON: This guy I met. I fell in love, he fell in like.
Why do we *fall* for people anyway? You *fall*, and then it *falls* apart. If you follow your heart. If you follow your heart, you might as well say, Come on, here's my heart, it's yours. Go ahead, tear it in two—seven months or twelve years, whatever it takes. *Get it over with.*
I love you. I love you, why isn't that enough?
But we have to do it. *Fall.* Or else, or else it's just . . . chess. Not love. Just (*laughs*) *math.* And all the time there's this dream that keeps sliding out of reach . . .

Listen to me. I'm a man of science. I was always on the outside, examining. But somehow I got trapped, inside. And . . . man. I should have specialized in school. Not just a G.P. A surgeon. So I could diagnose. Research. Nail down that specific gland that does it to us. *Love*. And slice it out.

You think we could live without it? I don't know.

Where does it go when it goes? That feeling. Love. Maybe it doesn't go. A powerful feeling, once you have it, it never really leaves you. That's why I'm starting to believe in an afterlife. Energy doesn't stop. Just goes away, somewhere else. (*He glances at Janie*) And maybe in that somewhere else we go to when we die, I can love the person I should love without all the twists of genes and glands and body parts getting in the way. Maybe that's heaven. That's my idea of heaven.

So. Work the steps. I admit I am powerless over my own . . . heart. And its power to hurt me. And the people I love. Or thought I loved. And still love, God help me cause I can't help it.

ALCOHOLIC and (*offstage*) **MARK, and JAY:** Thanks for sharing, Cameron!

(*Alcoholic exits*)

JANIE (*to us*)**:** There's no big finish here. No big dramatic flourish. We put our lives back together.

CAMERON: I had a great piece of ass, it meant more to me than it should.

JANIE: I meddled when it was none of my business.

CAMERON: I lied to people.

JANIE: I lied to myself.

CAMERON: And we put our lives back together. Oh, I ran into Jay a year or so later. Harris Teeter. Fresh fruits.

JANIE: I ran into Mark at the Publix. Pasta.

CAMERON (*to Janie*)**:** You did?

(*Grocery store: Jay and Mark join them*)

JAY: Hi, Cameron.

CAMERON: I almost turned away but I got it up for him. I said—how's Mark?

JANIE (*to Mark*): How's Jay?

JAY: Fine, I guess.

MARK: I don't know.

CAMERON: You guess?

JAY: We broke up last June.

MARK: We broke up.

JANIE: I didn't know.

CAMERON: You did?

JAY: I thought he might've called you.

CAMERON: No.

MARK: How's Cameron?

JANIE: Fine.

JAY: You know Mark, he's probably hooked up with somebody.

MARK: I miss him.

CAMERON: Why did you break up?

JAY: I'm not big on antiquing . . .

MARK: I was too embarrassed to call Cameron. After what happened.

JANIE: I guess.

JAY: So listen, Cam, if you're free sometime.

MARK: Can you do me a favor?

JAY: A coffee or dinner.

MARK: Cause you were always so nice to me.

JAY: I mean, water under the bridge, right?

MARK: Tell Cameron I said hi. I'd love to see him.

JAY: If you ever need a fuck-buddy.

MARK: I'm in the book.

JAY: You've got my number.

CAMERON (*to Janie*): He told you to tell me to call him?

JANIE: I forgot.

CAMERON: Janie—?

(*She holds her hand up to silence him and continues*)

JANIE: When I looked down, I'd smushed the tomato between my fingers.

(*Clerk appears*)

CLERK: You have to pay for that.

JANIE: I looked at the clerk, and I wondered what Timothy would have thought about all this.

(*Clerk turns into Timothy*)

TIMOTHY: I wanted you to rescue him.

JANIE: Rescue who?

TIMOTHY: Jay. You or Cameron, I thought one of you was strong enough to rescue him.

JANIE: From what?

TIMOTHY: From himself. From not being able to love enough. From not loving me the way I loved him.

CAMERON: Timothy—how could you let them—Jay and Mark—and you *watched?*

(*During this, perhaps, Jay and Mark appear in the shadows, re-enacting their "arrangement," slowly undressing each other*)

TIMOTHY: I watched because I could not believe that Jay would do that. In front of me. I found Mark for him. Your word, *pimped.* I gave Jay what he wanted. But it was a dare—a dare I hoped he would refuse.

He'd say, "But honey, you're all I need." Only he didn't. I invited Mark to dinner and told Jay, "Make your move." And prayed he would not make his move. I should have hated him for accepting my . . . offering.

But instead, his weakness became adorable to me, because he didn't know it was weakness. Kid in a candy store. Gorging.

And somehow I managed to transform his heartlessness into an amusing trait, like snoring or a cowlick. A thing you forgive and even love. That's marriage.

I should have been enough. But I was not enough.

And if I pushed them into each other's arms, who is there to blame when they found out that they liked it there?

(*Timothy goes. Jay and Mark disappear. Cameron and Janie alone*)

CAMERON: But this isn't about Timothy or Jay or even Mark.

JANIE: It isn't?

(*She looks at him. He looks at her*)

CAMERON (*to us*): I had to find a new apartment. I couldn't stay there. Memories of Mark. Janie invited me to move back in.

JANIE: The new wing, all to yourself, I mean it.

CAMERON (*to us*): She didn't mean it.

JANIE (*to us*): I didn't mean it. A year before, I would have meant it. It's weird. I walk through it now—the new wing—skylights, windows that face the rose garden, the transplanted rose garden. And not a stick of furniture in the whole place. Like a stage where the set designer was fired.

CAMERON: Or some avant-garde production.

JANIE: Beckett, Ionesco.

CAMERON: Theater of the Absurd.

JANIE: And we're stumbling through it like rhinoceroses. Rhinoceri?

CAMERON: But that was a while ago. My practice is thriving.

JANIE: My firm is unbeatable.

CAMERON: I ran into Kyle.

JANIE: I met a developer. Fred. He owns half of Buckhead.

CAMERON: Kyle is no longer Nurse Kyle, he's in med school. We bought a condo.

JANIE: I split my time between home and Fred's penthouse.

CAMERON: It's not like I'm settling. Kyle has so many—

JANIE: Fred has a teenage daughter.

CAMERON: —So many unexpected . . . *traits*.

JANIE: We shoe-shop together.

CAMERON: We have a dog. Cholera.

JANIE: Fred adores Brian.

CAMERON: And I have completely forgotten that business with Mark and Timothy and Jay.

JANIE (*sardonic*)**:** Which is why we stand here, telling and retelling our story like ghosts on a Ouija board. Only, all the names have been changed, to protect the internist.

(*Cameron begins to undress; he strips to his underwear during the rest of the scene*)

CAMERON: I don't feel naked all the time anymore. Just like I'm walking around in my underwear. When I heard about Jay and Mark, breaking up, I guess I thought I'd hear from Mark, but. . . . Good for him. Get on with his life. It's best for us both. But . . .

JANIE (*about Cameron*): I always thought he would come back.

(*Janie also begins to undress to her underwear*)

CAMERON (*about Mark*): I thought he would come back. But he won't.

JANIE: He can't.

CAMERON: Besides, I want him gone. I want him out of here. I want him dead sometimes . . . I *want* him . . . He's in my system. That most addictive drug. Love. That uncontrollable substance.

(*Pause, then they rally*)

JANIE: I'm going to Rome with Fred and Brian for Christmas.

CAMERON: Kyle starts his residency soon.

JANIE: And Cam and I—we're best friends.

CAMERON: But sometimes it's like staring at your own X-ray. Things you'd rather not see.

JANIE: The need.

CAMERON: The want.

JANIE: The ache.

CAMERON: The jones . . .

JANIE: It's an instant-recognition thing. Two people. Even strangers.

CAMERON: They can see it. That they've had their hearts ripped out.

JANIE: So we share that now. Even if it happened to us at different times.

CAMERON: There's that joke: Two guys out hiking. One gets bit on the ass by a rattlesnake:

JANIE: "Come on, man, you gotta suck the poison out"—

CAMERON: "If you don't suck the poison out, I'm gonna die!"

JANIE: And the other one says—

CAMERON: "I'll send flowers."

JANIE: There's only so many times you can suck the poison out. Then it's FTD.

CAMERON: But we're best friends.

JANIE: Only, we can't really stand to be in the same room anymore. Well, we don't need to.

CAMERON: Just either side of the doorway.

JANIE: The Brian exchange.

CAMERON (*about Mark*): God help me, but I was in love with him. And I was not enough.

JANIE (*about Cameron*): *I* was not enough. We are married now more than ever, in our wanting.

CAMERON: I can never forgive him—

JANIE: I can never forgive him—

CAMERON: For making me love him . . .

JANIE: Like he said.

CAMERON: We've learned so much.

JANIE: All the love—

CAMERON: The heartache—

JANIE: The three A.M.'s—

CAMERON: The past mistakes—

JANIE: Have I learned my lesson? Remind me what the lesson was. I'll get back to you.

CAMERON: You're my best friend.

JANIE: You're *my* best friend.

CAMERON: And it is not enough.

JANIE: It is not enough.

CAMERON: It will never be enough.

(*Pause*)

JANIE (*to Cameron*)**:** Enough?

CAMERON (*nods*)**:** Enough . . .

(*They hold hands and gaze out at the audience, hoping, perhaps, for some sort of recognition, or forgiveness, or release*)

PLAYWRIGHTS' BIOGRAPHIES

Samuel Adamson was born in Adelaide, Australia, and lives in London. His plays include: *Clocks and Whistles* (Bush Theatre, London); *Grace Note* (The Peter Hall Company at the Old Vic, London); *Drink, Dance, Laugh and Lie* (Bush Theatre in association with Channel 4, London); a new version of Chekhov's *Three Sisters* (Oxford Stage Company UK tour and Whitehall Theatre, London); and *Tomorrow Week* (BBC Radio 3). He was Writer in Residence at the Bush in 1997/1998 and Artist-in-Residence at Duke University in 2000. *Drink, Dance, Laugh and Lie* is published in the UK by Faber and Faber; the other plays are published by Samuel French Ltd. and Amber Lane Press.

Neal Bell's plays, including *Two Small Bodies, Raw Youth, Cold Sweat, Ready for the River, On the Bum,* and *Therese Raquin* (an adaptation of the Zola novel), have appeared in such theaters as the La Jolla Playhouse, South Coast Rep, Denver Center Theatre, Actor's Theatre of Louisville, and Playwrights Horizons In New York City. Mr. Bell has been playwright-in-residence at the Yale Drama School and has taught in Playwrights Horizons Theatre School in New York. Most recently the recipient of a Guggenheim Fellowship, Neal Bell has also received an Obie Award for Sustained Achievement in Playwriting.

John M. Clum is Professor of English and Professor of the Practice of Drama at Duke University. His recent books include *Still Acting Gay: Male Homosexuality in Modern Drama* and *Something for the Boys: Musical Theater and Gay Culture,* both from St. Martin's Press, and the anthology *Staging Gay Lives.* His play *Randy's House* has been produced in a number of professional and university theaters and he has directed over sixty professional and university dramatic and operatic productions. He was featured in the recent Channel 4 (Britain) documentary series *Stage Struck: Gay Drama in the Twentieth Century.*

David Dillon has been an award-winning producer, director, performer and playwright since 1978 and has worked extensively, though not exclusively, in both gay theater and musical theater. In addition to his first play, *Party,* he co-authored the lesbian version, *Girl Party,* with Chicago playwright Virginia Smiley and penned the sequel, *Third Party,* which combined characters from both versions. He has recently completed a new play, tentatively titled *A Family Affair*, and is working on several new projects as well. In addition to authoring *Party*, he directed the Chicago, New York, and Los Angeles productions and appeared in the show in Chicago, New York, and San Francisco. He currently resides in Los Angeles and can be found on the internet at www.daviddillon.com.

Steve Murray's produced plays include *Body Politic*, *This Passion Thing*, *Mileage*, *The Algae Eaters*, and *Rogue*. He is playwright-in-residence at Emory University's Theater Emory and is on the staff of the *Atlanta Journal-Constitution*.

Guillermo Reyes is Chilean born and a U.S. citizen. His *Men on the Verge of a His-Panic Breakdown* has been successfully performed all over the United States and won the Outer Critics Circle Award for Best Solo Performance in 1997. *Deporting the Divas* won the Drama-logue Award (San Francisco) for Best Play. Reyes is on the drama faculty at Arizona State University.